DATE DUE

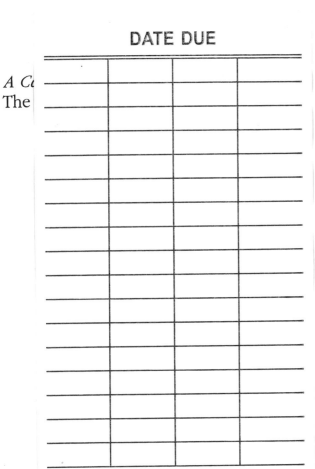

A C
The

Demco, Inc. 38-293

A Call to Action

The Films of Ousmane Sembene

Edited by
Sheila Petty

 PRAEGER

Westport, Connecticut

. by
estport, CT 06881
up, Inc.

ed States and Canada,
published by Flicks Books, England.

First published 1996

The Library of Congress has cataloged the hardcover edition as follows:

A Call to action : the films of Ousmane Sembène / edited by Sheila
Petty.
  p.   cm. -- (Contributions to the study of popular culture,
ISSN 0198-9871 ; no. 60)
  Filmography: p.
  Includes bibliographical references and index.
  ISBN 0-313-30279-0 (alk. paper)
  1. Sembène, Ousmane, 1923-   --Criticism and interpretation.
I. Petty, Sheila. II. Series.
PN1998.3.S397C36   1996
791.43'0233'092--dc20   96-28760

A hardcover edition of *A Call to Action: The Films of Ousmane
Sembene* is available from Greenwood Press, an imprint of Greenwood
Publishing Group, Inc. (Contributions to the Study of Popular Culture,
Number 60; ISBN 0-313-30279-0).

Library of Congress Catalog Card Number: 96-28760

ISBN: 0-275-95801-9

Printed in Great Britain.

Contents

Introduction

Sheila Petty

The history of world cinema began long before sub-Saharan Africans had the opportunity to participate in the production of this art form. In an essay entitled "The Igbo World and its Art", Chinua Achebe reminds us that "[a]rt must interpret all human experience, for anything against which the door is barred can cause trouble. Even if harmony is not achievable in the heterogeneity of human experience, the dangers of an open rupture are greatly lessened by giving to everyone his due in the same forum of social and cultural surveillance".[1] Like all art, cinema is the reflection of human experience, a journey into the search for Self.

As such a cinema, sub-Saharan African cinema has borrowed models and techniques foreign to its cultures, and is in the process of determining what constitutes its specificity and originality. Wole Soyinka once complained that "we black Africans have been blandly invited to submit ourselves to a second epoch of colonization – this time by a universal-humanoid abstraction defined and conducted by individuals whose theories and prescriptions are derived from the apprehension of *their* world and *their* history, *their* social neuroses and *their* value systems".[2] Usually, the consequence of such misapplications of "theories and prescriptions" is a contemplation of Self through the Other. Indeed, critical inquiries into the crisis of knowing the Self/Other have contributed to the debate around established notions about the subjectivity of history and human experience. Within the debate, V Y Mudimbe has examined the discipline of anthropology as an historical expression of the identity of the Western world's *imperium*:[3] "the pertinence of the inversed figure of the Same".[4] Mudimbe calls for the discipline's re-evaluation of subject-object relations, whereby the African who was once perceived as a simple functional object of study now thinks of herself/ himself as the "starting point of an absolute discourse".[5]

Although Mudimbe made the above statement in 1988, this notion of Africa and Africans as starting-points of absolute discourse has informed the entirety of African film practice, almost from its inception. No one body of work exemplifies this more than that of Senegalese filmmaker, Ousmane Sembene. The belief that expressions of Africanness should arise from within their original cultural contexts has been the driving force in his works, since this pioneering director began his film career in the early 1960s. Through his rich narrative structures, unique cinematic aesthetics and ideology, he has presented a forum for a multiplicity of African viewpoints on the changing nature of Africa since the beginnings of sub-Saharan African cinema. It is important to note that not only has Sembene been shaped by the historical context of African film production, but also he has been highly instrumental in shaping the evolution of the African film industry as a whole.

Sub-Saharan cinema was born out of Africa's "encounter" with Europe. Traditional African societal structures, previously self-sufficient, were disrupted by colonial foreign policy, which aimed to create subordinate trading partners that would export raw materials and import manufactured goods. Eventually, the colonizers attempted to impose the politics of development and modernization, as well as introduce Western education. This "encounter" with Europe opened up new systems of communication in what was primarily an oral civilisation, a storytelling society. Cinema therefore proved a new and exciting form of expression and communication.

Cinema first came to the French-colonized territories of sub-Saharan Africa in 1900,[6] when a French circus group projected the Lumière brothers' *L'Arroseur arrosé* (*The Gardener*, 1895) in a Dakar market-place. The early European films were admired and even feared for their potential to capture people in real-life situations. Distribution and exhibition expanded accordingly in major cities to meet the demands of this novelty. There was no question, however, of sub-Saharan Africans producing or directing films, even though their continent became a "fashionable" subject for ethnologists, researchers, missionaries and colonial administrators eager to document Europe's "Other".

It was not until 1953 that sub-Saharan Africa produced its first film. Mamadou Touré of Guinea shot a 23-minute short film entitled *Mouramani*, which glorifies the friendship between a man and his dog.[7] This production, however, remains relatively unknown, since most critics cite the 1955 Senegalese production, *Afrique sur Seine* (*Africa on the Seine*), by Jacques Melo Kane, Robert Carristan, Mamadou Sarr and Paulin Vieyra, as the first sub-Saharan African film. According to Manthia Diawara, this short film – which focuses on the lives of several students and artists living in Paris as they contemplate Africa's civilisation, culture and future – was made after the directors were denied permission to film their own countries in Africa.[8]

This, in itself, illustrates the great difficulty Africans had in accessing their own landscape and, by extension, their own art. In fact, after the publication of his first three novels, *Le Docker noir* (*The Black Dockworker*, 1956), *Ô Pays, mon beau peuple!* (*O My Country, My Beautiful People*, 1957) and *Les Bouts de Bois de Dieu* (*God's Bits of Wood*, 1960), Sembene realised that very few sub-Saharan Africans had access to their own literature, since publication generally required the use of European languages. In addition, the situation was complicated by high illiteracy levels, as education, an expensive process, was beyond the means of most sub-Saharan Africans. Sembene turned to cinema as a way to reach this larger and untapped audience. This decision led Sembene to Moscow's Gorki Studio in the early 1960s, where he studied filmmaking under the tutelage of Mark Donskoj and Sergej Gerasimov.

By the early 1960s, most sub-Saharan countries had gained independence, but this did not mean that black Africans suddenly possessed the infrastructure to produce films as they wished. The French had already begun control of distribution and exhibition south of the Sahara as early as 1926, when they established the Compagnie Africaine Cinématographique Industrielle et Commerciale (COMACICO), and again in 1934, with the Société d'Exploitation Cinématographique Africaine (SECMA). Diawara explains:

> They organized the market into three regions: the northern region comprising Senegal, Mauritania, Mali, and Guinea, with Dakar as its capital; the central region including the Ivory Coast, Togo, Benin, Upper Volta, and Niger, with Abidjan as the capital; and the southern region of Cameroon, Congo, Gabon, Chad, and the Central African Republic with its capital in Douala. From their central offices in Paris, COMACICO and SECMA sent copies of American, European, and Indian films to the capitals of the regions that determined the programs.[9]

This importation of films from other cultures is one of the major concerns that helped to shape Sembene's work. The influx of these films assisted in the destruction of traditional African culture and myths. As the contributors in this volume make clear, this cultural colonization had a powerful impact on Sembene's struggle to forge indigenous cinematic practices.

At an early stage, the colonial administrations recognised the power of film to shape public opinion. This led to a number of policy initiatives such as "Le Décret Laval", the purpose of which was to "control the content of films that were shot in Africa and to minimize the creative roles played by Africans in the making of films".[10] Although written documentation concerning the punitive use of this decree is scarce, its very existence nevertheless demonstrates the type

3

of philosophical racism encountered by Africans as they attempted to gain access to their own stories and screens. Even after independence, France continued to seek ways to "aid" its former colonies. The Consortium Audiovisuel International (CAI) was founded in Paris in 1961, in an attempt to produce African newsreels after the French style. Not surprisingly, national film industries did not emerge from this structure for several reasons. Firstly, the Consortium's mandate was to assist African governments in producing educational documentaries and newsreels only, thereby neglecting feature films. Secondly, all post-production facilities were located in Paris, making African participation in the post-production process difficult and expensive. Thirdly, foreign filmmakers (considered experts) were often hired to direct the newsreels, and thus Africans were seldom given the opportunity to control the productions themselves.

In 1963, the French government made yet another attempt to assist Africans in film production. A Bureau of Cinema was set up within the French Ministry of Cooperation to encourage Africans and provide them with the opportunity to create independent productions. Diawara explains that "[t]he Coopération could either act as the producer of a film and provide the African director with the financial and technical means, as well as the technicians, or the Coopération could wait until an independent director made the film, then pay for the cost of the production in return for some of the distribution rights of the film".[11] It is important to note, however, that the Bureau purchased the non-commercial rights to the films, and, as Claire Andrade-Watkins reminds us, a "major policy precaution at the Bureau was a strong preference for completed films or works in progress, meaning those which the filmmaker had already shot".[12] This policy precaution demonstrates that the Bureau not only was not truly facilitating production, but also evidenced a lack of faith in the ability of Africans to carry their own projects through to completion. By taking the precaution of largely purchasing completed films and thus hedging its economic risks, the Bureau offloaded onto African filmmakers the burden of finding finance and essentially assuming the risk of production themselves, without giving them the power normally commensurate with such risk-taking. Sembene has referred to this system as "mégotage", because the process of waiting for "scraps" from rich producers resulted in long delays in completing projects.[13] He was certainly justified in so doing: Sembene approached the Bureau to act as producer of La Noire de... (Black Girl, 1966), but their adjudicating committee turned the script down because of its political content. Ironically, the Bureau eventually purchased the rights to the film after Sembene managed to produce it independently.[14] Coupled with a distribution/exhibition system that was and is largely unsupportive of African filmmakers' aims and needs, the problem of financing remains part of a vicious circle that still hinders the African film industry today. This is the historical climate which fostered Sembene's film work. When his short film, *Borom Sarret* (1963), was completed, the French distribution company COMACICO offered him 100 000 francs CFA to purchase distribution rights, despite the fact that the film cost over 3 million francs CFA to produce.[15] These distribution difficulties and the attending economic hardship undoubtedly influenced his participation in various film lobby organisations. Sembene has certainly been proactive concerning the need to establish pan-African organisations aimed towards solving the difficulties of finance, distribution and exhibition faced by African filmmakers.

The problems of production and distribution intensified with the beginning of feature fiction production. Filmmakers could no longer be satisfied with seeing their films circulate only in the non-commercial sector, and they began to lobby for the protection of their rights by their own governments. By 1962, the North African countries of Algeria and Tunisia had nationalised their film industries; in 1966, Tahar Cheriaa, director of the Tunisian Cinema Service, created the Journées Cinématographiques de Carthage (JCC), where African productions could compete for the "Tanit d'or". Before the creation of the JCC, European festivals served primarily to launch African films: for example, Blaise Senghor of Senegal won the Silver Bear at the 1962 Berlin Film Festival for his short film, *Grand Magal à Touba*, and Sembene won the first film prize at the 1963 Tours International Film Festival for *Borom Sarret*.

Borom Sarret is the watershed event of Sembene's career as a filmmaker because the film constitutes his first success after expanding his artistic horizons beyond painting and writing, and into filmmaking. The film (for which Sembene founded his own production company, Domirev)[16] puts into play many of the themes and political concerns that infuse his whole body of work, resulting in the creation of an original African film aesthetic.

A socially committed activist, Sembene has been instrumental as a policymaker within African cinema. In 1966, at the Festival Mondial des Arts Nègres in Dakar, Sembene spearheaded discussions that would eventually lead to the decision in 1969, at the Algiers Festival Panafricain de la Culture, to create an organisation of African filmmakers known as the Fédération Panafricaine des Cinéastes (FEPACI). The federation was officially inaugurated the following year in Carthage, Tunisia. That same year (1970), the government of Upper Volta (Burkina Faso) nationalised its film industry and created the Festival Panafricain du Cinéma de Ouagadougou (FESPACO), where

African filmmakers could compete for the prestigious Yennenga Stallion prize. The goals of the festival are to promote the dissemination of African films and to encourage contact and confrontation of ideas amongst the filmmakers, as well as to contribute to the development of African cinema as a means of expression, education and consciousness-raising.[17]

Finally, in 1966, Sembene produced sub-Saharan Africa's first feature fiction film, *Black Girl*. It was hoped that from this moment onwards, the African film industry would take off in leaps and bounds, and filmmakers were concerned with the role cinema would play in the political, economic and cultural development of the continent. It was in the context of these concerns that members of FEPACI met in Algiers in 1975 in order to establish the "Algiers Charter of African Film". The charter stipulates that African film should be a vehicle for education, information and consciousness-raising, and not strictly a vehicle for entertainment. According to Diawara, "[t]he question for the FEPACI was how to insert film as an original fact in the process of liberation, how to put it at the service of life, ahead of 'art for art's sake' – in other words, how to film African realities in ways that could not be absorbed by the dominant cinema".[18] In 1982, FEPACI met again in Niamey to assess the situation of production, distribution and exhibition of African films. The outcome of this meeting, in which Sembene participated, was the "Niamey Manifesto" which emphasised the economic conditions of film production and distribution in Africa, while declaring film an historical necessity for the assertion of an African cultural identity.

As a cinema in search of Self, there has been much debate amongst filmmakers concerning appropriate modes of representing African cultural identity. For example, at the second FEPACI Congress of Algiers in 1975, many filmmakers condemned Cheikh Tidiane Aw's *Le bracelet de bronze* (*The Bronze Bracelet*, Senegal, 1974) and Daniel Kamwa's *Pousse-pousse* (Cameroon, 1975) for being too openly commercial and less committed to an overt condemnation of neocolonialism. The works of Sembene, Mahama Johnson Traoré and Med Hondo, however, were praised for their educational values.[19] Sembene himself has declared that "African cinema is a useful instrument for change born out of social necessity [which] is in the process of becoming the most important tool for the fertilization of a new African culture".[20] Significantly, more than a decade later, Gaston Kaboré underscored this argument when he claimed that "we have a perception of space, a certain notion of pacing and rhythm, and a narrative tradition that we can invest in our films...we can't be Africans and make films like Americans".[21]

This refusal of an Occidental aesthetic model infuses all of

Sembene's cinematic works, and indeed led to what might be considered as Sembene's own lasting contribution to African film: the emergence of a truly indigenous African cinema aesthetic. Sembene's pioneering use of narrative structure, cinematic grammar and unique African content in many ways broke the ground for present-day African cinema. The uniqueness of Sembene's vision is probed by the contributors in this volume, who present a critical overview of his entire film canon. Each deals with different aspects of the ideological/aesthetic issues central to an understanding of Sembene, both as a unique African voice and as a filmmaker of international acclaim.

In "The context of the African filmmaker", Roy Armes examines how cinema has developed in Africa, and provides an historical and political context in which to view the development of Sembene's career and work. Armes cautions that there is not one single history of African cinema, but rather a shared heritage of colonialism. Outlining the role played by the importation of foreign films, Armes delineates the domination of Africa's distribution and film production system by colonial and foreign powers, and demonstrates that this situation has historically disadvantaged the development of an indigenous film industry.

Ann Elizabeth Willey's essay, "Language use and representation of the Senegalese subject in the written work of Ousmane Sembene", traces Sembene's career as a writer from its beginnings to its current literary practice, and places in perspective the influence this medium has had on his film work. In particular, Willey demonstrates the powerful role that language plays as an expression of nation in Sembene's work and underscores his political use of language as an agent of protest.

Undertaking the challenge of retracing the development of Sembene's film aesthetics in his essay, "The creation of an African film aesthetic/language for representing African realities", Nwachukwu Frank Ukadike takes the position that Sembene's pioneering contribution to the œuvre of African cinematic practice lies in his ability to transform the conventions of dominant film practice. In particular, Ukadike cites Sembene's ability to transform film aesthetics by infusing them with oral tradition and unique African content, thus creating an indigenous aesthetic that speaks at once both to African audiences and to the world at large.

Philip Rosen's essay, "Nation, inter-nation and narration in Ousmane Sembene's films", posits that Sembene's films "explore the divisions as well as the unities generated by the simultaneity of nation and inter-nation". Rosen establishes that Sembene's enduring career is founded on his ability to exploit neocolonialist resources for nationalist purposes, without ceding ground on his ideological agenda.

Furthermore, Rosen illuminates Sembene's unique ability to mine sources both within and outside of his own nation to provide his work with an international context.

"Orality in the films of Ousmane Sembene", by Sada Niang, evaluates the importance of traditional oral storytelling devices in Sembene's narrative style. Niang exposes the ideological tensions created by the use of literacy skills as an exercise of oppression over an illiterate population. Specifically, Niang analyses the roles played by the *griot* and the infantryman, two typal characters drawn from oral tradition that reappear in many of Sembene's films, and demonstrates how these characters use rumours to open an ideological critique.

Sembene himself has been quoted as declaring that "[t]here can be no development in Africa if women are left out of the account",[22] and certainly it may be observed that women as characters in his films have played a vital role in shaping Sembene's vision of Africa as a nation. Sheila Petty's essay, "Towards a changing Africa: women's roles in the films of Ousmane Sembene", takes this notion as its central premise and explores the functions of female characters in Sembene's work, not only as gender constructions, but also as expressions of nation in and of themselves.

In "Ontological discourse in Ousmane Sembene's cinema", Frederick Ivor Case makes the argument that Sembene's work is focused on the dramatic presentation of alienation and the dispossessed. Case posits that Sembene's didactic purpose goes beyond ideological dogmatism and aesthetic conservatism by providing an environment in which subtleties of discourse are encoded in signs that take the "form of music, greetings, apparently simple cultural or religious acts, an object, or a given situation". By taking the central notion of "Being" (the state of existing culturally and spiritually within a community), Case outlines how Sembene's discourse develops and emphasises a unique expression of basic African values.

For African filmmakers, the 1990s present a continuation of the dilemmas that faced the industry in the 1960s. Sembene himself has faced off against unfair taxation of movie revenues by the Senegalese government by refusing to allow his most recent film, *Guelwaar* (1992), to be shown in Senegalese commercial cinemas until the tax is removed.[23] He remains committed to the continuation of social critique in African cinema, recently targeting foreign aid as an impediment to the development of true African economic and political independence. In Sembene's view, artists must refuse to sell themselves, and must prove that their role is important because their work reflects fundamental problems of historical origins, cultural disintegration and political anguish.[24] Sembene's challenge in the future is, as he says, "to remain African".[25]

Notes

1   Chinua Achebe, "The Igbo World and its Art", in *Morning Yet on Creation Day* (London: Heinemann, 1975): 65.

2   Wole Soyinka, *Myth, Literature and the African World* (Cambridge: Cambridge University Press, 1976): x. Emphases in original.

3   This term is borrowed from Kwame Anthony Appiah in "Is the Post- in Postmodernism the Post- in Postcolonial?", *Critical Inquiry* 17 (winter 1991): 353.

4   V Y Mudimbe, *The Invention of Africa: Gnosis, Philosophy and the Order of Knowledge* (Bloomington and Indianapolis: Indiana University Press, 1988): 180.

5   Ibid: 200.

6   Paulin Soumanou Vieyra, *Le Cinéma Africain: Des origines à 1973*, volume 1 (Paris: Présence Africaine, 1975): 15.

7   Ibid: 356. See also Mbye Cham, "Filming the African Experience", in FEPACI (ed), *L'Afrique et le Centenaire du Cinéma/Africa and the Centenary of Cinema* (Paris; Dakar: Présence Africaine, 1995): 200.

8   Manthia Diawara, *African Cinema: Politics & Culture* (Bloomington and Indianapolis: Indiana University Press, 1992): 23.

9   Ibid: 105.

10   Ibid: 22.

11   Ibid: 26.

12   Claire Andrade-Watkins, "France's Bureau of Cinema: Financial and Technical Assistance Between 1961 and 1977 – Operations and Implications for African Cinema", *Society for Visual Anthropology Review* 6: 2 (autumn 1990): 82.

13   Diawara: vii, quoting Guy Hennebelle, "Entretien avec Sembène Ousmane", *Afrique littéraire et artistique* 49 (1978): 124.

14   Diawara: 26.

15   Patrick G Ilboudo, *Le Fespaco 1969-1989 – Les Cinéastes Africains et leurs Œuvres* (Ouagadougou: Editions La Mante, 1988): 111. CFA stands for Communauté du Franc Africain.

16   Françoise Pfaff, *Twenty-five Black African Filmmakers: A Critical Study, with Filmography and Bio-Bibliography* (Westport, CT: Greenwood Press, 1988): 239.

17   Diawara: 130, quoting *9ème FESPACO: Cinéma et Libération des Peuples* (Ouagadougou: Secrétariat Général des Festivals Cinématographique, 1985): 24.

9

[18] Diawara: 42.

[19] Ibid.

[20] Pfaff: 243, quoting Sembene in *Essence* July 1978: 24 and *Africa* July 1977: 80.

[21] Gaston Kaboré, interviewed in the video *Regard sur le Cinéma Africain* (*A Look at African Cinema*, Quebec, 1990), directed by Philippe Lavalette.

[22] Ulrich Gregor, "Interview with Ousmane Sembene", *Framework* 7/8 (1978): 36.

[23] Elizabeth Mermin, "A Window on Whose Reality? The Emerging Industry of Senegalese Cinema", *Research in African Literatures* 26: 3 (1995): 122, 124.

[24] Paulin Soumanou Vieyra, *Le Cinéma au Sénégal* (Brussels: OCIC/ L'Harmattan, 1983): 153.

[25] Translated from the French: "il est très difficile, plus difficile que jamais d'être Africain". Ibid: 152.

The context of the African filmmaker

Roy Armes

A clear reflection of how cinema has developed in Africa is the fact that the divisions that confront us are largely those of colonial Africa. It is not by chance – and despite the fact that many films are made in local languages – that those who write about African filmmaking, and wish to link films, filmmakers and film-producing countries together in meaningful groupings, tend to use the shorthand of the language of the colonizer: anglophone cinema, francophone cinema, lusophone cinema. There is not a single history of African cinema, but a number of divergent patterns of development. What is shared is the heritage of colonialism.

The shared postcolonial experience

The postcolonial state functions in Africa much as it does elsewhere in the Third World.[1] The state formations inherited from colonial rule are hybrid forms, but they have many factors in common: they are not accountable to the ruled; they are interventionist and usually Europeanising; they are absolutist and invariably bureaucratic. Such states need a bilingual élite for their administration. The education of this élite gives it European values: a sense of nationalism even within the arbitrary boundaries bequeathed by the former colonizer, and at least lip-service to the notion of democracy. This élite therefore tends, at least initially, to turn its back on tradition, which is reduced to the function of, for example, the state dance troupe which entertains visiting dignitaries. Such an élite is not, however, without its own cultural production; indeed, in Africa, the élite finds its own exclusive expression (not shared by the mass of the people) in a literature written in the language of the former colonizer.[2] Filmmakers, like writers, bureaucrats and politicians, form part of this élite, and are inevitably influenced by its values.

This situation has, in fact, considerable implications for filmmakers. One factor to be taken into account is that the filmmakers are part of an élite, not participants in a mass culture. Almost all are university-educated or have studied formally at a film school; what one might call "naïve" filmmakers are rare, although they do exist, as the examples of Oumarou Ganda and Mustapha Alassane in Niger demonstrate. The various attempts to set up film schools in Africa have invariably been short-lived, and so the training which filmmakers receive will generally have been acquired abroad in one of the major cities of Europe – usually Paris, but sometimes Brussels, London or Moscow. Most film school courses last three years, and the years abroad imply, in specific terms of cinema, an awareness of the latest trends and fashions in world cinema. In wider terms, they imply sets of awarenesses and the existence of contacts binding them more to Europe than to the inhabitants of neighbouring African countries. In this respect, African filmmakers have benefited enormously from the long-term existence of two major biennial African film festivals – the Journées Cinématographiques de Carthage (JCC), founded in Tunis in 1966, and the Festival Panafricain du Cinéma de Ouagadougou (FESPACO), which has operated in Burkina Faso since 1969 – as well as their own African filmmakers' organisation, founded in 1969, the Fédération Panafricaine des Cinéastes (FEPACI), although, ironically, the official languages of the latter are French, English and Arabic.

A second shaping influence is the economic context in which African filmmakers are forced to operate. The Marxist theorization of capitalism – stemming from Baran and Sweezy, and taking in such economists as Andre Gunder Frank, Immanuel Wallerstein and Samir Amin – may or may not have general viability. However, its conceptualisation in terms of metropolis and satellite (or core and periphery), and its view of capitalism as a single, interlocked economic system, in which the development of the West can only occur at the expense of a parallel underdevelopment of the Third World, is certainly a very precise definition of how world cinema operates.[3] There is a single world market, dominated by Hollywood, which regulates the flow of films throughout the world. About half of Hollywood's gross receipts derive from its 70% share of gross world film rentals, and the Hollywood companies have shown themselves ruthless in their defence of their market share, as shown in the recent negotiations between the United States and the European Community over the GATT agreements.

Given this US dominance, the so-called film "industries" of the Third World – with the exception of the Indian film industry, which does dominate its own domestic market – are fragmented and distorted. Everywhere, including Africa, more profit can be derived from distribution and exhibition linked to Western companies than from production. Operating in collaboration with Western companies, local distributors and exhibitors have no need of local production. Imported films, which have already covered their costs elsewhere, will cost only a fraction of what is needed to produce an equivalent product locally. Indeed, distributors and exhibitors may well consider the very existence of locally-produced films (even if unsupported by them) as a threat to the profitability of their own operations, since – if successful – locally-produced films might change audience tastes. Imported films, on the other hand, build an appetite for more imported films, to the extent that the "natural" language of film comes to be perceived by audiences as a foreign film language: that of Hollywood. The implications for African filmmakers are severe: everywhere they are confronted with colonized screens, showing only imported films (often of appallingly low quality), with indifferent distributors, who scorn their work, and with an alienated audience, not in search of an expression of national culture, but eager for the cheap thrills to which they have become accustomed.

Various individual states – Tunisia, Burkina Faso, Algeria – attempted boycotts in the 1970s, but the results show that no African state on its own is sufficiently powerful to confront the might of Hollywood. Even for state-backed film production, there is no viable national market which can support the cost of even a modestly-budgeted film (except in the very different context of the Yoruba Folk Opera in Nigeria, which is discussed below). Export is needed for economic viability, but the inhabitants of neighbouring states are equally addicted to Hollywood-style films, and European markets are closed unless a European company has invested in the film.

At the early meetings of FEPACI, and at gatherings of filmmakers at Tunis since 1966 and at Ouagadougou since 1969, much emphasis was put on the potential role of the state in aiding production. In virtually all the fourteen newly-independent states of what had once been the huge French colonies of West and Equatorial Africa, national film corporations charged with fostering film production were set up: Société Nationale de la Cinématographie (SNC) in Senegal; Société Nationale Voltaïque du Cinéma (SONAVOCI) in Upper Volta (later Burkina Faso); Office Cinématographique National du Mali (OCINAM) in Mali; Fonds de l'Industrie Cinématographique (FODIC) in Cameroon; Office National du Cinéma (ONC) in Congo; Société Ivoirienne de Cinéma (SIC) in the Ivory Coast; and so on. However, with the notable exception of that in Burkina Faso, these corporations tended to be underfunded, unadventurous and overbureaucratic. None was able to sustain any real flow of films over, for example, a decade. In certain cases (notably in Dahomey, when the country was transformed into the Socialist state of Benin), the granting of a monopoly of production to a national corporation actually brought film output to a halt. In any case, film as a capitalist enterprise is in many ways alien to an African state's priorities. It has no evident utility value, unlike traditional dance (which can be fostered for formal state occasions), an élite literature (which can be studied in the state university) or dam construction (which can be cited as an example of state modernization).

Film in the context of national culture

In attempting to locate filmmaking within its context, it is illuminating to consider it in relation to three broad categories of culture, what one might term the traditional, the élite and the popular.[4] By "traditional" is meant that culture which is assumed to be transmitted from a precolonial past, and hence able to claim a greater authenticity than the more hybrid forms of postcolonial culture. Clearly, this is likely to be of interest to a filmmaker returning from years of exile to begin his or her filmmaking career. However, access to the traditional is by no means a simple task. The impact of colonialism, certainly in sub-Saharan Africa, has been to block this flow from past to future. As one way of imposing their own values on the colonized, and of controlling what was felt to be an alien force, the colonizers recorded and tabulated African customs and traditions. With the disturbance of the continuity of an oral tradition, the colonizer's record can too easily be seen as a helpful source of traditional values. However, such recording is by no means a neutral operation. It freezes a living tradition, transforming it into something timeless, static and unchangeable. In extreme cases, by transmuting it through a Western sensibility, the colonizer actually invents the tradition he purports to record.[5] The filmmaker seeking to reject Westernized culture and find inspiration in his/her own presumed past is therefore in danger of ending up with another Western construct: an invented tradition, a rootless folklore, or even a version of Europe's own mythical view of Africa.

"Élite" culture is perhaps best represented by the literature written during the colonial era, and especially after independence, by Africans using the language of the European colonizer. This is very much a product of a Western education, a literature for professors and university students, written – by definition – by writers linguistically largely cut off from their traditions. Indeed, a constant theme is cultural alienation, the drama of the "returnee", the literature of the Self as other. Such literature can, on occasion, reach a truly universal level of significance – witnessed by Léopold Sédar Senghor's membership of the Académie Française, and the award to Wole Soyinka of the Nobel Prize for Literature – but it is a form of culture full of paradoxes. It is an expression of African experience written in a language not used for domestic intimacy, tenderness or love. Moreover, since the mass of the African population is illiterate and certainly incapable of appreciating the nuances of a foreign tongue, such literature needs a European readership to be economically viable. There has been little direct cross-fertilisation between European-language writing and African filmmaking, apart from the towering example of Ousmane Sembene's mastery and continued exploration of both forms. However, even here it is notable that Sembene's greatest novel, *Les Bouts de Bois de Dieu* (*God's Bits of Wood*, 1960), remains unfilmed, and that all his mature films have been made from original scripts. The question of language is crucial here. The first films in West Africa – including Sembene's own pioneering *Borom Sarret* (1963) – were made in French. In some states, such as Cameroon, with its hundreds of indigenous languages, this continues to be the case. Elsewhere, filmmakers have turned to local languages in their pursuit of true self-expression. Ironically, this also helps the film's reception in Europe, where the necessity for subtitles is often seen as a mark of both the exotic and the authentic.

Filmmakers share many of the concerns and constraints of the novelists and playwrights. With their élite Westernized education and professional training, the filmmakers of West Africa often began their careers with self-questioning studies of alienation. For many, success is still to be measured by success at Cannes or in the "art et essai" cinemas of the Parisian Left Bank. Certainly, French distribution is necessary in most cases if a film is to be a commercial success; a film may, on occasion, receive warmer appreciation from Western audiences than from the alienated spectators in the great African conurbations.

"Popular" culture has flourished in many parts of Africa as the former colonies have moved into independence. It constitutes, as it were, the unofficial art of colonialism or neocolonialism, growing in those urban spaces where official control is weakest. Popular culture is a form that is always evolving, unfettered, syncretic. African pop music is perhaps the prime example of the way in which popular culture can borrow from élite culture, and draw on traditional forms, combine local rhythms with, for example, European orchestration, be firmly rooted in time and space, and yet use modern methods of diffusion: radio, records, CDs, and so on.[6] Although one can point to examples of exploitation by the large record companies, African pop music is diffused and indeed performed worldwide, and its professional exponents – unlike the *griots* of traditional culture – can make fortunes. Apart from the leaders of the Yoruba travelling theatre groups – who enjoy a pop star status, at least at home – wealth and popular notoriety are things to which few filmmakers in Africa can aspire. They are trapped in an artisanal mode of production, and forced to act largely as isolated individuals, coming together only on the African film festival circuit. African filmmakers are artists constantly in search of an audience.

The isolated filmmaker

African filmmakers operate in an environment in which there is no pre-existing context for film production.[7] Filmmaking in francophone West Africa began a mere 30 years ago, and so it is impossible to talk of a tradition of filmmaking. Equally, there is no standard procedure for organising production and no conventional source of film finance. Because of the low levels of production, not only are there currently no directories of actors or production specialists, but also experienced crew members and trained actors are themselves virtually non-existent. Film training has to be acquired abroad, and there are no practical models or theoretical definitions for an African film's dramaturgy or visual style.

Of necessity, African films are personal creations in a way that films can never be in the context of an industrialised film industry. The filmmakers will have to involve themselves with every aspect of production. It is they who must raise the production finance from state or private sources. Since usually a number of funding sources – some local, some European – will be required, this can be an exhausting and time-consuming task, involving the negotiation of co-production deals, the sale of international television rights, and so on. In order to have full control of their project, most filmmakers write their own film scripts, and in some cases also appear as one of the leading performers.

Even if there are a number of co-producers, the actual shooting will usually be organised through the filmmakers' own personal production company: Domirev for Sembene; DK7 Films for Daniel Kamwa in Cameroon; Afrocult Foundation for Ola Balogun in Nigeria; and so on. The same system applies to filmmakers living in exile, as is the case, for example, with the Mauritanian filmmaker, Med Hondo, whose Paris-based company is Les Films Soleil O. Once the film is finished, the filmmaker will probably have to become his own distributor, taking a hand in arranging local screenings, and, if the film is sufficiently lucky to be offered showings abroad, travelling as the film's sole publicist and salesman. If the film is successful, it is the filmmaker himself/herself who will travel from festival to festival, television station to television station, doing deals with potential distributors and television representatives. At the same time, there is the necessity of trying to find financial backing for a new project.

Because of these difficulties facing all African filmmakers, perhaps half of all African feature films are first features. Many promising newcomers receive no opportunity to make a second feature, and, for those who do get the chance, the wait between a debut film and a second feature may be extremely long: no less than fifteen years for the Ivory Coast director, Désiré Ecaré. As a result, only a handful of African filmmakers have directed even half a dozen feature films over a period of twenty or more years: Sembene, of course, Hondo, Balogun and, among the younger generation and in a much shorter time frame, Idrissa Ouedraogo from Burkina Faso. Yet, films continue to be made and the various regional cinemas of Africa show a great diversity of approach as far as production activity over the past 30 years is concerned.

The divergent paths of development

Virtually the whole of Africa suffered from the effects of colonization. Significantly, it is only in Egypt, which had a very distinctive pattern of economic development in the 19th and early 20th centuries,[8] that one can talk meaningfully of a film industry, with 2000 or more feature films produced since the 1920s, and an ongoing production of some 40 features a year. This industry has all the structural features of a conventional Third World film industry. An output of this level requires a substantial investment in distribution and exhibition, but the circuits set up will need far more than 40 or 50 features a year if they are to be profitable, leaving the industry open to competition from foreign imports, particularly Hollywood movies, which have already covered their costs elsewhere and can therefore be exploited in ways that allow them to dominate the film market-place. Dominated at home, the Egyptian producers in turn dominate their neighbours, so that audiences throughout the Arab world have come to see Egyptian styles and dialect as the "natural" language of an Arab cinema.

The effects of this can be seen in the Maghreb. Between 50 and 100 feature films have been made in each of the three countries – Algeria, Morocco and Tunisia – since independence. Often these are ambitious and creatively exciting works by independent-minded filmmakers, but they get little space on their own domestic screens, and find their best export markets to be in Europe rather than in neighbouring Arab countries.

At the other end of the continent, there is the film industry of South Africa, where – in the figures given by Keyan Tomaselli – some 700 fiction films were made between 1910 and 1985.[9] These, produced for the domestic market under the very special circumstances of apartheid, form a case apart. There are promising developments in the new multicultural South Africa, with plans to bring the experience of cinema to the inhabitants of the townships, and with South Africa taking its rightful place at the various African film festivals.

In the former Portuguese colonies of Angola and Mozambique, left-wing governments set up film institutes on the Cuban model; however, because of resource constraints and the turmoil of civil war, few feature films have been produced. The same is largely true of anglophone Africa, where – following the model of the colonial film units – most emphasis has been placed on informational and documentary filmmaking. The few feature films produced have been isolated independent efforts, often with English-language dialogue, given little screen-time at home, and barely exported abroad, although in the 1990s there have been promising signs of new feature film development in Kenya.

The one exception is the cinema stemming from the Yoruba travelling theatre groups in Nigeria. Taken round by the filmmaker himself on the theatrical circuit, and never exported or shown at the African film festivals, these films form a unique example of a cinema which is a part of popular culture with all the features so ably defined by Karin Barber: "primitive" and un-Western, but linked to the other modern urban communication media with which the groups are involved: book publishing, records and cassettes, radio, television and live performance.[10]

Nothing could be further from the developments in francophone Africa – principally the fourteen states formed at independence from the two huge super-colonies of French West Africa and French Equatorial Africa – which form the principal focus of attention here.

Francophone Africa: the distribution structure

Throughout Africa – as elsewhere in the Third World – commercial film distribution developed in almost every place where urbanisation led to the creation of a proletariat with money to spend on its entertainment needs. In Africa, often the companies involved were foreign-owned, and operated transnationally. Always the distributors showed themselves indifferent to local production initiatives. Their profits were based on the import and local distribution of foreign movies, and they saw no need to challenge the audience's taste with a different sort of product, when the change might threaten the profitability of their operation, with no obvious advantage to themselves.

In colonial French West Africa, and French Equatorial Africa, two companies established themselves in the immediate postwar period, and continued to operate profitably through independence and into the 1970s. COMACICO (A Mocaer) and SECMA (M Jacquin) were both Paris-based distribution set-ups owned through Monaco-based holding companies.[11] Between them, they had a virtual monopoly of film distribution in francophone West Africa, and indeed owned more than a third of the film theatres. They divided the African territory amicably between them, pursued the same policy of acquiring only the cheapest available films on the world market, and kept the costs of the films they needed low by refusing to compete when purchasing African rights. With a population approximately equivalent to metropolitan France, this African film market was comparatively small – 250 film theatres compared to 4500 in France, and a turnover amounting to only 5% of that of French metropolitan distributors. By operating through three regional distribution centres (Dakar, Abidjan and Douala), and by rotating films daily without regard to national boundaries, SECMA and COMACICO were able to maintain a profitable operation.

This situation continued after independence, which saw the division of the two giant French colonies into fourteen separate sovereign states. By the early 1970s, however, the duopoly faced increased competition. On the one hand, this came from Hollywood, when the Motion Picture Export Association of America (MPEAA) set up an office, AFRAM, specifically to distribute directly to the fourteen states, as well as to Zaïre, Rwanda and Burundi. On the other hand, SECMA and COMACICO faced opposition from the independent African governments, which began to set up their own national film import-export monopolies. Guinea led the way with the creation of Syli-Cinéma in 1969, followed by Mali (which nationalised the local COMACICO operation to form OCINAM), Upper Volta (later Burkina Faso), which set up SONAVOCI in 1970, and Dahomey (later Benin), where a similar import-export company, OBECI, was established. Syli-Cinéma went on in 1972 to develop close links with SOCOPRINT, a Swiss-based company specialising in trade with Guinea.

By 1972, the owners of the two companies were ready to sell. The French government decided that, as a first step towards Africanization, purchase by a French company was in order. It took the necessary steps, and in 1973 a newly founded company, SOPACIA, bought – at a cost estimated at around £7-8m – both SECMA and COMACICO. As the next step, SOPACIA sold off most of its film theatres, while remaining the principal film distributor. However, the rival companies, AFRAM and SOCOPRINT, continued to expand their efforts, and African states remained hostile. SOPACIA, although in fact making heavy losses, was as hated as the old duopoly had been. After a further restructuring, which led to the formation of the Union Africaine du Cinéma (UAC), the French interests were finally Africanized by being handed over to a consortium set up in the meantime by the Organisation of Francophone African States: the Consortium

Interafricain de Distribution Cinématographique (CIDC). This was intended to create a common market among the fourteen states. Also set up at the same time was a second organisation, the Centre Interafricain de Production de Films (CIPROFILMS), based in Ouagadougou, and from 1978 under the direction of the Niger filmmaker, Inoussa Ousseini.

The original intention was that the profits made by the distribution company, CIDC, should be used to fund African film production, through the parallel pan-African production organisation, CIPROFILMS. However, almost inevitably, the shift in ownership did nothing to overcome the unequal economic forces at work in the world distribution of films, and, in any case, things did not go smoothly among the fourteen states involved. CIDC did not make a profit. Most states did not reform their tax structures to allow the common market for films to come into operation, nor did they pay their contributions to CIDC. Many national cinema organisations saw distribution as a purely commercial operation, and in true bureaucratic fashion were uninterested in the cultural role of finding an audience for African films in Africa. The fact that, in most African states, film – like television – is the responsibility of a Minister of Information, rather than a Minister of Culture, merely exacerbated matters. At the same time, many local exhibitors refused to show African films – although many of those which were properly distributed achieved commercial success. There is a market for African films in Africa, as shown by the packed audiences in the largest cinemas in Ougadougou during the FESPACO festival. However, Burkina Faso is a country which has sponsored film activities of all kinds for over 25 years, and even here, once the festival is over, the cinemas revert to showing the standard imported product.

CIDC did not take on the cultural role it might have been expected to adopt. It had only 59 African films among the 1200 titles it distributed (barely 5%), when, in 1984, having lost the confidence of African filmmakers, its operations virtually came to a halt. Once more, the market was vulnerable to Hollywood films, now distributed by AFRAM through SOCOPRINT, which has shown no interest in handling films made by Africans. As Manthia Diawara has noted, in 1992 there were more American films shown in Dakar than French films, and all the manœuvring during the 1970s and early 1980s had come to nothing.[12]

The French Ministry of Cooperation's intervention

Filmmaking in francophone West Africa has multiple sources.[13] The documentary work of the French ethnographer, Jean Rouch, from the

1950s in Niger and the Ivory Coast had a great impact on those who worked with him. He encouraged his assistants to make films themselves (at a time when African Ministries of Information still preferred to use French technicians), and thereby helped launch the careers of Alassane and Ganda, two Niger filmmakers who did not attend film school but went on to make feature-length films. The need for newsreels and official documentaries by the fourteen state governments was met largely by the French government through the Consortium Audiovisuel International (CAI), which, from the early 1960s, provided basic equipment for filming in Africa, and set up post-production facilities in Paris. This arrangement was frustrating for the African documentary filmmakers (most of them Ministry of Information bureaucrats), since they were unable to edit their work. However, it did have the important consequence of provoking African government interest in filmmaking. Many states became financially involved when African filmmakers, following the example set by Sembene with the first true African feature-length film, *Mandabi* (*The Money Order*), in 1968, turned to fictional feature film production. As the states acquired television facilities in the 1960s and 1970s, these too became a focus for filmmaking activities. Many future feature filmmakers gained their first experiences in this way, making short propaganda films for their national governments.

However, the key to an understanding of film production in francophone West Africa is the role of the French Ministry of Cooperation, which, in 1963, set up a Bureau of Cinema, which for the next sixteen years played a predominant role in fostering filmmaking.[14] The Ministry was also responsible for CAI, but its most lasting impact was through the work of the Bureau, under the direction of Jean-René Débrix, who had previously worked in an administrative capacity at the French national film school, the Institut des Hautes Etudes Cinématographiques (IDHEC). The effort is a paradoxical one, since it is clear that the Ministry was not aiming to sponsor a commercially viable African film industry, producing works for conventional distribution to African film audiences in the existing network of film theatres. Instead, it set out to offer Africans a means of cultural expression, and at the same time to deepen their awareness of the filmmaking process through direct involvement with a professional technician in the editing of their work. In retrospect, the efforts of the Ministry must be judged as a unique, remarkable and highly controversial experiment in neocolonialism. In all, around 200 short, medium and feature-length films – the bulk of which were on 16mm – were made by African filmmakers before the scheme as such was discontinued, on the insistence of the African governments involved, in 1980. However, by this time – given the increasing political awareness demonstrated by African filmmakers – the scheme had already become something of an embarrassment to the French government, and funding was reduced year by year from 1974 onwards. Souleymane Cissé's *Finye* (*The Wind*, 1982), a forceful study of the methods used by African military regimes, which was to be edited at the Bureau, promised to cause considerable political problems for the Ministry, but, by the time its shooting had been completed, the Bureau had been closed.

Assistance from the Bureau of Cinema was not given to states or organisations, but to individual African filmmakers applying on a personal basis in Paris. The stated aim of the Bureau was to make no discrimination: anyone wishing to direct a film could apply, and, if the project was feasible, it would be funded. Funding could be obtained by a filmmaker on the basis of a script, in which case the Bureau would act as producer. However, the preferred option was to fund films for which footage had already been at least partially shot. In return for the funding, the Ministry acquired the non-commercial rights which were bought at a higher than normal price (30 000 francs for a feature film, instead of the 7-8000 francs offered to French filmmakers). This allowed the French government to distribute the films produced to educational and non-commercial organisations in France, and also to its cultural centres in Africa. No effort was made to relate this scheme to the existing commercial film distribution set-up in Africa, with the result that the commercial rights given to the filmmakers were worthless, since their films had no access to the market.

The scheme was in many ways generous, but it allowed no salary for the filmmaker personally, causing considerable hardship when the filmmaker had to live in Paris to collaborate on the editing. Often no cash at all changed hands, since the money was to be used essentially to fund the editing (with a professional freelance technician) at the Bureau's offices in Paris, and the subsequent post-production work. Moreover, given the expense of film production in general, the sum offered could never cover the full cost of the film's production. Indeed, the whole operation was underfunded, with, for example, only three to four weeks allocated for editing. Officially, there was no censorship – the Bureau funded all projects submitted to it (an easy decision, since it controlled the chances of the film being shown). The only project known to have been rejected by the Bureau was Sembene's overtly political medium-length film, *La Noire de...* (*Black Girl*, 1966), relating the tragic experience of an African maid taken to France by the French family for whom she worked.[15] After the film had been independently completed, the Ministry did, however, purchase the rights, presumably to control its distribution both in

France and in Africa. This was a tactic also adopted with other independently-produced politically aware works: Sembene's *Emitaï* (*God of Thunder*, 1971), Med Hondo's *Soleil O* (*O Sun*, 1969) and *Les bicots-nègres, vos voisins* (*Arabs and Niggers, Your Neighbours*, 1973) and Sidney Sokhona's *Nationalité: Immigré* (*Nationality: Immigrant*, 1975).[16]

The result of the Ministry of Cooperation's involvement with African filmmakers was a bizarre situation: a personal – at times almost "home-movie"-style – cinema, in which the filmmaker was the total author (by necessity, writer, director and producer, and occasionally leading actor as well). It was an African cinema conceived and finished in Paris, sometimes by someone who had spent three years studying filmmaking in Europe, but on occasion by someone with virtually no filmmaking experience at all; an African cinema readily available through the Ministry's excellent archives in Paris, but for which there was no commercial distribution in Africa; an African cinema which could be seen by Africans only in French cultural centres in West Africa. It is not by chance that the two men generally recognised as the greatest of black African filmmakers, the Moscow-trained Sembene and Souleymane Cissé, have been among the sternest critics of the Ministry of Cooperation's activities.

The current scene

Since this particular Ministry of Cooperation system ended in 1980, film production in francophone West Africa has taken on the same pattern as independent filmmaking elsewhere in Africa. The filmmaker seeks to put together funding from a variety of sources: personal resources, private investment, government aid, distributors' advances, contributions from foreign television companies, the participation of the French Ministry of Cooperation, and so on. As early as 1966, Sembene experienced the problem of working with a foreign producer when he made *The Money Order* in collaboration with the French Centre National de la Cinématographie (CNC), subsequently noting that "Europeans often have a conception of Africa that is not ours".[17] Today, the greatest potential threat comes not from government organisations, but from the impact of European festivals and television companies. It is not a question of censorship, but a more subtle – perhaps even unconscious – influence, leading the filmmaker to shape his film to suit the preferences of a European, rather than an African, audience. As Férid Boughedir has noted,[18] since the success of Souleymane Cissé's *Yeelen* (*The Light*, 1987), which won the Prix du Jury at the Cannes Film Festival, there has been a marked preference shown for the exotic, for films which match the European myth of

Africa as a place of mystery and magic. The European success of Ouedraogo's superbly crafted first three films – *Yam daabo* (*The Choice*, 1986), *Yaaba* (*Grandmother*, 1989) and *Tilaï* (1990) – is surely not unconnected with the fact that they are set in a timeless African pastoral world, totally remote from the dirt, noise and squalour of any large African city. By contrast, African films which offer a clear politically committed image of present-day Africa, or explore the realities of colonization receive scant European attention. Sembene's *Guelwaar* (1992) had only a limited release in France, while his impassioned political assault on colonialism, *Camp de Thiaroye* (*Camp Thiaroye*, 1988), was refused by the Cannes Film Festival and has received no distribution at all in France. The latter film, it may be recalled, is a rare example of a film deliberately made without any European involvement, being, instead, a coproduction between three African national film corporations: Société Nouvelle de Production Cinématographique (SNPC, Senegal), Société Anonyme Tunisienne de Production et d'Expansion (SATPEC, Tunisia) and Entreprise Nationale de Production Cinématographique (ENAPROC, Algeria).

The French Ministry of Cooperation no longer receives individual would-be filmmakers in its Paris offices, preferring to deal more directly with African governments and intergovernmental organisations, such as OCAM. Its immediate involvement with African filmmaking now takes the form of participation in the production costs of 35mm features destined for the conventional international market – it participated, for example, in the production of *The Light* and in Ouedraogo's first three feature films. The Ministry continues its overt policy of avoiding censorship, helping to fund Hondo's anti-colonial epic, *Sarraounia* (1986), for example. However, what the French government gives, it can also take away. When *Sarraounia* was released in Paris – the market in which it is most likely to recover its costs – it suffered a virtual boycott. Discussing the film in Paris in 1988, Hondo claimed that this was organised by the French Foreign Ministry, which set out to kill the prospects of a film which had the apparent support of the Ministry of Cooperation, but could be deemed offensive to the French military.

The French Ministry of Cooperation's activities continue to affect African cinema at all levels. It still supports its irreplaceable archive of early African filmmaking, but the control of this has now been transferred to an educational organisation, the Association Universitaire pour le Développement, l'Education et la Communication en Afrique et dans le Monde (AUDECAM). It has also recently sponsored a dictionary of African cinema, listing all the films made in what it deems its "sphere of competence", which naturally includes all 33 countries which were former French colonies in Africa and the

West Indies, but – interestingly – also takes in Angola, Mozambique and Zaïre.[19] The intervention in African filmmaking over the past 30 years of the French Ministry of Cooperation has been controversial, but its impact in shaping the context of the African filmmaker has undoubtedly been greater than that of any African government or organisation. Without question, it served to stimulate interest in cinema in a whole generation of African intellectuals, and prompted the support and recognition of the cinema's cultural role on the part of at least some African governments.

Notes

[1] Anthony D Smith, *State and Nation in the Third World: The Western State and African Nationalism* (Brighton: Wheatsheaf Books, 1983).

[2] Among the many books on African literature in European languages, two extremely useful studies are Dorothy S Blair, *African Literature in French: A history of creative writing in French from West and Equatorial Africa* (Cambridge; London; New York; Melbourne: Cambridge University Press, 1976) and Abiola Irele, *The African Experience in Literature and Ideology* (London: Heinemann, 1981).

[3] For further discussion of this point, see Roy Armes, *Third World Film Making and the West* (Berkeley; Los Angeles; London: University of California Press, 1987): 35-49.

[4] Karin Barber, "Popular Arts in Africa", *African Studies Review* 30: 3 (September 1987): 1-78.

[5] Terence Ranger, "The Invention of Tradition in Colonial Africa", in Eric Hobsbawm and Terence Ranger (eds), *The Invention of Tradition* (Cambridge: Cambridge University Press, 1983): 211-262.

[6] See Chris Stapleton and Chris May, *African All-Stars: The Pop Music of a Continent* (London: Quartet Books, 1987) and Ronnie Graham, *Stern's Guide to Contemporary African Music* (London: Zwan Publications and Off the Record Press, 1988).

[7] For a fuller discussion see Lizbeth Malkmus and Roy Armes, *Arab and African Film Making* (London; New Jersey: Zed Books, 1991): 3-62.

[8] Patrick Clawson, "The development of capitalism in Egypt", *Khamsin* 9 (1981): 77-116.

[9] Keyan Tomaselli, *The Cinema of Apartheid: Race and Class in South African Film* (London: Routledge, 1989).

[10] Barber: 73.

[11] This whole section is based on Pierre Roitfeld, *Afrique Noire*

Francophone (Paris: Unifrance, 1980).

[12] Manthia Diawara, *African Cinema: Politics & Culture* (Bloomington and Indianapolis: Indiana University Press, 1992): 115.

[13] In addition to Diawara, see also Nwachukwu Frank Ukadike, *Black African Cinema* (Los Angeles: University of California Press, 1994), and Dhruba Gupta, *African Cinema: A View from India* (Jamshedpur: Celluloid Chapter, 1994).

[14] In addition to Diawara, Ukadike and Gupta, see Claire Andrade-Watkins, "France's Bureau of Cinema: Financial and Technical Assistance between 1961 and 1977: Operations and Implications for African Cinema", *Framework* 38/39 (1992): 27-46.

[15] Diawara: 26.

[16] Ibid: 34.

[17] Ousmane Sembene, quoted in ibid: 32.

[18] Férid Boughedir, unpublished conference paper, "African Cinema and Ideology: Tendencies and Evolution", delivered at the Africa and the History of Cinematic Ideas Conference, London, National Film Theatre, September 1995.

[19] L'Association des Trois Mondes, *Dictionnaire du cinéma africain, Tome 1* (Paris: Éditions Karthala, 1991).

Nation, inter-nation and narration in Ousmane Sembene's films

Philip Rosen

Introduction: canons, auteurs and Sembene

There is a slight peculiarity to any discussion of conceptions of nation in the films of Ousmane Sembene. He has achieved the status of an *inter*nationally canonical filmmaker, outside as well as inside Africa. In the United States, for example, his films are invariably shown at the New York Film Festival; he is celebrated in metropolitan newspapers, as well as non-academic film magazines; and *Camp de Thiaroye* (*Camp Thiaroye*, 1988) was cablecast on Cinemax during Black History Month of 1995. On a more scholarly level, such diverse figures as Fredric Jameson, arguably the pre-eminent Marxist cultural theorist in the United States, and Clyde Taylor, a leading US critical authority on international black cinema, have used Sembene as a crucial examplar in key theoretical essays. Sembene is now not only a common topic at academic conferences, but also sometimes an honoured guest at them, including at least one which was solely on his work.[1]

Such international recognition for an African filmmaker has to be a step forward, but we have also learned the importance of being self-conscious about the rationales for canons. Sembene is indeed one of the crucial figures in world cinema of the past three decades. To say this usually involves a claim about the distinctiveness or representativeness of a filmmaker's aesthetic or signifying modes, and I will discuss aspects of these in this essay. However, it is also important to understand these modes as strategies devised within the historic, public, economic and technical situations in which a filmmaker finds himself/herself. This is the real film-historical utility of emphasising figures such as Griffith in the 1910s; Renoir in the 1930s; the constellation of international art cinema directors of the 1950s; Godard in the 1960s; and so on. Therefore, insofar as my understanding of Sembene is historical and "situational", it is implicitly in comparison to the very different situations and strategies of his international contemporaries such as Fassbinder (critical-national European art cinema), and Spielberg or Zemeckis (Hollywood's postmodern consumerist cinema of attractions).

It is of course of supreme importance that Sembene is also known, correctly, as a pioneering and self-conscious "Senegalese" and "African" narrativist. However, it must be understood that there is a sense in which the material situation of his filmmaking has always been international and intercontinental. He came to film already established as a francophone novelist and, while maintaining a pugnacious intellectual independence, could work through French neocolonial institutions aimed at creating a "francophone" cultural sphere in such as way as to enlist their material support for his filmmaking. The paradoxical result was anti-colonialist and arguably nationalist films, such as *La Noire de...* (*Black Girl*, 1966), supported by French resources. This has been a necessity right up to *Guelwaar* (1992), whose credits describe it as a French-Senegalese coproduction, but whose context is a globalizing media age, since such diverse partners as Germany's Westdeutscher Rundfunk Köln (WDR) and Britain's Channel 4 Television participated. On all these counts – critical success and canonization, film-historical significance, and infrastructural support for filmmaking – Sembene has therefore always been an international figure.[2]

Yet, as Nwachukwu Frank Ukadike has recently re-emphasised, the question of the nation-state has been one of the nodal problems for Sembene and his African filmmaking contemporaries. Ukadike argues that the work of key figures in the first generation of sub-Saharan filmmakers (Sembene and Med Hondo are his chief examples) is intimately tied to the concerns of such diverse anti-colonialist political thinkers as Nkrumah, Mondlane and several others, especially Fanon.[3] In some sense, Sembene's narrative work has always manifested awareness of the heritage of radical political theorization involving a militant, although often ambivalent, appropriation of the idea of the nation for anticolonialist struggles. It seems appropriate that one of his more recent films, *Camp Thiaroye*, is based on an incident recounted in Keita Fodeba's "African Dawn": Fanon himself held up this poem as a model work in his seminal essay, "On National Culture".[4] It is, however, crucial to add that all Sembene's films were made in a post-liberation period. What happens to the concept of the nation after a national liberation struggle? One of the basic premises and projects of Sembene's film work has been direct and indirect interrogations of the concept of the nation as an anticolonial concept in a postcolonial world.

However, perhaps the seeming paradox of Sembene's internationality and his situational concern with nationness is actually a productive contradiction. I would begin by noting that, even in African national liberation theory and practice, nationness is in some sense defined by inter-nationness. When a colonized "people" is conceived as the nation, it can only be labelled such in opposition – economic, political, cultural and/or military – to a colonizing nation-state. Furthermore, this determinant "externality" of the nation is intricated with "internal" divisions of class and cultural experience. Thus, political and cultural leaderships of anticolonial nations and newly liberated nation-states tended strongly to be drawn from that minority of individuals selected by the colonizing system for multilingual education and multicultural experiences. Even the most nationalist leaderships were sociologically separated from the very masses of people they named as the nation.

The first important consequence to be derived from this is that the nation as a concept serves as a place-holder for a desired "internal" political unity superseding local divisions of class, caste, ethnicity, gender and so on. The concept of nation therefore foregrounds the problem of social and political collectivity. The second consequence is that these divisions were also overdetermined by social and educational categories linked with *inter*nationality. For leading African anti-colonialist theorists and political leaders, a crucial problem became the relation of such political and cultural-intellectual élites to other components of their "nations". Fanon's "On National Culture" is a classic consideration of this relation to some of its "internal" and international complexities, but it is just one of many produced in national liberation theory.[5]

Sembene's films explore the divisions as well as the unities generated by the simultaneity of nation and inter-nation. A central *representational* issue in them is how to conceive and configure collective groupings and collective identities in order to make them available for interrogation by the resources of *film* narrative. For the nation is ultimately a conception of collectivity, albeit one both privileged and problematised by the recent political history of Africa.[6]

In this essay I will treat Sembene as an auteur, considering his films as a "synchronic" whole, but with some interest in shifts and developments in his narrative strategies. Sembene is a special type of auteur, one of those remarkable intellectual-cultural practitioners who emerged from the generation of African national liberation struggles into the post-liberation period with an internationally cosmopolitan experience and cachet.[7] From his anti-colonialist use of filmmaking resources made available by French neocolonial spheres to his current global recognition, the issue of the nation is both initiated and problematised by the institutional interchanges between nation and inter-nation at the heart of Sembene's filmic situations. These are inseparable from the political, historical and sociocultural issues manifested in the films.

How to situate Sembene? Is he something new and culturally

specific, a *griot* emerging from "the people" of national liberation theory, but for an age of mass media? Or is he something more familiar, an international auteur who gains his currency from recognition in Western art-house and university circuits? The answer is both, simultaneously. In his material, cultural and intellectual situation, and in his cinema, nation and inter-nation are mutual conditions for one another.

Journeys and spaces

Guelwaar, Sembene's most recent film, is set in Senegal. One character, Barthélémy, has lived in France and has taken on French citizenship. (This has historic reverberations in Senegal's privileged colonial relation to France.) Barthélémy, the son of the deceased economic nationalist, Pierre Henri Thioune (called by the honorific title, "Guelwaar"), takes two key journeys: one unseen by the audience, from the neocolonial metropole back to Senegal, and one which is dramatised, from his family's Christian home in Thiès to a rural Muslim village in the region, in search of his father's misplaced corpse. During this second journey, his escort, police commandant Gora, describes him to the village head as a white black man. Barthélémy denigrates Africa and Senegal in comparison to France, and he communicates only in French, rather than in Wolof. Yet, when he returns to the village as part of the entire Christian community of Thiès, Barthélémy undergoes a somewhat schematic narrative reversal and reasserts his Senegalese nationality. In one more twist, however, the change in this binational traveller-citizen positions him to protest, correctly, against internal Senegalese corruption stemming from the very fact of foreign aid, and not just from the misuse of food-aid money.

Barthélémy is not the central character of the narrative, which does not have a single focal protagonist, but his situation illustrates something general about Sembene's film narratives and treatments of sub-Saharan nationality. This is a constant awareness and play of geopolitical spaces and languages. As structures, both are actually determinate and delimiting; as processes, both are potentially fluid and unlimiting.

The kind of narrative event that negotiates geopolitical spaces in Sembene's films is the journey. Journeys proliferate in them, although not always with the positive change of Barthélémy. Journeys can in themselves have initiating narrative consequences, as in *Black Girl* and *Camp Thiaroye*, or sometimes simply *are* narrative consequences, as in the enforced dispersions of *Emitaï* (*God of Thunder*, 1971) and *Ceddo* (1976). Such journeys provide a narrative strategy for figuring the nation, whether critically or promotionally, in relation to internations and sub-national regions and groups.

Two categories of journeys echo and inflect one another, while tracing two levels of core-periphery geographies. One is external to the nation, as in Barthélémy's journey to and from France, and one is internal, as in his journey to the Muslim village. As we will see shortly, both external and internal journeys experience language as a pressure point, where space intersects social and cultural collectivity. As a consequence, distortion through translation, misunderstanding and even silence becomes as constant in Sembene's films as journeys.

In these films, therefore, journeys form and inform narrative space with sociopolitical meanings and hence narrative change – that is, temporality. In Sembene's work as a whole, one can distinguish three overlapping modes in such formings and informings. Firstly, the central narrative strand may be organised as a journey. This mode is especially strong in certain of his earlier films, such as *Borom Sarret* (1963) and *Black Girl*, which are focalized around central protagonists. Here the spatial displacements of a single major character govern much of the narrative progression. These displacements appear subjectivized via point-of-view narrative strategies, and yet they are heavily allegorized in more collective, political and social terms as the divisions between wealth and poverty, power and weakness.

A second mode of Sembene's journey formations makes journeys less the central strand of a narrative than important elements of a more complex narrative tissue; and yet, these journeys clearly retain something of a decisive or determining quality. This mode tended to develop as Sembene's filmic resources and narratives became more elaborate, and they may be associated with his development of stories involving larger ensemble casts after 1966. In *Mandabi* (*The Money Order*, 1968), a money order precipitates the disastrous days of the would-be patriarch of piety and polygamy, the none-too-bright Ibrahima Dieng. Not only must he take a series of wearying internal journeys to other areas of the city, and not only is he the target of an aggressive internal journey from the countryside by his offended sister, but also the film registers a determining external journey through a flashback motivated by the letter of the dutiful nephew in Paris, the source of the disruptive money order. Similarly, in *Xala* (*The Curse*, 1974), there is a point where the film elaborates the journey of El Hadji Abdoukader Beye *to* the countryside in search of a marabout who can lift the curse of impotence laid on him by a band of beggars. The beggars themselves have converged *from* the countryside on his place of business and home in the city, in order to wreak the revenge of the impoverished swindled out of their just share.

Camp Thiaroye might be placed in this mode, since the entire narrative is a consequence of a journey to the European war, and it

31

also includes internal journeys of the soldiers to the town and of Diatta's kin to see him at the camp. Furthermore, in *Guelwaar*, the internal journey of the Christians to retrieve the body of Pierre from the rural Muslim cemetery has several productive consequences besides Barthélémy's transformation, including a partial but engaging analysis of generational and ethno-religious divisions within the Senegalese nation by Muslim and Christian elders, and the epilogue, where Christian youths destroy foreign food-aid in a utopian presentiment of a 21st century Africa.

In a third mode, some films seem to decentralize such travellings with respect to the story progression, to the point where key journeys can become unspoken and unnoted by characters; and yet, they turn out to be devastatingly central to the narrative's meanings. An extraordinary example occurs in *Ceddo*. The enforced but unseen external journey of slaves, which figures the world-historical, disastrous diaspora of Africans to the Americas, is ignored by all speaking characters, but is strikingly marked for the audience by the non-diegetic sound of African-American spirituals from an otherwise unrepresented future.[8] In fact, despite *Ceddo*'s microcosmic spatial and temporal restriction to one ethnicity in one village in one historical conjuncture, it actually includes or implies a complex web of such journeys. The verbose presence of the imam, as well as the silent visual presences of the Catholic priest and the European trader, are consequences of already-accomplished external journeys of invasion. Some of the *ceddo* go into voluntary exile to avoid conversion. There is even something like internal journeying, with a privileged destination, namely the ritual space of individual combat established by the heroic *ceddo* challenger. Princess Dior becomes the agent and inspiration for collective rebellion only after a journey from the village to this peripheral space. In addition, except for the utopian ending, the historical losers – the *ceddo*, and the king and his court – are those who do not journey. A less startling but still telling example of the decentralized yet somehow determinant journey occurs in *God of Thunder*, where the village conscripts are forced on a collective journey to the European war.

Languages and nations

In *Camp Thiaroye*, made eighteen years later, it is as if the conscripts of *God of Thunder* return, but now as accomplished soldiers being demobilized at war's end. Yet, interestingly, this film is a Senegalese-Algerian-Tunisian co-production (co-directed with Thierno Faty Sow), and the draftees are not just Diola or Senegalese, but from all over France's colonial Africa. Among other things, the film interrogates some potential consequences of such journeys, rather than their causes. However, the most knowledgeable elaboration of those consequences is signalled through the imagistic, Leone-like flashback images and Fassbinder-like snippets of the song, "Lili Marleen". These bits of international stylistics in this international African coproduction about something like inter-regional and inter-ethnic African commonalities suggest that a supersession of nationality informs the film.

Yet, there is a certain implicit tension around any imputed pan-Africanist internationality. These stylistic techniques are associated with the memory of the only character who seems fully cognizant of the narrative's Césaire-like parallel between European concentration camps and colonialist practices in Africa.[9] The character possessing this knowledge is the emblematically-named enlisted man, Pays. His knowledge remains ineffective for he is mute, in contrast to the multilingual, internationally cosmopolitan intellectual, Sergeant Diatta.

The multilingual Diatta has a fairly direct predecessor in (unsurprisingly) *God of Thunder*. In this film, an earlier, less complex Sembene sergeant, Badgi, translates – very loosely – French officers' threats and speeches to the unspeaking conscripts and the anonymous village women who turn out to be the anticolonialist heroes of the story. However, in *Camp Thiaroye*, the sergeant is less an unquestioning subaltern than a complex cross-border figure. On the one hand, he takes pride in his service in the French Army and is socioculturally cosmopolitan (he knows Western literature and classical music, and corresponds with his French wife); consequently, however, he is well aware of French racism and identifies (up to a point) with the rebellious enlisted men. In *Guelwaar*, on the other hand, a more indigenous military subaltern, police commandant Gora, has the linguistic gift suitable for *internal* journeys, while the external traveller, Barthélémy, and the non-travelling villagers need his translation services.

Who has language, and who is silent? A colonized subject who can translate is one who has crossed some of the most pertinent borders, made some journeys; and therefore he or she is usually at some social, economic or geopolitical advantage. The one who cannot translate and move freely among languages is at a comparative disadvantage. The question of mastery of language, of translation and mistranslation, is as universal in Sembene's films as the motif of the journey. Translation should be understood broadly here, restricted not just to verbal facility from Wolof or Diola to French and back. Sometimes it appears as the question of literacy, as when Sembene himself plays the minor figure of the scribe who translates from speech to writing at the post office in *The Money Order*.

Sometimes translation is shown to be the very privilege of speech itself. This is foregrounded in *Ceddo* not only by the figurative and proverbial utterances of characters, but also by the use of *jottali*, wherein the praise-singer/*griot* has the duty of ceremonially mediating the public speech of the nobles. (The only one who effectively bypasses *jottali* is the immigrant imam who speaks Wolof as a foreign tongue.) In West Africa, however, the privileges of public language and rewording claimed by the *griot* simultaneously connote the possibility of distortion, so that silence may inversely connote nobility. Thus, in *Ceddo*, the court *griot*, Jaraaf, is a self-serving political schemer, as opposed to the impoverished *ceddo griot* who (although it seems a contradiction in terms) is often silent.[10]

In Sembene's films more generally, the linguistic gift is similarly double-edged and dialectical. Invariably, those who have journeyed spatially or linguistically may misuse or become blinded in some way by their privilege. As a result, they become separated from or oppose some of the key forces motivating the narrative. Those forces are usually associated with the needs of a less articulate populace. Thus, silence and even inarticulateness can be both a mark of political oppression and a form of privileged refusal, a refusal of the privileges of language. At the very least, they suggest the material interests of the silenced in a kind of overall knowledge not available to the multilingual and international. Some variations on this aspect of Sembene's narratives include the village women of *God of Thunder*, whose ultimately determining stand for the rights flowing from their labour and from custom is never stated by one of them; the massed *ceddo* whose interests are expressed only through a spokesperson whose words will in turn be denigrated by the court *griot*; the soldiers at Thiaroye struggling to find a common language and strategy in pidgin French, but whose basic point of knowledge should be the mute Pays; and even Diouana in *Black Girl*, whose apparent inarticulateness is belied by her interior monologue.

Those in a problematic relation to language turn out to be Sembene's protagonists. They are situated collectively: nationally or, at his most expansive, pan-continentally. This link to the national is in part geographical, since they are also those least likely to travel, especially on external journeys. When they do so, as with Diouana in *Black Girl* and the enlisted men in *Camp Thiaroye*, the results can be disastrous or explosive, or both.

The translator, on the other hand, is also a mediator, situated on borders. The mediator/translator figure is situated at junctures of geo- and sociopolitical divisions of knowledge, and hence power. It is a politically ambivalent, hence flexible, narrative function which can be split into different characters (the two *griots* of *Ceddo*; Barthélémy as external traveller, Gora as internal traveller and translator in *Guelwaar*), and is available for interrogating the general fact of "national" élites and subalternity.

Nations, characters, allegories

Who journeys, who does not, and why? Who speaks, who cannot, and why? These two questions are fundamental to setting Sembene's film stories in motion, and for figuring the processes of colonial and postcolonial economic and power relationships that are among his manifest topics. The conjunction of geographical, linguistic and political divisions and identities is also a fundamental tenet of many Western nationalisms. These questions therefore suggest a concern with nationness in Sembene, but they also return us to the progressive reappropriation of the concept of the nation in national liberation movements.

This also shifts the issue to a representational one. A central task for Sembene as film narrativist becomes the representation of collectivities, for "nation" is one. The most direct proposal for understanding Sembene's representational strategies with respect to nationness, therefore, would be to treat individual characters as narrative agents that allegorize collective aspects of African life and history.

This recalls Fredric Jameson's controversial claims about "national allegory". In Jameson's conception, which is chiefly with regard to novels, this allegorization involves a relation between the private and the public: stories of individualized characters or configurations figure a broader public, collective context whose signified is national. The term "allegory" thus designates a switching or, more precisely, a translation, from one code or level of experience to another, more repressed one. Among Jameson's examples are *The Curse* and *The Money Order* in both film and novel forms. He argues they are post-national liberation fables that critically unveil the sociocultural shifts determined by the universalization of the money form. Jameson's proposal that national allegory is a typical "Third World" textual strategy almost immediately came under heavy and seemingly justified attack as prematurely homogenizing Third World experiences and literatures, and as simultaneously underestimating the heterogeneity of literatures produced in the geographical first-world.[11]

Yet, the notion of allegory as a kind of translation from manifestly individual characters to collective concerns persists in studies of non-first-world cinema. For instance, Clyde Taylor, a very different kind of thinker to Jameson, promotes a dialogic, heteroglossic "postaesthetics", involving representational methods which spectatorially and epistemologically surpass individualization. He invokes *Ceddo* as an example, praising it for a heteroglossic multiplicity that opens up spaces for the spectator to interrogate contradictions; however, part of his praise is that the film avoids merely "mechanical" allegory. For our purposes, this is a back-handed way of acknowledging the utility of the concept of allegory in these matters. In fact, for Jameson also, figures of allegorization are fluid and not monologic, split among several characters and narrative elements. Moreover, both thinkers use Sembene texts as models of non-Western signification concerned with collective representation, an arena designated by the term "allegory".[12]

Who journeys and who cannot, who speaks and who cannot? The fictional worlds of Sembene construct a web of distinctions and processes to explore these questions. However, any possible answers must always be understood in relation to the collectives of which characters are members, as well as to the impersonal, non-individual forces impinging on them. His stories often proceed through the actions, discourses and decisions of individual characters. Allegorization is thus as good an initial term as any to designate the concerns in Sembene's narratives with representational and political constructions of collectivity.

Questions of representation thus lead to the parts of the characterology which Sembene has developed in his films over the years, but they also lead to narration and filmic style. I will identify three broad narrational currents in Sembene's films, with narration conceived as the formal means by which the story-world or narrative is organised and communicated to the spectator. I will (somewhat awkwardly) call them "centrally focalized narration", "relatively focalized narration", and "decentred collective narration". In each case, I will discuss style in relation to the epistemological status of character and "allegory".

Centrally focalized narration in *Borom Sarret* and *Black Girl*

Sembene's earliest international recognition in cinema was achieved with *Borom Sarret* and *Black Girl*. A peculiar representational achievement of these remarkable films, made on shoestring budgets, is that they heavily utilize selected stylistic techniques developed in Western narrative cinema for purposes of psychologization, and yet their overall significations seem more political and sociological than psychological. As already noted, the central narrative strand in both is an individual character's journey (internal in the first, external in the second). Furthermore, both films emphasise their journey constructions by heavily focalizing their narratives around that single, more or less "national" character.

The dominant means of this focalization in *Borom Sarret* is the soundtrack, which, together with non-diegetic music, emphasises the interior monologue of the driver. In *Black Girl*, it is a complex combination of interior monologue, eyeline and point-of-view match editing, and flashbacks motivated as Diouana's memories. By long-established convention in first-world cinema, these should add up to a heavily subjectivized narration.

Sembene in fact made these films during a period in international film history when much of European art cinema aimed at pushing such conventions to their limits. Consider Alain Resnais's *La Guerre est finie* (*The War Is Over*, 1966), released in the same year as *Black Girl*, which is also a journey narrative with political subject-matter made in the French cultural sphere. For most of Resnais's film, the narration is locked into the subjectivity of an individual character. Thus, story order is almost completely determined by the concerns and perceptions of that character. Of course, it is an option in mainstream cinema to focalize in this way. Furthermore, however, Resnais ambiguates the audience's knowledge of events by pushing focalization to a greater extreme by selective blurring of the opposition between diegetic subjectivity and objectivity. (Is a given sequence of images actually happening? Does it happen at some other chronological point in the narrative? Or is it a character's fantasy?)

The War Is Over thus presents itself as devising a non-mainstream mode of representation. A Jameson would still describe it as "modernist", for it sustains the determining quality of the interiority of the individual subject. This subject remains the semantic anchor and simultaneously the key epistemological and representational problem for the narrative as a whole. Thus, political collectivities are sometimes a topic of dialogue among individual characters, but the main representational issue for the filmic narration is the status of individual consciousness.[13]

On the other hand, while Sembene's early films appear concerned with designating individual subjectivity via similar narrational impulses, they do not lock spectatorial comprehension into an individually unique set of perceptions, memories, dreams, fantasies and desires. Instead, the characters are translated into something more socially and politically generalizable. The subjectivity of a central character does seem to determine story order – the very progress of the narrative – and often achieves direct visual and sonic representation through resources of film style. Yet, the resulting narration and therefore that subjectivity are ultimately shown to be in some way insufficient to the narrational purport.

At least two convergent strategies contribute to this: the objective significance of settings, and the ultimate inadequacy of any single character as narrational and epistemological anchor. As to the first of these, I have already noted that the very concrete location *mises en scène* in *Borom Sarret* and *Black Girl* (together with the terms of the story, of course) delineate Third World urban dichotomies between wealth and impoverishment. The location shots of Paris in *The War Is Over* simply provide a place over the border from Spain to stage Diego's consciousness. However, in Sembene's early films the quasi-documentary shooting of the Dakar slums or Marseille bears the historical weight of colonial divisions which generate and impinge on characterologies. That is to say, the films are informed by a contradiction between the subjectivizing narration and a *mise en scène* whose objective and generalizing significance becomes increasingly evident. In *Borom Sarret*, for example, the affluent high-rise residential districts of Dakar, which are in stark contrast to the urban impoverishment recorded in the rest of the film, become themselves virtual subjects of the narration, and "expel" the cart driver through the agency of a policeman. Therefore, while the narration is heavily focalized around a character and his/her journey, space is almost never subjectivized as it is so elaborately in *The War Is Over*, for it still surrounds and may rise up to oppose the central character as an outside, geopolitical force, rather than as an internal perception.

This kind of narration establishes a principle important for many of Sembene's films. The film style functions in such a way as to imply awareness of "international" norms even in the most "national" films. Techniques that commonly function to promote individualizing narration in Western cinema unexpectedly but systematically lead to concerns beyond the individual. These techniques themselves therefore designate a kind of symptom of the character's limitations, and the spectator is invited to judge and position the overall situation in ways in which the central character cannot. This is because the individualized consciousness and/or practices of the protagonist divide her/him from the kinds of understanding or self-understanding that might lead to politically and individually desirable changes. Hence the focalized character turns out to be an inadequate semantic or epistemological anchor.

The consequent switch from individual to a more collective postcolonial awareness clearly bears comparison to the related operation which Jameson calls "national allegory". *Black Girl* even includes a scene and brief documentary shots of an official ceremony at a national monument to those other travellers to Europe who became Sembene protagonists in later films, the *tirailleurs sénégalais*. However, as Jameson and Taylor would caution, if this is allegory, individual characters do not stand in a simple one-for-whole, instance-for-concept relation to entire populations. How could they, given their limitations? Even the most highly centralized characters are set off against other characters by material interests and desires. This establishes another basic principle operative throughout Sembene's film work: peoples and nations will be rendered in terms of division as much as any absolute collective harmonies.

Sembene's story worlds invariably reveal a variety of interests and diegetic positionalities among characters or groups of characters within a given nation. This means that there are differential sets of knowledges and understandings within the story world, and yet none of them is necessarily all wrong. Again, it is just that none is quite sufficient to the narrative meanings as a whole. In *Borom Sarret*, a street *griot* cons the driver out of his meagre earnings, almost hypnotizing him with ridiculously irrelevant praises of glorious ancestors. The *griot* never appears again, yet his cynically functional exploitation of regional and national traditions is just as indicative as is the fact of the cart driver and his economically marginalized labour. Or rather, their *relationship* indicates a nation in the throes of a class-bound, neocolonialist, political-economic structure, and (as Jameson says of *The Money Order*) of the invasion of superficially "traditional" practices by the modern money form. In the end, despite the centrally focalized narrational techniques, it is the web of such *relationships*, together with all the other interrelationships of the film, penetrated by enforced poverty and divisions of interest and power, which signifies collective determinants.

The principle of division among the people is thus intimately related to the principle of the insufficiency of any single character in narrational knowledge, in power, and/or in a combination of the two. In a sense, therefore, if the geopolitical *mise en scène* counters and critiques the stylistic emphasis on the individual subjectivity of the central characters, other characters might be described as a second level of such "objectivity". Of course, they are also implicated in Sembene's geopolitical spaces and also shown to be sociohistorically situated agents. However, the ultimately insufficient knowledge of any individual character is a key epistemological provocation. The films imply the necessity of supra-individual, relational, collective perspectives, even as they seem to make individualized consciousness a privileged object of representation.

In *Black Girl*, the number of such characters and social and national positionalities already begins to increase, although without the expansive, quasi-novelistic characterology which will become fundamental to Sembene's later films. Examples include Diouana's politically articulate yet masculinist boyfriend; her mother who (together with Diouana) helps initiate the exploration of silence in Sembene's films; others from the Dakar slums; and all the French

39

bourgeois characters. Whether their narrative presences are strong or relatively peripheral, these other characters figure a set of interrelationships which "allegorically" situate the experiences and consciousness of the title character, whose subjectivity is so emphasised by stylistic means.

The French wife is worth discussing as an especially rich, complex figure interestingly related to configurations of journey and language, as well as to the principle of division crucial in Sembene's œuvre. In directly oppressive contact with Diouana more than any other character, she can be read as a class figure, not only because she is herself implicated in a bourgeois colonialist family, but also because, like a good petit bourgeois functionary, she is a kind of subaltern who governs the colonized labourer in the domestic sphere. However, there is also an odd and inverted parallel between her and Diouana, which suggests a division of interests even within the French bourgeoisie. Her oppression of Diouana contributes to her own oppression by her bourgeois husband – who is himself a neocolonial functionary serving larger interests. Adding gender to the mix of class and colonial exploitations, one might say that it is her job to mediate, activate or "translate" the power of her husband and his superiors to Diouana. The film thus suggests that bourgeois and colonialist power is manifested in a patriarchal order. However, as the Frenchwoman is in an uneven and contradictory relation to this constellation of power relations, she is never able to articulate or analyse her own resentments, so that there are echoes in her of the silence of the oppressed.

The film is most concerned with Diouana's greater oppression and limitations, and so it provides direct access to Diouana's consciousness and hers alone. Nevertheless, the wife points up the unspoken structural echoes throughout the fictional world, right down the line of power relations emanating from the exploitation of newly liberated Senegal by French economic interests (the Dakar slums; the material interests of the French ingenuously expressed in polite bourgeois conversation), to the wife's position (her frustrated submission expressed in arguments with her husband, displaced into bullying her children and Diouana), to Diouana's consciousness (her initial desires to journey to France; her admiration for the French family; the very magazines she reads). On the most general, allegorizing level, this suggests that the ultimate analytic priority of the postcolonial experience is international, material class relations, as intersected by patriarchal structures. These will be central in any account of the new nation or, for that matter, the new individual citizen.

Oppressed and yet aligned with oppressive forces, she is in some surprising ways structurally comparable to the subaltern sergeant-translators in the later "military" films (*God of Thunder*; *Camp Thiaroye*). In *Black Girl*, the mediator/translator figure has not fully developed into the rich intersection of journey and language of the later films. However, the wife is the key subaltern, and the gender components of her position indicate that the characteristics of the mediator-translator could be combined into a complexly liminal figure.

Relatively focalized narration: *The Money Order* and *The Curse*

By the late 1960s, narrational strategies and the characterology of Sembene's films had undergone something of a development. This is most obviously marked by the fact that point-of-view camerawork and interior monologue techniques tend to be greatly attenuated, so that the impression of subjective narration which they articulated in previous films is virtually eliminated. For purposes of discussion, we may divide his newer narrational strategies into two broad currents, which I am calling relatively focalized narrations and decentred collective narrations. Relatively focalized narration governs the postcolonial satires, *The Money Order* and *The Curse*, as well as the short film, *Taaw* (1970).

In these films, the narration is still strongly focalized, at least in the sense that they are dominated by the problems of an individual character whose difficulties reveal a network of impersonal economic, social and political relationships: Ibrahima Dieng in *The Money Order*; the title character in *Taaw*; and El Hadji Abdoukader Beye in *The Curse*. However, the subjectivizing *stylistic* elements of the early films are only occasionally employed. Motivation of editing and camerawork as optical point-of-view, interior monologue or dream is no longer basic to the narrational principles of the whole film, and is instead reserved for special moments. A formal result is that focalization becomes more dependent on organising story order and presentation according to the problems and trajectory of the central character, while the style seems much more "objective".

The "allegorizing" impulse of the centrally focalized narratives had operated narrationally through two dynamic formal contradictions. Firstly, a film style emphasising the subjectivity of an individual character confronts concrete, sociopolitically significant settings that lead the viewer towards social relationships. Secondly, the consciousness of the protagonists confronts the subjectivities of other, stylistically peripheral characters. With the relatively focalized narrations of *The Money Order* and *The Curse*, the first is de-emphasised, and the second made more overt. It is true that the semi-documentary location shooting of Dakar in these films – especially *The Money Order* – maintains the striking sense of socio-economic and political geographies of the earlier films. However, since subjectivizing stylistics are now more muted, the challenges to the central character by other characters become more direct and merciless. A central character such as El Hadji Abdoukader Beye in *The Curse* may even be shown up in dialogue by others, such as the daughter and the beggars.

In fact, there are now occasional and sometimes sudden departures from the dominant focalization of the films, and we are shown things which the main character could not know. Examples in *The Curse* include the mercenary discussions among the party-goers, the wedding night conversation between mother and daughter, and scenes among the beggars in El Hadji's absence. Such brief glimpses of the acts and perceptions of other characters may still afford only partial knowledge. (It is so with the party-goers but not with the beggars, who hold the hermeneutic and sociopolitical secret of the narrative.) However, any departures from the main focalization certainly reinforce a sense of the insufficiencies of the central character's consciousness. Something implicit in the method of the earlier films is now more explicit: subjectivity itself is ultimately conceived as an objective sociopolitical force among other objective sociopolitical forces shaping and limiting the centrality of any individual subject.

The inadequacy of individualized consciousness thus remains one of Sembene's major thematic and formal concerns. In his earliest films, Sembene almost completely ordered the story according to the concerns and knowledge of a single central character, and had reinforced this with some fairly extreme forms of stylistic focalization, but the point was to establish the principle that the pretensions and interests of any character as an individual must be shown up as false and insufficient. "Allegorizing" comprehension was thus provoked by the implicit relativization of an apparently centred narrative.

In the later, relatively focalized category, there is more distance from the central characters than was possible by the centrally focalized method. One consequence is that the satiric possibilities of limited consciousness tend to come forward. The whole method might even be described as a distancing tactic, not only in a Brechtian sense, but also in other narrational senses. For, while the films appear to present their stories as following the concerns of one central character, they openly provide the spectator with multiple perspectives from which to judge that character.

This suggests the implications of this narrational method and characterology for the exploration of collective, social or "national" formations. Social and political interrelations may be represented as the interaction among narrational *perspectives* anchored in the interests and limitations of different characters. This insistence on social interaction merges with satiric tone in such a way as to be an excellent instrument for a clear, even fable-like critique of the new formations of nation-state that followed the political liberation of Senegal and much of Africa. "Distancing" in this sense can even mean that the narration occasionally steps outside the narrative. The most direct example of this is the agitprop montage which concludes *The Money Order*. As Dieng and his wives express puzzlement at the postman's insistence that they must change things, the montage completes the revelation of the insufficiencies of poor Dieng's consciousness by resuming brief fragments of the preceding story that demonstrate the necessity for change.

However, if multiple perspectives suggest the tensions and divisions that make up a collective formation, it is not clear that focalization around a central character, whether predominantly conveyed through subjective stylistics or through story order, is logically necessary. Why not directly represent collectivities? This leads us to the third narrational current in Sembene's films, and formally his most radical.

Decentred collective narration

In films released after 1966, Sembene's scripts demanded an ever-increasing number of characters. This enabled increasingly complex explorations of social and national differentiations, positionalities, limitations and divisions. However, at a certain point, the large-cast strategy turned out to be more than a quantitative change. The films crossed a "qualitative" threshold, and one can identify a new method of filmic narration, which I call decentred collective narration. In these films, Sembene reconfigured aspects of his representational modes of collectivity, division and politics, which remain constant concerns in all his films.

Decentred collective narration was first developed in his historical films of the 1970s, *God of Thunder* and *Ceddo*, but extends into his later films, *Camp Thiaroye* and *Guelwaar*. Among these, *Ceddo* and *Guelwaar* stand out for their settings. *Ceddo* is Sembene's only historical film to date which is not a testament to anti-colonial struggles within living memory, while *Guelwaar* – which returns to some of the tone, if not all of the substantive analyses, of the pre-*Ceddo* sociopolitical satires – is the first Sembene film with a contemporary setting that fits into the category of decentred collective narration.

This category is defined by two fundamental but simple principles. The first is negative: whole narratives are not organised by focalization around an individual character as they are in the two previous categories. The second is that at least some collectivities are visually, sonically and narratively presented as such. This means that the interests, limitations and difficulties of collectivities are no longer implicit. Instead of being signified in an aesthetically interesting tension with an apparently individualized narrative method, as they had been in his centrally focalized and relatively focalized narrations, they become the *explicit* foundation and topic of the story. The indirection that Jameson calls "national allegory" (and, perhaps not coincidentally, associates with relatively focalized narrations) seems flanked, if not abandoned.

In the new method, therefore, narratively privileged collectivities are sometimes actually seen as massed groups. A paradigm is the great meeting of all factions of the nation in *Ceddo*, a film in which the new narrational methods are fully and remarkably perfected. In this film, even when collectivities are not seen as such, individuals speak to one another as part of the group. This is brilliantly foregrounded by the use of ritual speech (*jotalli*) and the mediation of the *griot*. Sembene's view of language as a social, historical and political function here achieves one of its most remarkable manifestations.[14]

Yet, in this method, Sembene's narration continues to avoid securing meanings in even the most privileged of diegetic agents. Like the individual protagonists of Sembene's earlier films, his collectivities almost always encounter essential difficulties articulating and/or pursuing their interests (except at certain utopian moments). Indeed, the principle of division within or among collectivities is a fundamental source of narrative tensions. The other two methods are focalized through individuals, but promote collective understandings by exploring the epistemological insufficiency of the individual character as individual. In decentred collective narrations, the insufficiency of collectivities is not because they are collectivities, but because they are not fully and consciously realised as such.

Of course, direct representation of collectivities is foreshadowed in Sembene's earlier, non-historical films – for example, the slum population of *Black Girl* and the beggars of *The Curse*. In these instances, such dispossessed groups are ultimately proposed as the only possible epistemological anchorage. However, it is not until *God of Thunder* that groups directly presented as such become key actants and concerns of the story throughout the narrative. The groups, however, tend to be sub-groups to the nation as a whole. Thus, the strongest but not the only examples in *God of Thunder* are the village women and, to some extent, the conscripts, both of whom are seen most often collectively and under guard. On the other hand, all the Diola are never seen together. Even at the end, when the men and women finally unify in their resistance, they must unite across space by song and drum, and are presented through crosscutting. In *Ceddo*, the privileged example are the *ceddo* themselves, but, in this film, almost everyone is represented as part of a group. (Even the King is filmed surrounded by family or aristocracy – until the last time we see him.) In *Camp Thiaroye*, it is the demobilizing soldiers. *Guelwaar* is particularly complex, since the Muslim and Christian sub-groups that should add up to the nation are themselves internally divided by a series of implicit hierarchies of interest and power (male-female, economic, political, and so on).

Sembene's endings always propose a logic or image different to that governing the story. The decentred collective narrations are particularly striking in holding up alternatives to national divisions. When Princess Dior kills the imam in *Ceddo*, she seems to unite aristocracy and people across caste and gender lines; however, this concludes the film so abruptly and with a sociopolitical logic so different to those previously articulated by characters, that this ending actually grounds the film's historical analysis in a utopian challenge to the audience. In *God of Thunder* and *Camp Thiaroye*, privileged groupings achieve a kind of partially unified collective practice; however, the results are catastrophic as well as heroic. (However, *Camp Thiaroye*'s epilogue hints at a continuity of journeying and liberation struggle after the catastrophe.) *Guelwaar*'s ending distantly recalls that of *Black Girl*: the Christian youths, always seen as a group and never as individuals, destroy foreign food-aid, and a superimposed title clearly identifies this as a utopian goal for 21st century Africa.

Thus, while predicating themselves on direct representation of collectivities, Sembene's decentred collective narrations paradoxically retain and even sharpen the analytic principle of social division familiar from his other films. Rather than an achieved unitary harmony, collectivity is still defined as a problem. Rather than being grounded in an essentialized identity available to a nation or society, collectivity is always in an ongoing process of formation and deformation, a process which threatens to weaken or even dissolve it (as in *Ceddo*). This is underscored in endings which, with greater or lesser degrees of strength, often present the possibility of a positive, liberating sociopolitical unity as a counter-factual, utopian prefiguration.

What of Sembene's filmic style in this narrational mode? Teshome Gabriel has argued that a filmmaker's primary commitment to representing and addressing oppressed collectivities would entail reconstructing filmic time and space in ways that emphasise groups, relations and stories, rather than individual heroes, individual completed actions, and technical virtuosity, as in Western mainstream cinema. He identifies third cinema with a contemporary impulse towards collective representations, and argues that it draws on popular and folkloric aspects of cultures in order to emphasise the relations of people to one another and to their lands.[15] Certain of Sembene's attitudes – for example, towards the concept of the folkloric – may be quite different. However, it seems clear that even in his earliest, centrally focalized narrations, Western stylistic techniques were overtly employed to be undermined in connection with the sociopolitical critique of individualization and interiorization. The decentred collective narrations are films where alternative stylistics are most intensively developed.

The project of inventing non-Western stylistic modes appropriate for postcolonial collective representations is probably most refined and systematic in *Ceddo*, but it is most challengingly explicit in *God of Thunder*. In this first of the decentred collective narrations, individualized focalization is so greatly attenuated as to be generally non-existent. This is so with respect to both story order and style. In terms of cinema rhetorics, *God of Thunder* thus has claim to being Sembene's most aesthetically radical film (although it should be paired with *Ceddo* in this respect). I am thinking not only of shifts in its diegetic registers between historical reconstructions and conversations with the gods, or of the peculiar interruption of the film by its credits long after the narrative is under way. There are also the film's particular constructions of time and space.

Bazinian formulas, such as the long take or paucity of close-ups, are not sufficient descriptions of certain aspects of this film. Take the extended duration of certain scenes, such as that in which two conscripts are captured by *tirailleurs* waiting for them on a road. Shot with few cuts, mostly in frontal long-shot of a dirt path that recedes into the horizon, this is a visual narration that seems to emphasise the land as much as the action. We see two instances of a key action, the capture of Diola young men, but, for the most part, the camera refuses to close in and attend to individual reactions of captors or captives. The temporality and spatiality of the scene refuses anchorage in any character interiority, even though it seems ultimately to privilege the two Diola boys who serve as (significantly silent) witnesses and participants throughout the film.

In its evocation of popular memory and a "folkloric" relation to the land, in its partisanship (however critical) on behalf of a politics of the people, and in its address to such a people, *God of Thunder* seems to instanciate Gabriel's third cinema aesthetic: priority is given to clear storytelling not dependent on the Western time and space of individualism and individual action, the close-up, the individual hero. The construction of a radical alternative in *Ceddo* is even more stylistically complex and flexible, for it utilizes non-individualizing but analytic editing strategies at least as much as long-take strategies.[16] Yet, "Western" cinema stylistics are never completely eliminated even from Sembene's most radically unique films. They are not nearly as crucial as they were in the centrally focalized narrations, but some do seem to remain options with varying functions. For example, they may flash up briefly, even startlingly, but with a politically emblematic function. In *Ceddo*, superficially "interiorizing" examples include the priest's dream of a Christian West Africa (which is, however, more than just *his* dream), and Princess Dior's late dream of offering the *ceddo* warrior water. But also, Western stylistics may show up in more subtle ways – for example, in occasional optical point-of-view editing, or in slight variations of dominant Western shot/reverse-shot constructions. However, instead of being aligned with concern for the individual in the usual ways, here they are often subtly redirected.

Such stylistic figures function differently in these films partly because they are less dominant, but also because the narration as a whole is no longer consistently focalized around a single character or even a single group. As a consequence, even the most subjectivizing stylistic techniques no longer operate to privilege single characters. This suggests that opposing or negotiating Western film stylistics remains an issue in Sembene's decentred collective narrations, but the fact that the story is only governed by the action of collectivities displaces their significance.

As an example, take the sequence in *God of Thunder* where two sisters row a boat searching for their draft-resisting brother because the French authorities are holding their father hostage against the brother's return. For once, even this film uses strongly marked point-of-view editing, in the shots where the camera takes in the approach of the sisters through reeds from the perspective of the hidden brother. Yet, there is virtually no *psychological* interiority in play. In the first place, the (non)focalization of the narrative as a whole does not mesh with the technique; there is no other point where the film concentrates on the brother and his sisters, and so their motivations and interior states (aside from those immediate ones verbally expressed in this mostly non-dialogue sequence) are never stated or investigated. Secondly, even within this sequence, focalization fluctuates; we are with the sisters on their project (focalization by story order, but not by optical point of view), then with the brother hiding (optical point of view). Thirdly, the sequence is just one episode in a larger narration consisting of both brief individual focalizations (but without point-of-view editing) and unfocalized segments. Furthermore, all these modes convey a story whose progress is determined by problems of collectivities which we directly see. The combination of fluctuating focalizations with non-focalized segments is what suggests the term *decentred* in describing these collectivized narrations. Sembene's two most recent films continue the large-cast, decentred collective impulses developed in the 1970s, but his critical use of Western stylistic codes has become increasingly complex and flexible, since they no longer seem to designate specially marked moments, and yet continue to be questioned without hypertrophying as they had in the centrally focalized narrations. An excellent example is the private diatribe of Nogoy Marie Thioune at the missing corpse of her politically righteous husband in *Guelwaar*, which first reveals the undertone of patriarchal authoritarianism that was inseparable from his political virtue. Her speech is coded as "private" expressiveness, much of it emotionally delivered and intimately filmed in shot/reverse-shot. However, the reverse-shot from her is to her husband's burial suit laid out on the bed – that is, not even to his corpse but to his missing corpse (!). Therefore, although she physically and grammatically addresses her husband, her complaints turn out to be a monologue.

Once we recognise the terrible humour, there remains something intriguingly oxymoronic in the very conception of filming a monologue in shot/reverse-shot. Nogoy's most intense emotions can only be felt and expressed if she addresses them from and to social positions of wife and husband. If this is individual psychology, it is psychology as a social symptom. For the filmic mode by which her internal emotion is externalized demonstrates a division between the domestic and the political, the private and the public, within which Nogoy exists. In addressing her doubly absent (not present, but also not alive) husband, she adheres to this division, a community value which paradoxically denies her needed support from the community that honours her. That she will never reveal her disputes with her husband publicly insures, as usual in Sembene's work, that the narration does not anchor itself in an individual character, and simultaneously poses a sociopolitical analysis of her problem.

It is worth noting that Sembene's most recent film thus continues the sociopolitical conception of gender relations, overdetermined by the history of modernization and gender roles in Africa, that is consistent throughout Sembene's cinema, from as early as *Black Girl*. This scene also indicates that, despite their stylistic originality, the decentred collective narrations have formal impulses in line with the centrally focalized narrations. For they do sometimes use even the most standardized Western stylistic techniques against themselves, to demonstrate collective processes and divisions.

It also turns out that, even if the individual-collective opposition does not work as predicted by Jameson's conception of national allegory, the films are still to some degree "allegorical", in that they are predicated on the problems of an overarching national collectivity. *Guelwaar* is clearly a commentary on contemporary Senegal. The film presents it as an example of a sub-Saharan postcolonial nation-state, caught in the interplay between the political economy of the global, and the social, cultural and political divisions within nationality. Whether at the level of historical and political referent or of cinematic style, therefore, Sembene's films have continued to explore the inseparability of nation and inter-nation.

Conclusion: cinema, nation, inter-nation

We have seen that, as a formal proposition, in Sembene's fictional worlds there must be at least two separated spaces of action which characters can traverse. Thus, his stories tend strongly to be articulated around journeys, whether or not those journeys seem immediately central to the main story-lines, for that traversal need not occur onscreen. These separated spaces are available to model core-periphery relations, which can be figured as internal or external to local geographies and sociopolitical institutions. These distinctions and the journeys themselves may be relatively implicit (as in *Ceddo*) or explicit (as in *Black Girl*). Crucially, however, the films show the interrelation and interdependence of internal and external spatial distinctions – for example, on the one hand, Senegal vs. France, and, on the other, the slums of Dakar vs. its affluent sections, or countryside vs. city.

Language and translation are practices that serve as nodal points for the cultural, political and class interrelations among such spaces. Differences in linguistic ability mark not only the distinction between external and internal, but also distinctions within the external and the internal. There are key divisions among various registers of speakers, as well as an overarching one between the speakers and the silent or inarticulate. Possession of linguistic power can be mapped onto the referential or connotative distinction between élites and non-élites familiar from national liberation theory. Thus, as is clearly demonstrated in *Camp Thiaroye*, Sembene's linguistic and spatial divisions are available for addressing the classic postcolonial question of the relation between colonizers and colonized, as well as political-intellectual leaderships and the people or nation.

We have also seen that all Sembene's modes of filmic narration – centrally focalized, relatively focalized and (the most original, especially in the 1970s) decentred collective narrations – refuse epistemological privileges to diegetic agents. This is so whether the filmic style is most overtly geared towards the subjectivity of an individual character, or towards the overarching political and human fact of collectivity. This refusal is inseparable from Sembene's politically critical refusal to narrate the postcolonial nation as a unified, achieved collectivity. In his films, the divisions and inequalities composing a "nation" make the whole situation unsayable, and often unknowable, by any of its members.

In one sense, the narration itself takes on the virtuous silence of Pays, or of the women of *God of Thunder*, who never speak their analysis, but only sing and act – that is, "perform" – their situation. This is tied to the fact that only images of what is *not*, Sembene's utopian collectivities, can ground the politically critical evaluation of what *is*. In another sense, this leads to claims by Jameson and Taylor for a multiplicity of allegorical configurations and spectatorial activity promoted by Sembene's films. It is not surprising that Sembene's films have been discussed in terms of West African problem tales as well as Brechtian aesthetics.[17]

Throughout this essay I have also tried to emphasise that Sembene devises stylistic strategies in relation to his work on filmic narration. Since discussion of film style is the discussion of configurations of images and sounds, it is pertinent to conclude with some brief thoughts on the status of cinema implied by Sembene's films. This returns us to the postcolonial situation of the first generation of sub-Saharan African filmmaking.

To a great degree, treating Sembene as a self-consciously African artist is unavoidable and necessary. This is evidenced by the fact that certain of Sembene's key narrative motifs are actually widespread in sub-Saharan cinema. One important instance is the journey narrative. A wide range of work by other filmmakers could be adduced. One early example is *Sambizanga* (Sarah Maldoror, People's Republic of Congo, 1972), which scenically elaborates on Maria's near-epic journey from a village to Luanda in search of her imprisoned anticolonialist husband. A recent example is *Samba Traore* (Idrissa Ouedraogo, Burkina Faso, 1992), a story articulated around the title character's return to his village with stolen money from the city. On another level, critics and scholars have made much of the relation of African cinema to the narrative heritage of African oral traditions, and much still remains to be said about it. For example, supporting the pertinence of Jamesonian national allegory, Ukadike argues that allegory is an aspect of the oral tradition, albeit one which became politically mobilized in post-liberation black African cinema.[18] Clearly, the use of journey motifs in Sembene's films could be attributed to a number of "African" cultural factors, not least among them African epic traditions and journey narratives. It is important, however, to keep in mind the self-consciousness of the process on the part of Sembene and many of his contemporaries.

If we ask about the *particularity* of Sembene's narrative strategies within this provisional African specificity, the overlaying of the journey motif by linguistic performances and issues stands out. As a novelist in French before he was a filmmaker, Sembene is well aware of the vexed issue in sub-Saharan African literatures around the relation of African writers to non-print, indigenous languages. Because the novel and short story assume Western print apparatuses, African prose writers often have conceived of themselves as appropriating and negotiating Western print languages in contexts where they are colonial imports and impositions. (Some of the non-literary political implications of the language issue are dramatised in certain scenes of *The Money Order*.) Hence Ngũgĩ's famous decision to write in phoneticized Gĩkũyũ, which could be orally transmitted to local populations. Sembene himself is sometimes said to word the dialogue of certain of his characters so that his French reads as if it were directly translated from Wolof.[19]

This question of print language may serve as a kind of model for a series of analogous concerns or parallels. We could cite the overriding fact of the African oral narrative tradition, for it is also widely accepted that prose by African writers tends to manifest profound cultural experiences with the oral epic and tale. In them, therefore, the modern Western generic heritage of the novel and short story may itself undergo modifications or refunctionings. Like the colonially implanted official European print languages, written genres are narrative "languages" in dialectical and historically shifting interaction with older genres or narrative "languages" in a looser sense.

For self-consciously sub-Saharan cinema, we may draw another "linguistic" analogy. To a certain degree, anticolonialist and post-national liberation filmmakers confronted cinema as a foreign, colonial imposition dominated by Western production money, distribution networks and modes of representation. The point is not that the cinematic apparatus is an irretrievably imperialist technology, which would imply an anti-modern, essentialist technological determinism. Sembene's demystifying remark that "cinema, when you know it, is a very simple thing" straightforwardly notes the availability of film and all Western technologies for postcolonial reinflection and appropriation.[20] In this context, the question of refunctioning cinema is not conceived through clichéd oppositions of modernity/tradition, and heavy technology/light technology. Rather, it has to do with Western "film language", the dominant conventions for configuring images and sounds as narrative. These could be refunctioned based in part on experiences of indigenous African narrative, on pre-existing artistic and linguistic genealogies within contemporary political, social and aesthetic conjunctures.

The status of cinema in Africa has probably not been as widely debated as that of the novel. However, like the novel, cinema itself is a matter of cultural, economic and geopolitical borders and flows, the transmissions, appropriations and revisions of "languages". I would suggest that the conception of cinema manifested in Sembene's films is consistent with his rejection elsewhere of Senghorian *négritude*. Rather than an ambition to devise an essentialist indigenous cinematic identity, the stylistics of all his films imply a consciousness pointed towards critical confrontations, oppositions and negotiations with mainstream Western forms. Yet, it seems to me that he has indeed invented some radically distinctive strategies with respect to style and narration, something especially striking in certain of the decentred collective narrations. Of course, these self-consciously draw on indigenous traditions and values – but not only these – over and against the reified individualism readable in Western film forms.

The concept of the nation is an important aspect of this cinematic process. To make the point, I would extend these analogies with the language question to the nation-state itself, and consequently to the political-cultural exigencies of constructing "national identities". From the perspective of colonized sub-Saharan Africa, the notion of the national citizen was at the origin of modern revolutionary politics. At the same time, the nation-state, with its centres of modern power and capital tied to both domestic and international economic, military, cultural and administrative-bureaucratic flows, was the political "language", genre and/or "technology" *par excellence* of colonialism. The fact of such intercontinental flows could thus suggest that, like narrative and cinema, the nation-state as a model of political organisation is also potentially open to being refunctioned and reformed. Hence the appropriation of the concept of the nation in national liberation struggles as a way of unifying effective political opposition to invading colonialisms, and as a way of interrogating internal divisions in their interaction with international forces – and hence, it is nowadays more controversial to add, the contradictory but continuing heritage of the nation-state in the international, postcolonial context. However, *Guelwaar*, at least in part, seems to insist on this last point.[21]

Language and novel, cinema, nation-state: these nodes suggest the paradox or dialectic of nationality at work in the films and career of Sembene. In his films, the nation becomes unthinkable, unrepresentable without the inter-nation. The journey and language motifs situate his films at the junctures of relations and differences between the foreign and indigenous – or rather, they enable the films to explore differences and the foreign at the heart of the indigenous.

They also describe Sembene's situation as intellectual, artist and filmmaker, as postcolonial, as political epistemologist – as, one might say, mediator-translator.

This distinctive figure in Sembene's film characterology – the French housewife, sergeant-translator, *griot* and so on – can be a subaltern, a go-between, an artist, an intellectual... He/she is situated astride the very principle of collective relationality itself: the frictional points of contact not only between colonizer and colonized ("external" frictions often associated with external journeys), but also among divided elements of a nation or society – class, ethnicity, religion, gender, region ("internal" frictions often associated with internal journeys); and therefore the configuration of all relationships as a network of geopolitical, sociopolitical and historical junctures; and thus the mutual determination of "external" and "internal".

Sembene's often-quoted remark that he is a *griot* for the new era takes on rich connotations in relation to this figure. The distinctiveness of narration and style in Sembene's films are strategies emanating from his situation, which is both national and international. However, in addition, the *griot* as mediator/translator remains subject to the partiality of knowledge that plagues virtually all Sembene characters. It is implicated in the extreme in the dialectic of the linguistic gift discussed above: the opposition between the fluid ambivalence of the verbose, and the oppressed but potentially liberatory positionality of the silent. In that silence and in the rebellions it sometimes portends in Sembene's films, one still hears the voice of national liberation theory at its best, and its utopian but critical commitment to something called "the people".

Notes

[1]   See Kenneth Turan, "Out of the Real Africa: Acclaimed Senegalese director Ousmane Sembene gets a rare retrospective at the Nuart", *The Los Angeles Times*, 1 January 1995, calendar section: 30, 33-36; Michael Atkinson, "Ousmane Sembène: 'We are no longer in the era of prophets'", *Film Comment* 29: 4 (July-August 1993): 63-69; Fredric Jameson, "Third-World Literature in the Era of Multinational Capitalism", *Social Text* 15 (autumn 1986): 65-88; Clyde Taylor, "Black Cinema in the Post-aesthetic Era", in Jim Pines and Paul Willemen (eds), *Questions of Third Cinema* (London: British Film Institute, 1989): 90-110; Samba Gadjigo, Ralph Faulkingham, Thomas Cassirer and Reinhard Sander (eds), *Ousmane Sembène: Dialogues with Critics and Writers* (Amherst: University of Massachusetts Press, 1993).

[2]   On Sembene's use of French institutions supporting "francophone" cinema, see Claire Andrade-Watkins, "Film Production in Francophone Africa 1961 to 1977: Ousmane Sembène–An Exception", in Gadjigo et al (eds): 29-36. More generally, see Manthia Diawara, *African Cinema: Politics & Culture* (Bloomington and Indianapolis: Indiana University Press, 1992): chapters 3

and 5; and Nwachukwu Frank Ukadike, *Black African Cinema* (Los Angeles: University of California Press, 1994): 61-62, 68-70.

3   Ukadike: 92ff.

4   Frantz Fanon, "On National Culture", in *The Wretched of the Earth*, translated by Constance Farrington (New York: Grove, 1981): 227-235.

5   For a sense of how widespread consideration of these problems was, compare Fanon to Amilcar Cabral, "National Liberation and Culture", in *Return to the Source: Selected Speeches of Amilcar Cabral* (New York: Monthly Review Press, 1973): especially 46-48, on culture, nation and class, and 54-55. I owe this last reference to Neil Lazarus.

6   Another inquiry could compare and contrast representational methods in Sembene's novels with respect to collectivity.

7   However, it is important that Sembene's trajectory was more unusually unofficial. For example, his international education led through the French Army and labour unions to the Gorki Studio, rather than through the Dakar-Paris educational apparatus.

8   Some functions of this music and the absences it designates are discussed in Philip Rosen, "Making a Nation in Sembene's *Ceddo*", *Quarterly Review of Film and Video* 13: 1-3 (1991): 160-161, 166.

9   See Aimé Césaire, *Discourse on Colonialism* [1950], translated by Joan Pinkham (New York; London: Monthly Review Press, 1972).

10   See Mbye Baboucar Cham, "Ousmane Sembene and the Aesthetics of African Oral Traditions", *Africana Journal* 13: 1-4 (1982): especially 35-38, for *jottali*. See Christopher L Miller, *Theories of Africans: Francophone Literature and Anthropology in Africa* (Chicago: University of Chicago Press, 1990): 79-85, on Mande practices and the connotations of excessive speech vs. silence.

11   Jameson: 85. The heavy generalizations about "the" Third World in this essay came under significant critique almost immediately. See Aijaz Ahmad, "Jameson's Rhetoric of Otherness and the 'National Allegory'", *Social Text* 17 (autumn 1987): 3-25.

12   Fredric Jameson, *The Political Unconscious: Narrative as a Socially Symbolic Act* (Ithaca, NY: Cornell University Press, 1981): 17-102 and 103-150, and Jameson (1986). See Taylor, especially 106-107, on *Ceddo*. The limited confluence of Jameson and Taylor around Sembene is interesting because of their divergences. Taylor rejects the universalization operations of Enlightenment thought as irremediably aligned with colonialist and racist enterprises, while Jameson seeks to hold onto elements of the slippery Enlightenment heritage of Marxism. In addition, Taylor rejects that art-historical succession of canonized aesthetic movements, such as modernism and postmodernism, which are central to Jameson's claim that the apparent realism of Third World literary texts is actually the vehicle for an allegorization that is an alternative to Western modernism and postmodernism. There are many examples of the currency of "national

allegory" in recent film studies, in Jameson's sense, but also in other senses. See, for example, Alex M Saragoza with Graciela Berkovich, "Intimate Connections: Cinematic Allegories of Gender, the State and National Identity", in Chon A Noriega and Steven Ricci (eds), *The Mexican Cinema Project* (Los Angeles: UCLA Film and Television Archive, 1994): 25-32; and the approval of the notion, however hesitant and with acknowledgement of Ahmad's critique, in Ella Shohat and Robert Stam, *Unthinking Eurocentrism: Multiculturalism and the Media* (London; New York: Routledge, 1994): for example, 275.

[13]   For a pertinent account of the narrational strategies of this film, see David Bordwell, *Narration in the Fiction Film* (Madison: University of Wisconsin Press, 1985): 205-233.

[14]   For a close analysis of these matters, including considerations on the kind of style Sembene devises to carry this narrational load, see Rosen: especially 148-159.

[15]   See Teshome H Gabriel, "Third Cinema as Guardian of Popular Memory: Towards a Third Aesthetics", in Pines and Willemen (eds): especially 57-61.

[16]   For a closer analysis of some of these mechanisms in *Ceddo*, see Rosen: 153ff.

[17]   For Sembene and the problem tale, see Cham.

[18]   Ukadike: 25. See the pioneering articles (at least in English) by Cham, and Manthia Diawara, "Popular Culture and Oral Traditions in African Film", *Film Quarterly* 41: 3 (spring 1988): 6-14, as well as related contributions to the present volume. According to Cham: "Unlike Achebe, who integrates known Igbo oral narratives within the narrative of some of his works... [Sembene] selects and adapts certain formal features of the oral narrative tradition in order to construct his work" (27).

[19]   The reference, of course, is to Ngũgĩ wa Thiong'o, *Decolonising the Mind: The Politics of Language in African Literature* (London: James Currey, 1986): especially 63-86. See also Sada Niang, "An Interview with Ousmane Sembène by Sada Niang: Toronto, July 1992", in Gadjigo et al (eds): 89-95; and Frederick Ivor Case, "Aesthetics, Ideology, and Social Commitment in the Prose Fiction of Ousmane Sembène", in Gadjigo et al (eds): 4-8. In fact, a comparison between Ngũgĩ and Sembene on the language question would be more complex, and would require linguistic expertise which I do not possess. Despite some seeming differences on questions of colonial print languages, Sembene has an history of dealing in written Wolof – for example, in the Wolof-language journal, *Kaddu*.

[20]   Noureddine Ghali, "An Interview with Sembene Ousmane", *Cinema 76* 208 (April 1976), translated in John D H Downing (ed), *Film & Politics in the Third World* (New York: Autonomedia, 1987): 46.

[21]   One of the most thought-provoking arguments on this ambivalence of the nation-state and its historical relationship to colonialism, anticolonialism and the postcolonial situation is Benedict Anderson, *Imagined Communities: Reflections on the Origin and Spread of Nationalism* (London: Verso, 1991).

Orality in the films of Ousmane Sembene

Sada Niang

Two types of characters appear in almost all the films of Ousmane Sembene: the Senegalese infantryman and the *griot*. The former occupies centre-stage in *Borom Sarret* (1963), *Emitaï* (*God of Thunder*, 1971), *Ceddo* (1976), *Camp de Thiaroye* (*Camp Thiaroye*, 1988), whereas the latter appears in all of these, in addition to *Mandabi* (*The Money Order*, 1968), *Xala* (*The Curse*, 1974) and *Guelwaar* (1992). In their various embodiments, both underline major concerns which run throughout Sembene's films: popular history, and the need for pertinent frameworks of mass communication built on various features of orality. Invariably, Sembene has defined himself as a modern *griot* using literature and film to communicate with his compatriots on issues directly related to their daily lives.[1] Typically, his films expound on the common experiences of mostly illiterate characters living at the margins of Senegalese society, yet constituting the majority of the population.

Although most critics praised Sembene for having produced the first feature film in an African language,[2] Mbye Baboucar Cham[3] showed that *The Money Order, Ceddo* and *The Curse* all used tropes such as repetition, and character types such as the trickster, both of which originate from and are still highly functional in oral tradition. Two years later, Françoise Pfaff pointed out that Sembene's films articulate themselves through music, gestures and spaces.[4] Finally, in 1991, using *Wend Kuuni* (*God's Gift*, 1982) as an example, Manthia Diawara further elaborated on the interconnectedness of written and oral forms of communication, reported on the problematic relationship between literature and cinema in Africa, and then documented the use of "orality" as an organising principle in *God's Gift*.[5]

Drawing from linguistics and communication theory, I will argue that features of orality in Sembene's films are language-bound and code-bound. In portraying an opposition between written and oral forms of communication, Sembene documents the transformation of African men and women into outsiders. From *Borom Sarret* to *Guelwaar* (1992), these marginalized characters have reclaimed a position on the outskirts of an irrelevant mainstream. Later, I will argue that, in the absence of any widespread competence in the written registers of any language, Sembene's characters centre their drama on the propagation of and protection from rumours. Finally, I will show that, for these illiterate and marginalized characters, the use of oral discursive patterns of communication is both socially and aesthetically empowering.

In *Borom Sarret, La Noire de... (Black Girl*, 1966), *The Money Order, God of Thunder* and *Guelwaar*, oral and written forms of communication are two language-specific codes, ideologically charged and dramatically set against each other. Sembene's films systematically link writing with official documents in French (tax voucher, passport, money order, identity card, voting card, cheque, birth certificate, death certificate, or requisition for food levy). These "papers", as Dieng and his wives refer to them, mediate between a removed state and the majority of its illiterate citizens. They are kept in deep, sweaty "bubu" pockets in *The Money Order*; firmly held in the hands of the distant "patron" in *Black Girl*; handed from one Army officer to a Legion officer in *God of Thunder*; and angrily requested and snatched by the police chief in *Guelwaar*. Amongst the local population, those who are made to carry them cannot or do not read them. Whenever they produce them, their hands tremble, the features of their faces tense up, and their terrified eyes implore the kindness of a police officer or clerk busying himself[6] with some administrative task (*Borom Sarret*; *The Money Order*).

Similarly, those who devise these "papers" are much rumoured about, but seldom seen. Their appearance is usually staged in closed office spaces, past secretaries and assistants, and behind desks and telephones. Their presence in open spaces brings simmering social conflicts to a boil, as in the case of the public row at Mbarka's store, of the confrontation between the police officer and Borom Sarret in *Borom Sarret*, and, finally, in the numerous scenes between Gora and the Muslim community of Baye Ale in *Guelwaar*. Even though the texts inscribed on these "papers" are never made explicit in any of the films, they trigger fears expiated in prayers and rituals (*Borom Sarret*), cause depression and suicide (*Black Girl*), and jeopardize a precarious social peace (*Guelwaar*). Indeed, in most of Sembene's films, the word "kayit" (Wolof for "paper") acquires a malefic connotation. To sign it, is to inflict events of tragic proportions upon oneself, unless one is wearing a uniform while doing so.[7] To ignore it, by putting it aside, brings about personal humiliations and public strife (*The Curse*; *Guelwaar*).[8] Finally, to claim what it declares is duly yours provokes the suspicion of other members of the community, sends the victim through a Kafkaesque journey in various government offices, and leaves him or her wretched and revolted (*The Money Order*). It is therefore no wonder that the main instruments for the propaganda of the written code (schools, libraries, newspapers in French) are absent from Sembene's films.

In *Borom Sarret*, the written code is seldom present. It fleetingly appears on "cars rapides" (local mini-buses) to signify affiliation with a trade union, or the geographical origin of their owners. For the cart driver and his wife, it is synonymous with imposition and exclusion, theft and violence. Praying early in the morning, Borom Sarret raises his voice to implore the protection of Allah against the written "laws of the country":

> I implore the divine protection of Allah, the merciful one. May he protect me and my family from the laws of the country and the unbelievers, amen, amen, amen!

His first paying customer is stopped from burying his dead child for lack of proper documents:

> Guard: Brother, it's not the right paper!
> Man: I am a stranger here!
> Guard: Borom Sarret, don't go in! Go get the right paper!

Later, as Borom Sarret is stopped by a police officer for violating municipal traffic laws, he too realises that written laws have made him subject to space restriction in his own country:

> Police officer: Get down quick! Quick! Your papers! Have you got a pass to come here? Borom sarrets are not allowed here!

While the officer is issuing (writing) the ticket, he steps on Borom Sarret's war medal and refuses to budge. As he silently protests, Borom Sarret is shouted at, handed a ticket, deprived of his means of livelihood, and, in a manner suggesting the predicament of Dieng in *The Money Order*, sent on a long journey home, on foot.

There are many examples of this type of device in Sembene's other works. For example, in *The Money Order*, the unexpected arrival of the money order triggers a relentless and dehumanizing paper chase. El Hadji's demise in *The Curse* is partly due to his failure to comply with the terms of the contract he signed as a member of the Chamber of Commerce of Dakar. In *Camp Thiaroye*, the three French officers preparing to execute the fraudulent money exchange attempt to dismiss Major Diatta's passionate tribute to his men by circulating a paper with the word "Communist" in capital letters.

Guelwaar, produced almost 30 years after *Borom Sarret*, presents some of the same character types and situations: public transportation is still effected by horse-pulled carts, and, in the last scene of the film, Pierre Henri Thioune's remains are returned to a Catholic cemetery in a cart. At the Muslim burial grounds, parents and relatives of Pierre Henri are denied access. Furthermore, Thioune's house may be sturdier than his counterpart's three decades ago, and food perhaps not as scarce, yet his prostitute daughter (Sophie), who supports the family with the revenues of her trade,[9] recreates the moral ambiguity of the last scene in *Borom Sarret*. Finally, in both films, literacy skills are used by men in uniforms to exercise control over an illiterate population.

I would like to suggest that at no other time in his career as a filmmaker has Sembene so forcefully made the case against the repressive and restrictive nature of writing and written texts as in *Guelwaar*. In a flashback scene at the beginning of the film, Pierre Henri Thioune is shown in the police station lodging a complaint against "hooligans" seeking to disrupt weekly meetings held by the women of his parish at his house. As Gora, the police superintendent, sits and listens to him, the camera lingers on a folder bulging with written documents, bearing the caption: "Pierre Henri Thioune alias Guelwaar: dissident".[10] Typically, the contents of such documents are not revealed. Yet, in what looks like a dispute stripped of its preliminary stages, Thioune contrasts these with the endless possibilities of speech. Responding to the superintendent's query on the reasons for the meetings at his house, gesticulating and occasionally stopping for greater effectiveness, he says:

> Gora, it's no secret. Everyone knows what they discuss. They talk about their families, they talk about famine. They talk about drought. Don't you know that rains have been scarce this year? They talk about the misappropriation of aid which is sold or distributed to [government] party members. They talk about illicit wealth creation. They talk about the theft of public funds. They talk about death and mourning ceremonies, christenings. They talk about Christian solidarity and our faith. These are the kinds of topics they talk about, and they are not hiding from anybody to do so.

For his efforts, Thioune receives a warning from Gora which he immediately dismisses with derision.

In *Guelwaar*, oral forms of communication are both textually and socially enabling: they sustain a wider variety of topics than any of the written documents in the rest of the film, articulate democratic participation rather than control, and forge alliances. Through orality, the marginalized characters in society redefine themselves as citizens, charting a new course for themselves against the literate law-makers. Indeed, in a semiotic reversal characteristic of Sembene's films,[11] technologically-equipped, silent and closed spaces have become the hiding places of those who read and write. Gora in *Guelwaar*, the businessmen in *The Curse*, the French Army officers in *Camp Thiaroye* and *God of Thunder* – all increasingly find themselves besieged by their former victims. Gora's various evictions from the villagers' houses, and his retreat as order breaks down at the meeting at the Ciss compound, contrast with the confidence of the police officer in *Borom Sarret*, and with the arrogance of empire in the final shooting scene in *Camp Thiaroye* or *God of Thunder*, and point to new developments in Senegalese society. Indeed, the advent of political assassination in *Guelwaar* signals the weakening of those who read and write in French, when faced by increasingly articulate and fearless opposition in the local languages.

In the previous scene, as a retreating Gora finally suggests that a written deposition of Thioune's complaints be taken, an agitated Pierre Henri quickly produces a signed summary of his complaint, warns the police superintendent about the consequences of not resolving the issues troubling his community, and walks out of the police station.

Pierre Henri Thioune in *Guelwaar*, Rama in *The Curse*, Major Diatta and most of the Senegalese infantrymen in *Camp Thiaroye* usher in a new generation of characters for Sembene. No longer are they confined to what Walter Ong has called "primary orality".[12] With variable ease, these characters straddle between the registers of a script-bound French language and the pervasive orality of their own languages. With them, fear of the written, which so paralysed Borom Sarret and so brutalised Dieng, has been replaced by a defiance sustained by the knowledge that language is nothing but a tool, and a code nothing but an articulation of it. Indeed, for Moor Ciss and Pierre Henri Thioune, the value of the written text is strictly confined to its ability to conserve facts and keep the authorities at bay. Facts are neither created by script, nor should they be changed because of them.[13]

In *The Money Order*, *The Curse*, *God of Thunder* and *Guelwaar* socially pertinent meaning rests on the pillars of oral discursive strategies, and one of the most important of these is the use of rumour. The textuality of a rumour is fluctuating and may bear changes according to speaker, situation or discursive objectives. Invariably, it is carried in Wolof or Diola in Sembene's films, but may also be realised in standard French or any variety thereof (including français petit-nègre). Its propagator is usually not the main interested party and is often not identified. Finally, a rumour may generate another one, exist concurrently with it, or completely die down.

Sembene uses rumours as creative instances which forge communities, pretexts for reviewing interpersonal relationships, discursive events defining political goals, and as a means of information-sharing and control.

Fears, discomforts or community disruptions are established by the rule of the written, and are first articulated through oral modes of communication. In *Borom Sarret*, the tension brought about by the written laws of the country permeates the film from beginning to end. The early hours of the day at Borom Sarret's house are grim, desolate and fearful, as a nervous cart driver slips his amulets on, prays for his protection, and is reminded of the dire living conditions endured by his wife and child.

In *The Money Order*, news of the money order is propagated by Dieng's wives and equally illiterate neighbours. None among them, not even the literate Mbarka, requests proof of the existence of the money order. Yet, throughout the first 30 minutes of *The Money Order*, Dieng is like a public relations officer parsimoniously controlling the information surrounding the money order: he quietly walks back to his house to be briefed by his wives, angrily chastises them for their lack of discretion, and deftly keeps the news of the money order to himself as he requests the much-needed bus fare from Mbarka. As the shopkeeper informs him that fifteen kilograms of rice had been put aside for his wives, and further suggests that he should come and withdraw the merchandise on his return from the post office, Dieng becomes alerted that news of the money order has already spread by word of mouth:

> Mbarka: I have put aside fifteen kilograms for you.
> Dieng: Aah!
> Mbarka: Ah no! I cannot give you more than that. Stop by to pick it up on your way from the post office.
> Dieng: Alright! Give it to my children when you see one of them.[14]

Rumour control also seems to be a major concern for Pierre Henri Thioune's family after his death: Aloyse breaks the news of his father's death to his mother in the middle of the night, in a dark room, after having walked across a dark yard. The following morning, apart from the few "sarrets" dropping off friends and relatives, the general atmosphere is one of complete detachment, and is conveyed by the long shots of various angles of the house. Accompanied by the sound of Catholic hymns sung in Serer, a steady stream of co-parishioners is met by Aloyse at the entrance to the house. As the youth section of the parish approaches the gate and offers their sympathies to Aloyse, both he and the priest learn that the rumours of the disappearance of his father's body have already travelled far throughout the neighbourhood. Annoyed, Abbé Léon restricts the number of youths allowed to see the widow of Guelwaar, in order to protect her from the rumours, and orders that the cross they intended to plant on the dead man's grave be left outside.

In *God of Thunder*, even before its onset, the villagers know about the impending French expedition, and warn each other, preparing for the days to come: crops are hidden, and young men fearing forceful drafting in a "war that is not theirs" flee into the forest. Of those remaining men, a few adults and adolescents stand guard over the village in trees resembling the miradors of *Camp Thiaroye*. In the morning, as the dust rises from the section of Senegalese infantrymen advancing towards the village, drums are ominously sounded, piercing intermittent flute notes sent through the air.

El Hadji's predicament in *The Curse* is not encoded in written language, but eventually becomes known to everybody in the city. The news spreads in a chain: firstly directly shared, behind closed doors, among literate members of the business circle; then quickly spread from the illiterate Bayden to a close female associate; from Modou (the driver) to Serigne Mada; from the group of illiterate beggars to various other men or women; and finally, from an anonymous source to El Hadji Abdoukader Beye's literate daughter. Rama eventually confronts her mother with the news. Significantly, neither the magazine-reading Oumi nor the French-speaking secretary at El Hadji's store seems to share in the rumours surrounding the businessman. Yet, these two women – outsiders as it were – will dissociate themselves from him as soon as he loses car, money and sexual potency.

Indeed, in *The Curse*, with the exception of the early morning meeting between Dieng and the President, and of the Bayden and her two associates, none of the instances of news-sharing described above is explicitly portrayed in the film. Yet, that they did take place is seldom questioned by audiences. On the morning of what was to have been a memorable night, a grim-looking Modou meets his "patron" and helps him bear the humiliating burden which has plagued him. Two days later, as the remedies of the President's marabout failed to produce any tangible results, El Hadji Abdoukader Beye himself confirms that Modou had been informed of the events from the very beginning:

> Abdoukader Beye: Modou, I didn't sleep last night, thinking about the marabout you proposed yesterday. I don't believe in these marabouts anymore.

Modou: Boss, you can trust this one. He is the marabout of my village. He has accomplished miracles, he is a holy man.
Abdoukader Beye: I trust you! Let's go then!
Modou: You won't regret it, boss.

On the same fateful morning, beggars on crutches and knees converge towards the pavements opposite Abdoukader Beye's office, and quietly position themselves in front of his store window, while the musical score of the film extols the virtues of leadership built on self-help and creating opportunities for others.

In Sembene's films, rumours build and reaffirm social ties. They convey information where no official will venture, articulate resistance, as in *God of Thunder*, and define political goals, as in *Guelwaar*. Above all, they are the privileged mode of information-sharing and control of illiterate characters: rumours spread by those who read or write are usually false, and threaten the existence of the latter. *Camp Thiaroye* is a good example. Both infantrymen and French officers in this film know the terms under which the former were enlisted in the French colonial Army. Sembene once again produces no paper traces of such a contract: yet, the existence of such documents, orally explained to the infantrymen at the time of their departure, is neither questioned nor denied by those involved in the tragedy of their repatriation. The existence of such a written document, read and properly interpreted, then filed and ignored by the higher ranks of the French colonial Army, generates a rumour. Its new textuality is oral, open and made to fluctuate according to the desires of the military superiors. I would like to argue, however, that this rumour backfires, because those involved in its propagation are literate and, indeed, might have drafted the initial documents. Furthermore, unlike any such type of discursive structure we have encountered so far, the propagators of the rumours in *Camp Thiaroye* are its main beneficiaries. French is the only language available to them; however, because the code elected to carry the rumour is oral, it is similar to all the other instances we have referred to previously.

As the soldiers are mustered in the square of the camp, a tense general uses threat, the fear of military reprisals, flattery and a smiling face to spread rumours contrary to what the Senegalese infantrymen had been promised in Dakar, France and Morlaix. The news that they would not be compensated as promised – despite all their sacrifices, all the years lost in the defence of France, and, indeed, all their friends who died for the French Republic – brings a swift response from no less than their most credible witness, Corporal Diarra: "General, I be lie. One tousand French franc fit give you five hundred Africa money; I be true I de talk!"[15]

Diarra speaks in a dialect of French created by the *tirailleurs* and understood by all those present. As a stunned General approaches and threatens him, he is surrounded by a group of infantrymen, taken hostage and dragged to the barracks, screaming for help.

Finally, following Philip Rosen's analysis of *Ceddo*,[16] I would like to suggest that, for illiterate characters such as Dieng in *The Money Order*, the use of oral discursive strategies is socially and aesthetically empowering. For, as much as he is forced to delegate his will whenever dealing with government offices, he regains his full autonomy wherever knowledge of the expressive resources of the Wolof language is the only communicative requirement. In *The Money Order*, Dieng is trapped, bullied around but never taken in by his fellow Wolof neighbours, all of whom are illiterate. In the following scene, he outwits a suspicious Sow, who, weary of the rumours of the loss of the money order, expresses his surprise and indirectly accuses Dieng of selfishness:

> Sow: As far I am concerned, the rumours of the theft are surprising.
> Dieng: So goes the world these days. Nobody trusts anybody any more. Moral rectitude has become a thing of the past.
> Sow: We should all put our grains in the same basket so as to have at least one basket.
> Dieng: But if all the grains put together cannot fill a basket, there will still be a basket.
> Sow: Nowadays, it is very difficult to gather enough.
> Dieng: Aah!, that is right but you can be sure that water will never, never, never rise [on its own] or return where it originated from.[17]

Riddle for riddle, Dieng systematically turns ambiguous insinuations of Sow's interlocution against him. He first rejects the doubt cast on Méty's story that he (Dieng) had been mugged, by questioning the confidence Sow has in himself and in Dieng's wives. Sow, discovering his blunder, redirects his remarks towards the need for community solidarity. However, here again, Dieng, familiar with this type of esoteric language, intimates to him that such solidarity implies that everybody, whatever their material fortune, contributes their assets. Finally, as Sow abandons his metaphor and reverts to literal language to hint at how difficult times have become, Dieng rejects his "friend's" implied plea for assistance by revealing to him what both of them know: whatever assistance Dieng might give Sow will be lost to his own family forever.

In the films of Ousmane Sembene, orality provides a critical framework within which the history of the continent is re-examined from the point of view of the common people. It is a didactic method for signifying to Borom Sarret, Dieng and their neighbours their marginalized existence, and, through *Guelwaar*, the need to resist such marginalisations. Finally, it is also a means for building appropriate and fulfilling dramatic events for African audiences.

Notes

[1] See Mbye Baboucar Cham, "Ousmane Sembene and the Aesthetics of African Oral Traditions", *Africana Journal* 13: 1/4 (1982): 25-40. See also Nwachukwu Frank Ukadike, *Black African Cinema* (Los Angeles: University of California Press, 1994): 90-104.

[2] Ferid Boughédir, *African Cinema from A to Z*, translated by D A Woodford (Brussels: OCIC, 1992): 163.

[3] Cham.

[4] Françoise Pfaff, *The Cinema of Ousmane Sembene: A Pioneer of African Film* (Westport, CT: Greenwood Press, 1984): 63-68.

[5] See Manthia Diawara, "Oral Literature and African Film: Narratology in *Wend Kuuni*", in Jim Pines and Paul Willemen (eds), *Questions of Third Cinema* (London: British Film Institute, 1989): 199-201.

[6] In Sembene's films, all the civil servants fulfilling various administrative functions are male.

[7] In *The Money Order*, Dieng, a product of a world where the word is paramount, signs away his money order to his nephew Mbaye and immediately loses it. In contrast, the police officer in *Borom Sarret* and Amath in *The Money Order*, both of whom are clothed in attire which identifies their affiliation with the regime in power, do not further jeopardize their security by affixing their signature to documents.

[8] In *The Curse*, each civil servant or bank employee executing a writ against El Hadji or denying him a request does so with a document in hand. Similarly, his exclusion from the lucrative circle of the members of the Chamber of Commerce is made official by each businessperson affixing his signature to a circulating petition. In *Guelwaar*, the act of "ignoring" the contents of an official document can hardly be held against the villagers, since they are all illiterate. Nevertheless, the ensuing crisis is extremely acute, and threatens the very fabric of their community.

[9] With Abbé Léon walking behind her, Hélène exposes the extent to which the well-being of both her and Sophie's families depends on the fruits of their trade: "...so I became a registered prostitute. Every week, I go to the doctor's office for a visit. I can't speak for others but the thought of AIDS scares me stiff. Still, every month I send money to my family. None in my family has to beg. My younger brother has enrolled for his first year of

medical studies. I must help him. I paid for my father to go to Yamoussokro for the consecration of Notre Dame de la Paix. Father, you see this [she points to her necklace], he brought it back for me. He told me that the pope has blessed it. Sophie too has paid for her father's pilgrimage. You know where he went? Jerusalem."

10   "Pierre Henri Thioune dit Guelwaar: élément incontrôlable".

11   In *The Money Order*, Dieng is shown several times retracing his steps to the heart of the city. In *The Curse*, on the morning after his failed nuptial night, El Hadji walks alone as the film's soundtrack replays the musical score of the previous night's celebrations. As El Hadji retraces the itinerary of the wedding procession back to his office, his secretary sprinkles a deodorant liquid in a sewer drain in front of the office's front door. Seconds later, another woman empties her dishpan in the same drain. Diawara has argued that "African oral narratives abound in digressions, parallelisms, flashbacks, dreams". See *African Cinema: Politics & Culture* (Bloomington and Indianapolis: Indiana University Press, 1992): 11. Finally, for Isidore Okpewho, "repetition is...one of the most fundamental characteristic features of oral literature". See *African Oral Literature: Backgrounds, Character, and Continuity* (Bloomington and Indianapolis: Indiana University Press, 1992): 71.

12   Walter J Ong, *Orality and Literacy: The Technologizing of the Word* (London: Methuen, 1982): 6.

13   In *Guelwaar*, an angry police superintendent is called a "madman" by illiterate villagers who refuse to accept the fact that the death certificate in their possession belongs to a different man to the one they think they have buried.

14   The text in Wolof is as follows: Mbarka: [...] deeseel naala fukki kilo jiroom. / Dieng: AAh!... / Mbarka: Ah déét manuma laa joxx lu ëpp. Boo joogé post ba rekk saalaw nga jaar fi ma jox laa ko. / Dieng: baax naa, kon book boo gisee ken ci sama doom yi nga joxal maa kokë.

15   "Ma seneral, Pas veritement ça. Mille francs français pour cinq cents francs afriki! C'est ça la veritement."

16   Philip Rosen, "Making a Nation in Sembene's *Ceddo*", in Hamid Naficy and Teshome H Gabriel (eds), *Otherness and the Media: The Ethnography of the Imagined and the Imaged* (Chur, Switzerland: Harwood Academic Publishers, 1993): 147-172.

17   Sow: Mandéy Jeng, saac gi may dégg doynaa waar lool! / Dieng: Adunaa bindoo nonu. Fi mu neek ken wooloo tul ken ndax ken jubul! / Sow: Daynani, pepp yëpp nu dajele leen ci andar ngir ak andar. / Dieng: Wayee bu dara matul andar it, andar pepp yëpp it, andar laa rekk. / Sow: Wànde nakk jamano ji nu tolloo, jaffeñ nga ce am am gu mat, gu anda ak doylu. / Dieng: Aah!, li nga wax deggë lë, waye nëlë wër ni ndox, du jogé mukk mukk mukk wala moo delu muk femu jogé woon.

Towards a changing Africa: women's roles in the films of Ousmane Sembene

Sheila Petty

Change, a catalyst for all human inquiry, is often documented through observations of representations of women's positions in society. In the case of sub-Saharan Africa, many nations experienced myriad societal and cultural changes as they gained independence and sought to deal with the political and economic disruptions wrought by European colonization. This notion of change has informed almost every film of the sub-Saharan African cinema since its birth in 1953, and Ousmane Sembene's cinematic works are no exception. Indeed, from *Borom Sarret* (1963) to *Guelwaar* (1992), his films are commentaries on changing African societies, and increasingly reflect his preoccupation with the corruption of indigenous African culture and with the link between Westernization and economic dependence in Africa.

Women of the African continent are among the first to suffer the effects of an unequal international economic order, and development projects, when instituted, have not always worked to the advantage of women because their contributions are often viewed as supplementary rather than central.[1] For Sembene, however, "[t]here can be no development in Africa if women are left out of the account",[2] and he is perplexed by the idea that "[i]n a modern Africa women can take part in production, education, but they are still refused the right of speech".[3] Because Sembene recognises the crucial role women play in Africa's development, he gives voice to African women's concerns in his films, and these concerns are depicted through female characters in the films' narratives. This essay focuses on an analysis of female characters in an effort to consider their functions in the films' narratives, and thus their importance in Sembene's vision of Africa's future.

Although the characters I intend to analyse are female, my aim is not to discuss them simply in terms of gender construction, but as fictional constructs within political, sociocultural and historical contexts that perform specific functions in the films' narratives. As Assiatou Bah Diallo, head writer at *Amina* magazine, once observed, it is impossible to speak of a monolithic black woman in cinema. According to Diallo, it is more fruitful to speak of a multiplicity of images of women in African cinema, in view of the fact that these women on the screen bear witness to a constantly changing society.[4] Privileging gender analysis runs the risk of obscuring the larger African reality portrayed by African filmmakers. Thus, gender experience should be considered as one aspect of African female characters' identities, but not the determining factor. This is particularly true of Sembene's films. Female characters occupy a variety of positions in his narratives, and no easy generalization can be made. They are not all agents of change, nor are they all victims. They represent a multiplicity of voices in Sembene's filmic ideology, and to understand this ideology one must listen to all the voices.

Throughout his life, Sembene has opposed the forces which he considers germane to cultural alienation in Senegal: French colonialism, Senghor's negritude and promotion of "la francophonie" (the French-speaking commonwealth), and American imperialism.[5] Although he is eager to alert his audiences to the dangers of cultural alienation, Sembene's mandate is more far-reaching than mere consciousness-raising. Rather than simply informing his audiences about change, he is anxious to provoke his audiences to act – to stand up and refuse economic and cultural imperialism:

> [W]e are left with a society which is growing more and more impoverished, emptying itself of its creative substance, turning more and more to values it does not create...if America is calling the shots in Senegal at present, it's because those who govern Senegal allow this to happen. So we find ourselves with a society on its knees, waiting for America to provide. Never, ever, ever, in the space of ten years, have I felt so humiliated by my society as now...A society can't live on handouts. A society that has its own culture can confront all sorts of calamities and adversities with its head held high.[6]

In order to provoke action, Sembene uses typal characters in his cinematic works, each of whom embodies a different strategy for dealing with the changing nature of modern Africa. Thus, rather than striving to create "positive" or "negative" images of Africans, Sembene creates characters who are defined by their functions in the narratives, each type acting as an agent or representing a point of view or choice of action and its subsequent consequences within the African reality.

In considering the broad context of Sembene's cinematic works, *Xala* (*The Curse*, 1974) provides the clearest example of a multiplicity of voices or points of view, thus demonstrating the splintered nature of neocolonial/postcolonial Africa. *The Curse* was produced twenty years after the birth of sub-Saharan African cinema, at a time when many Africans were becoming frustrated with the nationalist project of neocolonialism. Although national movements emphasised a return to tradition and the unearthing and reappropriation of an African identity in order to reattain nationhood, Independence itself was farcical because a colonial mentality continued to pervade African consciousness:

> [T]he national bourgeoisie that took the baton of rationalization, industrialization, and bureaucratization in the name of nationalism, turned out to be a kleptocracy. Their enthusiasm for nativism was a rationalization of their urge to keep the national bourgeoisies of other nations, and particularly the powerful industrialized nations, out of their way.[7]

The Curse is very much a critique of this "kleptocracy" and its subsequent consequences for the whole of Senegalese society. Sembene constructs his critique by creating a typal character, El Hadji Abdoukader Beye, whose function is to embody neocolonial Africa. El Hadji, a member of the bourgeois élite of Dakar, discovers that he is afflicted with the curse of sexual impotence, the *xala*, when he marries his third wife. The spectator learns, ultimately, that this curse is the result of El Hadji's pursuit of material enrichment and social advancement at the expense of his compatriots. He is quite prepared to sacrifice his "Africanness" and grasp neocolonial power by standing on the backs of his fellow Africans. However, the reasons for this and the emotional forces that have shaped him are never explained in the film. As a typal character, El Hadji is defined by his function in the narrative and not by the psychology of his character in the classical Western sense. This is entirely appropriate to the structure of *The Curse* because Sembene's main goal is to subvert the emotional involvement typical of classical Hollywood narrative cinema, and provoke the audience intellectually to question the implications of embracing neocolonialism.

In order to consider possible solutions to Senegal's cultural bankruptcy as a neocolonial nation, Sembene has created three female typal characters whose functions are to confront El Hadji, each reflecting a different position or point of view. Awa, El Hadji's first wife, appears as the embodiment of traditional African values (Mother Africa) in both her dress and her behaviour. Oumi, the second wife, embodies the materialistic, seductive temptress (Africa in its present neocolonial state) who leaves her husband at the first sign of financial insecurity. Interestingly, it is El Hadji and Awa's daughter, Rama, who represents the space in between Awa and Oumi, and embodies Sembene's own sociopolitical ideology at that point in his career.

Rama attempts to create a synthesis of the contradictions of her traditional upbringing and Western education, and thus represents both a respect for Africa's past and a vision of its future.

Sembene uses the narrative device of El Hadji's third marriage to expose the conflicting ideological positions of the three women. Although they are united in their opposition to the marriage, the women are divided in their reasons for opposition. For example, Oumi opposes the marriage because she is jealous and greedy. However, Rama, who is a student and advocate of Africanization, refuses to attend the wedding reception because "every polygamous man is a liar". As a patient and traditional woman, Awa accepts El Hadji's third wife as his prerogative, even though it causes her much pain. She is conscious of her social obligations regarding her position as first wife, but also the consequences of leaving such a position – when Rama encourages her to divorce El Hadji, Awa remarks: "You think I'd find another husband? I'd be third or fourth wife with luck." Awa's position as first wife confers on her a certain status in Islamic society and the significance of this position has a definite cultural meaning for Sembene's Senegalese audience. For example, El Hadji's desire to consult Awa when things go awry is not only a result of her long-suffering patience, but also reflective of her position as first wife.

Although Awa submits to the rules of a polygamous society, she is not without power, and Sembene underlines the subtlety of this cultural construct in a key scene in which she is alone with El Hadji. When El Hadji implores Awa to get out of the car with him to greet Oumi, their brief exchange is presented in a shot/reverse-shot construction. All shots keep El Hadji in the left third of the frame, leaning into the car towards Awa. The reverse-shots centre Awa in the frame in medium close-up. This underscores her position as the privileged narrative agent because El Hadji maintains a weakened position within the frame, whereas Awa is centred and thus balanced in the composition of the frame space. She pointedly reminds El Hadji of the Islamic marital laws which state that, as second wife, Oumi must come to her.

Through her status-seeking greed and love of all things Western, Oumi provides a most striking contrast to Awa. Interestingly, it is her materialism that links Oumi most closely to El Hadji, and Sembene underscores this visually in the scene that follows Awa's refusal to leave the car. El Hadji enters Oumi's bedroom and sits on the bed, while Oumi, who is fixing her wig, proceeds to insult Awa (whom she believes has encouraged the marriage) before demanding money from El Hadji: "I don't have a cent. Since you're spending, I will too." Ironically, the couple who shares the same neocolonial ideology also shares the frame space of every shot in the scene. However, Oumi tends to dominate the space in the frame because she sits higher than El Hadji and consistently leans into his space as she berates him. This positioning also forces the spectator to question El Hadji's moral strength: is he really in control of his situation as he appears to be, or is he a "follower", mindlessly complicit with the system?

Awa and Rama are "linked" by their desire to preserve Senegalese cultural heritage; for Awa, however, this means practising traditional values, while Rama is eager to reject those values which she believes will impede the development of postcolonial Senegal. What separates Rama ideologically from her mother is her Western education, and this is underscored through a combination of two scenes. When Rama suggests to her mother that she talk to El Hadji about his *xala*, Awa is appalled that Rama would even consider such a disrespectful act. This gulf between the two women is created by their different cultural positioning, and is not representative of their personal feelings for each other. Sembene demonstrates that a similar gulf exists between Rama and El Hadji in a parallel scene in which Rama confronts her father alone in his office. Generally, a shot/reverse-shot construction works to suture the viewer into the emotions of the characters because their space is perceived as being linked psychologically. In this sequence, Sembene subverts this perception by using a shot/reverse-shot structure that violates the 180° axis rule. Rama and El Hadji face each other across his desk but never match eyelines, thus giving the impression that they are talking past each other, both personally and ideologically unable to see eye-to-eye on the "future of Africa".

Interestingly, their contrasting ideologies are further emphasised through the *mise en scène*. In this scene, El Hadji is seated in front of a political map of Africa (with borders established during colonialism), while Rama is seated in front of a pan-African map (without political borders). This implied split in their positions is furthered when El Hadji offers Rama a glass of French mineral water, which she refuses because it is imported. By placing the bottle, which represents France, between them on his desk, Sembene makes literal the metaphorical and ideological gulf that separates father and daughter. This gulf is personified when El Hadji addresses Rama in French and she replies in Wolof. When he angrily demands to know why she is speaking Wolof, Rama simply gets up and replies, "Papa, have a good day" as she takes her leave. At this point El Hadji attempts to dissolve the barrier between them by offering Rama money, but, in so doing, he only creates another boundary reminiscent of those on his political map. Rama is not interested in financial gain, only in her mother's happiness and the family's solidarity.

According to Sembene, Rama "is like a step forward in a society which must find a synthesis. It must do so, but how? One can no longer be traditional but neither can one completely resign oneself to European ways."[8] Although she clearly embodies Sembene's vision of a truly independent Africa, Rama represents but one voice and therefore one choice of action in the totality of his "Senegalese dialectic".

Because this dialectic involves an examination of all structures and their meanings, Sembene chooses various aspects of Senegalese society to examine in various films. Thus, he must tailor his characters to suit the ideology he is probing and presenting. For example, according to Sembene, his first feature-length film, *La Noire de...* (*Black Girl*, 1966), denounces three realities: French colonialism which persists in a new form of "African slave trade"; the new African class which is neocolonialism's accomplice; and the existence of a certain form of technical cooperation.[9] As in *The Curse*, *Black Girl* probes the consequences of embracing neocolonialism through the downfall of a major character: both El Hadji and Diouana seek solutions outside themselves and thus outside their culture.

Recognition of this situation in *Black Girl* is revealed by a narrative construction containing a forward timeline and a back-story narrated through flashbacks in order to tie together all the story elements. Diouana, who cannot speak French, expresses herself through interior monologues, while an offscreen voice narrates her thoughts in French to the spectator: "It all started in Dakar. No one wanted a maid."[10] Diouana makes the rounds of all the European homes to no avail, and finally has no other recourse but to join the group of unemployed domestic workers gathered in the maids' square, waiting for prospective employers to pass. Sembene uses a high-angle long shot to portray the group of young women moving from one pavement to another, following the buildings' shadows; although this is a device clearly used to indicate the passage of time, it also serves to foreshadow the eventual diminution of Diouana's identity. Finally, when "Madame" arrives, a dozen young women rush towards this "providence", but Diouana holds herself aloof. Madame examines the women as if she were choosing a vegetable at the market. She scrutinizes Diouana, utters the word "you" in her direction, and turns to leave. Elated, Diouana dances for joy announcing to everyone that she is working for Europeans.

When viewing Sembene's films, one must take into consideration the fact that he is constructing his narratives first and foremost for Africans; certain narrative information will therefore be more immediately recognisable to someone within the culture than to a Western viewer. The European family with whom Diouana finds employment is a "coopérant" family. To a Senegalese audience, this term carries a specific meaning: Diouana's employer is an advisor in the programme that France created after Independence to assist in the development of Senegal's technical infrastructure. Although Diouana's employers are obviously well-paid and enjoy an elevated social status in Dakar, they are still foreigners and treat Diouana much differently in Africa than in France.

An example of this occurs when Madame gives Diouana her discarded clothes, and Diouana mistakes this simple act of charity for an act of kindness and friendship. It is only when she is in France and outside her culture that Diouana is forced to confront the inherent inequality of their social positions. Diouana's inferior social standing as a maid is implicit when viewed within the social/cultural context of Dakar: as a foreigner in an environment familiar to her maid, Madame cannot afford to be ungenerous to Diouana, and the latter never questions the power relations between giver and receiver. However, when Diouana and Madame arrive in France and Madame is surrounded by her own peers, all pretence of equality is dropped and Diouana's "lowly status" as black servant is made very explicit.

By presenting a contrasting interplay of power relations between Diouana and Madame, Sembene is implying that there is a heavy price to pay for "helping hands". Diouana suffers a loss of identity and dignity because "she who receives" ends up beholding to "she who gives": in France, separated from the support system of family, friends and culture, Diouana is forced to become entirely dependent on the largesse of the "coopérant" family, rather in the same way that Senegal at the time was reliant on France for technological infrastructure. Both Diouana and Senegal fail in looking outwards to France for resources they could cultivate within themselves, and, as a result, are exploited by colonialism.

Sembene is portraying the loss of unity and the importance of community life which is instrumental in helping individuals cope with hardship. He wants the viewer to identify with this issue rather than with the character's individual psychology, and he has created Diouana as a typal character whose function in the narrative is to demonstrate the consequences of embracing the "myth of France". Trapped on one side by her own unrealistic expectations of France, and on the other by the unrealised expectations of her friends and family, Diouana attempts to reclaim the culture on which she turned her back by snatching from the wall the mask she had bought and given to her employers in Dakar. This mask is the only remaining link between Diouana and her culture. Ultimately, it becomes a symbol of both defiance and hope. When Monsieur returns Diouana's belongings to her family, he is followed out of the quarter by her younger brother who is wearing the mask. In effect, Sembene is suggesting that Senegal's youth will eventually empower themselves and all Senegal by accepting the "mask" and defining their identity from within. Although the narrative contains psychological content, the minimal use of close-ups tends to subvert the psychology of Diouana and distance the spectator from what might otherwise be viewed as a melodrama. Diouana recognises her situation when she declares: "I'm their prisoner. I don't know anyone here. No one in my family is here. That's why I'm their slave." This leads to her refusal to be complicit with the very system she embraced: "Never will I be a slave". Although Diouana's recognition of her entrapment is presented through a short series of close-ups, the low camera angle and declarative tone of voice subvert notions of psychological excess and woman as victim trope by empowering both Diouana's image and her words. Diouana's suicide therefore is ultimately an act of defiance rather than of desperation.

Similarly, in *Niaye* (1964), Ngoné War Thiandum commits suicide out of a refusal to be complicit with a system that is breaking down in the face of corruption and debasement of traditional values. Ngoné War Thiandum is of noble ancestry and lives her life in accordance with the traditional ethics of honour practised by her distinguished predecessors. When her unmarried daughter becomes pregnant, it is discovered that the child is a result of incest, forced on her by her father. Ngoné War Thiandum is affronted by this unnatural act, and the refusal of the village elders to punish her husband creates a tension between herself, the community and her daughter. Her individual honour has been compromised in the eyes of society and she refuses to live with this shame and loss of dignity; this ultimately results in her suicide.

Her distressing situation alienates her from the other village women, complicit in their silence, and this is underscored visually in a scene in which Sembene contrasts long shots of a solitary Ngoné War Thiandum waiting to consult her female *griot*, with shots of village women performing domestic tasks as a group. Sembene refuses to employ the cinematic grammar that would foreground Ngoné War Thiandum's individual emotional distress at her predicament. Instead, he opts for long shots and voice-over narration of the events by the village *griot* in order to force the spectator to consider the larger ideological concerns of hypocrisy and debasement of traditional values.

In an attempt to suppress evidence of the incest, the villagers force Ngoné War Thiandum's daughter, Khar Madiaga Diop, into exile with her child. En route to Dakar, the young girl is tempted to abandon the baby but reconsiders when she sees a flock of vultures circling above the crying child. By choosing to take the child with her and thus accepting responsibility for her actions, Khar Madiaga Diop serves as a metaphor for Sembene's vision of a future Africa.

Sembene contrasts this portrayal of a splintering solidarity in *Niaye* with a reverse process in *Emitaï* (*God of Thunder*, 1971). In this film, which depicts the oppression of a Senegalese village by the French colonial Army during the Second World War, it is the women who attempt to reverse the erosion of traditional societal values by providing action and solidarity in the face of the crisis.

The film opens with the passive surrender of all the young men in the village to forced conscription. The following year, the French colonial Army imposes a tax of thirty kilos of rice per villager to feed the troops. This presents the villagers with a dilemma: rice is sacred to the village culture, thus making it necessary to resist handing it over to the colonial government, but the villagers' means of resistance is limited because the god Emitaï forbids violence. The narrative conflict hinges on forced change. In order to survive, the villagers are compelled to question their traditional practice in the face of modern oppression.

The elders meet together in the sacred forest to make their sacrifices and await guidance from the gods. Because they are looking to an outside agent to solve the dilemma, their resistance can be regarded as passive in nature. The passivity of the men clearly demonstrates that they are not responding to the changing circumstances by evolving themselves, but are instead relying on outmoded methodologies. Sembene has always regarded the necessity to adapt to changing circumstances by taking action into one's own hands as critical to the creation of modern Africa. In *God of Thunder*, he is not criticising masculinity or traditional practice *per se*, but rather the passive reliance on an outside force.

Sembene contrasts the men's passivity with the active resistance of the women. He provides an interesting structure for analysis because the women function not as individuals, but as a collective heroine, and demonstrate that the traditional value of solidarity can be a point of resistance. Thus, Sembene indicates that tradition is valuable, provided it remains responsive to change and does not prevent a culture from taking active responsibility for its own evolution.

In *God of Thunder*, the women do not wait for the gods to provide inspiration or direction: they actively resist the colonial Army by hiding the rice. This solution succeeds in subverting the double bind faced by the women because it prevents the French from taking the rice without the villagers' having to resort to violence. The actions of the men and women are presented as being in direct opposition to each other ideologically and cinematographically. Sembene illustrates this near the beginning of the film in a series of short sequences that places all three forces into opposition. The first scene begins at night with long shots of the procession of women concealing the rice. The men are shown standing passively on the sidelines watching and commenting: "The women are going to hide the rice. We can't let the white men have it. They are right; better to die." This is followed by another series of long shots of the women's procession during the following day, intercut with long shots of the conscripted soldiers marching. The women move screen left to right within the frame and the soldiers move screen right to left, placing them in opposition to each other through editing. Sembene uses a tilt from top to bottom of the baobab tree to link this sequence with the scene of the elders' council in the sacred forest. The visual dialectic is strengthened because Sembene uses horizontal movement within the shots depicting the women and the Army, then breaks the plane by using vertical movement in his transition shot. Finally, he emphasises the passivity of the men within the same sequence by using static camera set-ups during the elders' council, contrasting with the movement of the women and the Army.

Recognising that the women were instrumental in hiding the rice, the Army officers attempt to destroy the women's resolve to protect the rice through torture. They force the women to sit in direct sunlight without water or cover; this action, however, rather than breaking the women, only leads to their defiance and the strengthening of their position as a group. When one of the men buys his wife's freedom by giving up his family's portion of the rice, she refuses to go with him and remains with the group.

By creating a collective heroine, Sembene is signalling to the spectator that the action of *God of Thunder* is ideological rather than personal. This is reinforced by the use of silence and speech in the film. The women rarely speak and Sembene contrasts their silent action with the men's paralytic oratory, seeming to suggest that talking is useless when action is warranted.

A very powerful moment occurs during the women's torture. Two of the young village boys try to ease the women's suffering by bringing them water. Sembene shows the women drinking through a series of close-ups, and, although these are shots of individuals, their very number serves to underline the group's suffering as a whole. The boys are eventually chased off by the conscripted soldiers and the women respond by all singing together. This burst of communal sound contrasts with their previous silence, providing an extremely powerful illustration of their collective defiance and solidarity.

Although women play a peripheral role in *Mandabi* (*The Money Order*, 1968), Sembene's portrayal of Ibrahima Dieng's wives, Méty and Aram, lays the groundwork for *God of Thunder*'s collective heroine. In contrast to *The Curse*, in which the wives conflict with each other, Méty and Aram are united in the protection of their family's interests. In this sense, they show the same solidarity as do the women of *God of Thunder*. *The Money Order* is concerned more with the recognition of one's own potential to effect change than with the need to take direct action, the element that dominates *God of Thunder*. *The Money Order* brings its characters, including Méty and Aram, to an awareness that the corrupt system within which they live requires change, and it ultimately empowers them to take the first step themselves.

Married to a man who has been out of work for four years, Méty and Aram are obviously concerned about the family's financial situation. The arrival of a money order from Dieng's nephew in France sets off a chain of reactions that ultimately brings the family far closer to the brink of disaster than they were before the money order arrived. On the surface, it would appear that the object of the narrative quest is to cash the money order. However, Sembene reveals a much more complex agenda as he portrays the pitfalls of easy money and consumer credit in neocolonialism by creating a wonderfully ironic discourse based on the optimism, greed and bureaucratic red tape generated by the uncashed money order. Even before Dieng learns of the money order's existence, Méty and Aram tell the local shopkeeper and receive credit to buy food for the whole family. This has the unfortunate effect of broadcasting their family's new "wealth" to the entire neighbourhood, and soon they are besieged with demands for loans.

The Money Order illustrates the difficulty in applying a Western feminist grid to an African construction. A Western feminist argument could be made that Méty and Aram are oppressed by the patriarchal construct of polygamy: certainly they are clearly shown by Sembene as having to resort to conspiracy in order to subvert Dieng's authority as male head of a Muslim household. However, it should be questioned whether such a reading is efficacious in understanding *The Money Order* as a text. Sembene has presented much stronger critiques of polygamy: in *The Curse*, for example, the inciting incident of the narrative is focused on the disruption caused by El Hadji's third marriage. It can be further argued in this case that El Hadji's extended family is largely dysfunctional because of the infighting for power among the households of his various wives. In *The Money Order*, Sembene once again uses the cultural construction of polygamy for its "metaphorical potential",[11] but, in this case, the marriages are not sites of disjunction: rather, they are sites of conjunction, a collective space in which Dieng, Méty and Aram receive support and protection. Thus, the expression of polygamy in *The Money Order* is a constructive one and actually more traditional in its nature than the marriages in *The Curse*: Méty and Aram work together in solidarity for the greater good of the family, rather than splintering along lines of self-interest.

Applying a Western grid without allowing for cultural differences can result in a colonization of the text's larger meaning. This is particularly problematic when considering Sembene's work, because his ideological notion of culture is central to understanding how his films function as cultural documents. When questioned about *The Money Order* and his own position on polygamy, Sembene has replied: "I am against polygamy but my concern was not to deal with this subject in this film. Its unity of action would have suffered from it."[12] Thus, it can be fairly assumed that Méty's and Aram's roles as women within the narrative construction are not geared towards an examination of polygamy as an oppressive institution. To read them as such is essentially to miss the point that Sembene is trying to make: all Africans, regardless of gender, have the potential to change their society.

As character constructions, Méty and Aram generally function within the narrative as forces dedicated to saving Dieng from absolute disaster, and thus on a symbolic level represent the notion of traditional solidarity. This is illustrated when Dieng discovers that he needs a photograph to obtain an identity card, and Aram willingly sacrifices her gold necklace to raise the money. Later, in a desperate attempt to deflect demands from their neighbours, Méty and Aram take advantage of Dieng's beating by the photographer to claim that he was robbed of the money order: as Méty says, "a lie that unifies people is better than truth". Although the wives lie to protect the family's interests and demonstrate solidarity and loyalty to Dieng in the face of disaster, Sembene is implying that this is less a survival strategy than an ironical construct, because their actions are not sustainable over the long term. In a sense, the wives are misdirecting their energies by using their solidarity to support a corrupt society, rather than to revolutionize it.

Sembene uses the act of lying to underscore the corruption of the entire society. Dieng says to the postman: "Honesty is a sin in this country". This is ironical because Dieng lies to his wives who, in turn, lies to him who are lying to his friends; thus, no one is dealing honestly with each other. Méty and Aram are victims of a system with which they are complicit, and they are included in the solution that Sembene is proposing when he has the postman remark, "We shall change this country...You, your wives, your children, we'll all change it". Dieng and his wives are responsible for both their actions and their outcome, and thus are also responsible for initiating the changes necessary to improve society. Because both Méty and Aram are included in the postman's exhortation, it is clear that Sembene sees the process of change as being inclusive of both men and women. By focusing on the question of the individual's role in change, rather than centring on the action of change, Sembene ultimately leaves the audience pondering their own participation in the creation of a new Africa. With the release of *Ceddo* in 1976, Sembene takes the notion of women's involvement in nation-building one step further. In *Ceddo*, the principal action concerns the conflict that occurs with the penetration of Islam into a traditional animist culture. Sembene layers *Ceddo*'s structure by adding a Christian missionary and a slave trader, thus collapsing a number of important historical timelines into a single setting. As a fictional construct, *Ceddo* is not meant to be a direct historical representation of these events which took place at different intervals in African history, but the film can be regarded in a metaphorical sense as an effort to reclaim African history in an African voice.

The *ceddo* are defenders of traditional cultural identity. The central action of the narrative focuses on the *ceddo*'s rebellion against their oppression by Demba War, the king. Demba War has come under the influence of the imam, and this has resulted in the erosion of the *ceddo*'s traditional rights.

The film opens with the kidnapping of Demba War's daughter, Princess Dior Yacine, by a young *ceddo* rebel, whose intention is to hold her captive until the king restores the *ceddo*'s rights. The kidnapping of Dior could be read as an expression of male violence against a female victim. However, by privileging her gender over other aspects of her construction, there exists a danger of appropriating Sembene's narrative intent. Dior's importance to the *ceddo* rebel lies more in her social status than in her gender, and this is underscored by the function that her character plays in the narrative structure. Sembene uses the contact between the *ceddo* and Dior to provide a strategy for direct ideological debate on the issues that would otherwise not have existed. Furthermore, by subjecting Dior to the same type of disenfranchisement of rights as the *ceddo* are currently experiencing, Sembene sets the stage for her eventual recognition of the inherent injustice of the *ceddo*'s situation.

The princess's capture serves as a narrative device to expose Sembene's central thesis concerning the loss of cultural identity and roots. The chevalier Saxewar, to whom Dior is betrothed, declares that it is his duty to rescue and marry her. Madior, the king's nephew, is incensed to learn that, since Islam forbids his culture's traditional practice of matriarchy and matrilineal succession, he will no longer inherit Dior as his legitimate spouse. Biram, the king's son, is jubilant because, under Islamic patriarchy, he will inherit the throne and Dior. Thus, even expressions of masculinity are disrupted by the incursion of Islam and, interestingly, Sembene undercuts all these expectations because Dior chooses to liberate the *ceddo* and, in so doing, liberates herself.

Dior embodies the notion of Africa at "ground zero". Like Rama in *The Curse*, she is interested in preserving her culture and roots, but she must take drastic action in order to do so. She is not objectified in the Western sense because, unlike Western constructions of women in film, her power is not centred in her sexuality. Like the *ceddo*, she is using every means at her disposal to escape her oppressor: she resorts to a sexual advance towards the *ceddo*, not out of desire or fear, but out of a strategy for escape, borne out by her attempt to kill him.

There has been some critical discussion regarding the significance of Dior's dream sequence, where she appears to dream of union with the *ceddo* rebel. Françoise Pfaff points out that it is both Dior's "feelings of independence and womanly love"[13] that are expressed in the dream, but Pfaff's discussion of the cultural issues, such as class, makes it clear that the dream has an ideological resonance beyond that of simple sexual attraction. An argument could be made that Dior is admiring of the *ceddo* not for his sexual properties, but because he personifies all that is ideologically honourable in a warrior: in effect, Dior's acceptance of the *ceddo* in the dream could signify her symbolic acceptance of the *ceddo* in reality. To a certain extent, this could be textually supported by the contrast Sembene creates between the young *ceddo* rebel and the other men trying to possess Dior's political influence. However, the absence of consistency within the narrative structure creates a paradoxical ambiguity, perhaps intentional, that can only be resolved by the spectator taking a position as an individual.

It could be observed that Dior is confined to a passive role in the narrative because much of it takes place with her as a witness, rather than as an active participant. However, by constructing Dior's position as "witness", Sembene has created a position that in fact empowers her to take control and act directly. Like Méty and Aram in *The Money Order*, Dior is brought to the threshold of change through recognition of the basic injustice of her societal situation, but, unlike Dieng's wives, Dior actually crosses the threshold of recognition into action during the confrontation with the imam and the Islamic forces. During the forced conversion of the vanquished *ceddo*, Dior is returned to the village by the imam's men. In a series of long and medium-long shots, Sembene shows Dior walking slowly past the *ceddo*. She snatches a rifle from one of the imam's guards and turns to point it at the imam. The *ceddo* protect her by throwing themselves in front of the imam's men and taking the barrels of the rifles into their own mouths. Filmed in long shot and centred in the frame, Dior fires at the imam, striking him in the genitals. He falls and Sembene cuts to a medium close-up of Dior staring down at the imam. The camera zooms in to a low-angle close-up and Dior looks up, in fourth wall address directly confronting the spectator with her action. Because of the deliberate pace with which the overall sequence develops, the shooting of the imam is a calculated action on Dior's part and is the natural culmination embodying all that she has experienced during the course of the narrative. Dior throws down the rifle in long shot and then moves slowly past the imam's disciples, making direct eye contact with them. The final shot of the film depicts Dior approaching two disciples: they part to let her pass and she moves beyond them yet again to gaze directly at the audience.

Sembene has chosen this type of presentation to empower the princess, not only as a woman, but also as an agent of change. Clearly Dior's action is constructive for, unlike the passive men in the film, she acts out against her aggressor. Her direct gaze is a call to action, not from a gendered character point of view, but from the point of view of Senegal. As Sembene himself has observed: "When the princess kills the imam, it has great symbolic significance for modern Senegal. This action is contrary to present ideas and the role that women now hold."[14]

In *Ceddo*, Sembene recodes narrative closure from a play of power and containment into a device that forces the audience to consider the action that Dior Yacine takes in order to throw off the yoke of oppression. Interestingly, Sembene uses this device to similar ends in his first film, *Borom Sarret*. This short film, focusing on the misadventures of a cart driver in Dakar, is set in newly-independent Senegal and puts into play the type of neocolonial critique that will provide a foundation for Sembene's entire body of work.

The character of Fatou, Borom Sarret's wife and the major female character of the film, is most instrumental at its conclusion. When Borom Sarret returns home at the end of the day without money or his cart, Fatou hands him their baby and leaves the courtyard, assuring him, "We will eat tonight". Borom Sarret's query, "Where is she going at this hour?", remains unanswered in the final shot, and it is inferred that Fatou will prostitute herself before allowing her family to go hungry. The ambiguity leads to an active spectator, as interpretation of her action is left up to the audience to infer the response and consider the solution. Fatou's determination to take action and alter their situation provides an interesting contrast to the two young beggar boys who appear at the door of the courtyard as she leaves. Fatou is prepared to make whatever personal sacrifice is necessary so that future generations will not have to beg.

If Sembene's position on the issue of self-sufficiency is implied in

Borom Sarret, it is transparent in *Guelwaar*, his most recent and politically explicit film. Set in present-day neocolonial Senegal, the film deals with the mistaken burial of the Catholic, Pierre Henri Thioune (called Guelwaar, which means "the noble one" in Wolof), in a Muslim cemetery. Because the film's narrative structure is fractured into many points of view, no single character or action is definitive in and of itself. What predominates, however, is Sembene's critique of foreign aid, which, according to Françoise Pfaff, was later grafted onto the story of the burial mistake.[15] Thus, when attempting to analyse the characters of Nogoy Marie (Guelwaar's widow) and Sophie (Guelwaar's daughter), one must consider their functions within Sembene's ideological framework. Once again, Sembene has constructed representations that resist gendered readings in the Western feminist grid. This is particularly true of Sophie who supports the whole Thioune family as a prostitute in Dakar. Sembene creates a tension between Nogoy Marie's attitude towards her daughter's profession and Guelwaar's position that it is better to prostitute oneself than beg for a living.

The temptation exists to read Sophie's situation as an experience of gender oppression. However, Sembene subverts this possibility by using the character of Guelwaar to present her situation as economic oppression rather than pure sexual oppression. Although it could be argued that the two forms of oppression are interdependent, Sembene depicts Sophie as a survivalist in an African reality. In fact, Sembene affords Sophie real power, for she is not only self-reliant, but also able to support her entire family.

Sophie's own personal thoughts and feelings regarding prostitution are never foregrounded. Rather, Sembene provides this information indirectly during the funeral wake in a conversation that takes place between Father Léon and Sophie's friend, Hélène, also a prostitute. This represents a departure from a classical presentation in which the viewer would expect the evidence to come directly from Sophie. However, through the character of Hélène, Sembene is demonstrating both the hypocrisy of society and the proliferation of prostitution as an economic strategy. For example, in a series of two-shots, Hélène and Father Léon slowly move in a circle, always away from each other. Hélène is forced to talk over her shoulder to the priest, giving the impression that they are not connecting. She declares that when she obtained her high school diploma there were no jobs, resulting in her decision to become a registered prostitute. Interestingly, this information underscores the fact that she is a responsible person: as a registered prostitute, she must submit to weekly medical check-ups that screen for the AIDS virus.

Hélène's function in the narrative is purely ideological, and, although she does not reappear after this scene, the discourse on prostitution continues throughout the film. Sembene uses her character as a device to present the spectator with complete discourse on the circumstances surrounding her prostitution: as Father Léon is a stranger to Hélène, he must be given rather more detail than would be required if they had a long-standing relationship. This allows Sembene to create a narrative space in which he provides the spectator with the expositional information that neither Hélène nor Sophie is alone in her predicament. Because Father Léon listens very carefully to everything Hélène says and does not pronounce a harsh judgment on her, he demonstrates an understanding of the ideological schism that Sembene sees existing in Africa: Hélène is a devout Catholic but a practising prostitute, and these should be mutually and morally exclusive. However, because of economic necessity both of these states coexist.

In the character of Nogoy Marie, Sembene demonstrates that the mystical is always close to the African consciousness. After Guelwaar's death, Nogoy Marie hears him "calling" her three times, but is unable to understand why. In the bedroom, she addresses her confusion to Guelwaar's presence, symbolised by his suit on the bed. The camera frames her in close-ups, centred in the frame space and looking down at the suit, but pulling away to screen left. This affords a certain tension to the close-ups, reflecting Nogoy Marie's mixed emotions and symbolically placing her ideology in conflict with that of Guelwaar as she questions the circumstances leading up to his death.

At the cemetery, Nogoy Marie experiences a flashback of her past life with Guelwaar that offers a narrative opportunity to flesh out this conflict. Guelwaar is about to set out to attend a foreign aid distribution meeting when Nogoy Marie discloses to him that Sophie is a prostitute. The remainder of the encounter is presented in a modified shot/reverse-shot structure which begins with Guelwaar replying, "I'd rather she were a prostitute than a beggar...rather she was dead than a beggar". In an extreme close-up, in which Nogoy Marie is centred in the frame, she counters, "What about my dignity as a mother? I'd rather live off charity than know what my daughter does in Dakar." The camera then pulls back to a medium two-shot to show Guelwaar stretching out his hand in front of her and declaring: "Woe betide the one who holds out his hand and waits for others to feed him and his family". Guelwaar's hand, acting as a metaphorical barrier between the couple, becomes larger than life as the camera moves in to a low-angle medium close-up in which Guelwaar repeats his idea: "Pierre Henri Thioune would rather die than wait for another man to feed his family".[16] Again, in an extreme close-up, Nogoy Marie offers the counter-argument couched in personal terms: "Behave like your fellow men. Free yourself from your armour of pride. Learn to live like others do."

Central to Guelwaar's ideological position is the notion that Africa is a beggar and is beholden to those who give handouts. During his speech at the aid meeting, he declares: "Famine, drought and poverty, do you know why they happen? If a country is always taking aid from another country, that country will always only be able to say one thing...thank you, thank you, thank you." In a metaphorical sense, all narrative blocks preventing recuperation of Guelwaar's body lead to Nogoy Marie's recognition of the validity of Guelwaar's ideological position. In terms of narrative structure, this recognition is implied: the viewer infers from Nogoy Marie's placement in crowd shots and at the Muslim cemetery that she is "witnessing" everything. Thus, in the final scene, when she is asked by the elders to stop the youths from trampling on the foreign aid, she replies: "The sacrilege isn't what the children are doing. It's what you didn't say. You made an agreement with that man who is lying back there and then went back on your word. *That* is sacrilege." Nogoy Marie's declaration and confrontation of the elders therefore bring Sembene's ideological structure full circle: by underlining their failure to act, Nogoy Marie places the responsibility for their situation (and Africa's) directly on the shoulders of the elders. In this way, Sembene is returning to territory first claimed by Fatou in *Borom Sarret*. Changing Africa can only be effected from inside Africa, by Africans.

The journey from *Borom Sarret* to *Guelwaar* demonstrates that Sembene perceives his society to be comprised of individuals each capable of contributing to the growth of the society, despite – or perhaps because of – the notions of difference that lie between them. Thus, in Sembene's ideological project, men and women are equally charged with the responsibility of change. Sembene creates constructs of women's representations both within culturally traditional feminine models and outside them, underscoring his position that participation in change can have equal but different expressions, each determined by the roles embodied by the individuals involved.

An understanding of the roles women assume in Sembene's work must be predicated on a recognition of the vital importance that cultural determination plays in the structure of his ideology. Considering Sembene's project of reaching those within his society prevented from accessing his novels by illiteracy, his strategy of presenting a multiplicity of spectator positions within his narratives offers an insight into the complexities of contemporary Africa. This applies equally to male and female character constructs: there is no pretence in Sembene's work that his female characters speak for all African women or even all African experiences. Rather, Sembene's ideological discourse advocates the development of cultural self-awareness and the empowerment such awareness brings, regardless of gender, and thus each female representation within his narrative structures speaks to a unique vision of what Africa might become.

* * *

The author is indebted to V Borden, C Cunningham and D L McGregor for discussion on the topic of women in African cinema.

Notes

[1] Fatou Sow, "Senegal: The Decade and Its Consequences", translated by Anne C Rennick and Catherine Boone, *Issue: A Journal of Opinion* 17: 2 (summer 1989): 35.

[2] Ulrich Gregor, "Interview with Ousmane Sembene", *Framework* 7/8 (1978): 36.

[3] Ibid.

[4] Assiatou Bah Diallo, "L'Image de la femme dans le cinéma africain", *Vues d'Afrique: Les Journées du Cinéma Africain 1989* [festival catalogue]: 17.

[5] Ousmane Sembene, quoted in "'If I Were a Woman, I'd Never Marry an African'", interview by Fírinne Ní Chréacháin, *African Affairs* 91 (1992): 241.

[6] Ibid: 244.

[7] Kwame Anthony Appiah in "Is the Post- in Postmodernism the Post- in Postcolonial?", *Critical Inquiry* 17 (winter 1991): 349-350.

[8] Françoise Pfaff, *The Cinema of Ousmane Sembene: A Pioneer of African Film* (Westport, CT: Greenwood Press, 1984): 158, quoting Jean and Ginette Delmas, "Ousmane Sembene: Un Film est un Débat", *Jeune Cinéma* 99 (December 1976-January 1977): 16. Pfaff's translation.

[9] Guy Hennebelle and Catherine Ruelle, "Cinéastes d'Afrique noire", *CinémAction* 3 (1978): 116.

[10] Pfaff (114-115) makes an interesting point: "One has yet to emphasize that the use of French does harm to the authenticity of the film since Diouana is certainly not expected to think in French but rather in Wolof or some other African language spoken in Senegal, especially since she is illiterate (in 1965, less than 1 percent of women in Senegal were able to write or even to speak in French). In this instance, however, Sembene had to satisfy his French sponsors since *Black Girl* as well as *Borom Sarret* are Franco-Senegalese productions."

[11] Florence Stratton uses this expression in *Contemporary African*

85

Literature and the Politics of Gender (London; New York: Routledge, 1994): 137.

[12] Pfaff: 130, quoting Guy Hennebelle and Catherine Ruelle, "Cinéastes d'Afrique Noire", *L'Afrique Littéraire et Artistique* 49 (1978): 177. Pfaff's translation.

[13] Ibid: 175.

[14] Ibid: 174, quoting Ousmane Sembene, interviewed in *Seven Days* 10 March 1978: 27.

[15] Françoise Pfaff, "*Guelwaar*", *Cineaste* 20: 2 (1993): 48.

[16] An ironical argument could be constructed to demonstrate that Guelwaar is violating his principle of self-sufficiency by accepting aid from his daughter. However, it could also be argued that the notion of family within Sembene's ideology is to provide solidarity and support for the whole extended family.

Ontological discourse in Ousmane Sembene's cinema

Frederick Ivor Case

At the very centre of Ousmane Sembene's prose fiction is his essential concern with the individual and his/her daily struggles in the context of the prevailing, religious, social, political and economic realities that determine community mores. Although this essay is not focused on the intratextuality of Sembene's prose fiction and his cinema,[1] it is necessary to point out that the humanistic preoccupations of his writings are to be found throughout his cinema.

Within the contemporary African context that predominates in Sembene's cinema are the contradictions of colonialism and its racist consequences, as well as the promises of independence with its attendant capitalist exploitation of those who have no work and no voice. By presenting the frustrations and hopelessness of the dispossessed, Sembene articulates a consistent discourse of the victimised. There is an unmistakable didactic purpose in Sembene's cinema that must not be confused with ideological dogmatism or aesthetic conservatism. Indeed, as we shall see in this essay, there are subtleties of discourse that the spectator, who is also listener and participant, must unravel.

Every discourse is, by its nature, axiological and therefore implicitly or explicitly ideological. The consistency of Sembene's discourse resides in the nature of the ontological questions raised by fundamental transformations in the social and economic conditions of life. The choice of categories that characterises Sembene's cinema is based on his individual perspectives of the world presented through the medium of African realism, which is not to be confused with verisimilitude. Although Sembene's prose fiction depends on the words on the written page and their evocations in the imagination of his readers, the discursive process of his cinema fully exploits articulation through images. This is not to say that dialogue or interior monologue is not important. Verbalised discourse, silence and music are essential to the aesthetic and thematic processes of Sembene's cinema.

However, the cinema is an art form that depends very heavily on metalinguistic phenomena. Although Sembene's cinema contains many explicit and implicit verbal statements on being-within-a-community, it is often through situations that full ontological meaning is revealed. The use of a variety of semiotic devices and the frequent silences that break up the dialogues oblige us to turn our attention to the signs that he has produced for us to read. These signs are often the very means of enunciation and can take the form of music, greetings, apparently simple cultural or religious acts, an object, or a given situation. It is these signs as well as the dialogue that constitute the process of Sembene's cinematographic discourse, and it is primarily through these signs that his ontological thought is expressed.

The societies portrayed by Sembene's cinema are often African with an overt expression of Islam.[2] It is not surprising, therefore, that expressions of Being are revealed through factors that are, in essence, both non-Islamic and Islamic at the same time. Islam in Senegal is generally most tolerant of cultural diversity which permits pre-Islamic African cultural factors to present themselves in ritual as well as in belief.[3]

Culture and religion are interdependent aspects of Being, and they are imposed by the community as much as they emanate from the individual. The state and the bureaucratic administration of its political and financial needs ensure that culture and religion are put to the service of political expediency. It is when culture and religion, as political expediency and community processes, act against the rights and interests of the individual that there is often a dynamic process of a decisive nature, in which the individual is either crushed or a large section of society rises in revolt.

The tension that exists between those who exercise and abuse power and those who are the victims constitutes the dramatic basis on which much of Sembene's work is focused. In a society that is built on a coherent set of beliefs and a common spirituality, the sociopolitical tensions of systemic degradation and exploitation relate directly to the state of Being of the individual.

Sembene's cinema reveals several perspectives of the dynamic of sociopolitical tension. Through analyses of the state of Being of his protagonists, Sembene explores spirituality as it is revealed in its widest sense.[4] Sembene's ontological thought is to be understood within the specific framework of contemporary social problems. Being is in every way determined by the sociocultural and economic contexts, and is sometimes independent of religion as a set of codified beliefs.

In Sembene's work, ontological dislocation is not the result of some abstract, philosophical search for Self. Ontological dislocation is engendered by socio-economic dislocation, accompanied by the abuse of male power. Since the society that Sembene describes is held together by deep-rooted principles of community, the interdependence that gives it meaning is in itself a powerful ontological statement. The signs by which men have come to identify themselves and their Being are often superficial and fragile externals that exist only for and by themselves and no longer connect their male possessors with the positive power that only community can confer. Therefore, men, in particular, begin to define themselves independently of their context. Although the words describe a function and a concept – father, husband, teacher, imam – the male protagonist dares to attempt to define and to determine the Self. The result is often a semantic gap, since the word denotes without reference to its connotative context. It is the connotative element that confers ontological meaning and depth to the semantic term.

Significantly, at the end of *Borom Sarret* (1963), the protagonist has become a carter without a cart. The words "borom sarret" mean the owner and, by association, the driver of a cart. Similarly, *borom kani* could be the owner of the pepper or, by association, someone who sells pepper. *Borom xamxam* means a person who possesses (great) knowledge. In this way, we understand the extent to which the protagonist of *Borom Sarret* leads a life that is in every way determined by his cart. It is from and through this cart that he is defined. We never learn his real name, since everyone who addresses him does so with reference to his cart. We learn that his wife's name is Fatima, and, although her physical presence in the film lasts no more than about one minute, her social presence is felt throughout the carter's day. He leaves home in the morning with her blessing for the day and with her implicit reminder that he is expected to provide the needs of his family. For his lunch, the carter eats the kola nut that Fatima gave him, and, as he wends his way home empty-handed, he wonders what he will say to his wife. As he lives through his day, the urgent mission that his wife has given him resonates as he meets failure after failure and squanders the little money that he has earned.

Fatima's personality predominates at the end of the film, as she leaves the child with her husband and sets out to resolve the dilemma of their daily sustenance that he has been unable to resolve. During the day, the husband's activities seem to lead him aimlessly from one situation to another. The presence of Fatima at the beginning and at the end of the film is marked by a sense of direction and purpose. Mbye Cham[5] makes a similar point concerning the role of the Princess Yacine Dior in *Ceddo* (1976). In these cases, the woman in the film represents a strength of character and a moral resolve that have to be acknowledged.

The kola nut that Fatima gives her husband is a stimulant chewed on by people in their hunger or in their search for the energy to continue their work. As a symbol, it may be used in a variety of social circumstances – for example, the conclusion of business and marriage negotiations. Therefore, the wife's simple act of caring at the beginning of the carter's day can be seen as a pact that she has made with him. He betrays this trust, however, by giving too generously to the *griot*, who is singing the praises of the carter's noble ancestors. Although he gives generously to the *griot*, he does not give to those less fortunate than himself. He does not even bother to answer the deformed beggar who asks him for alms; later on, the man with the dead child is abandoned at the gates of the cemetery with the body, because the father does not have the appropriate official papers for the burial.[6]

The carter appears not to have the moral sense associated with the Islamic society to which he belongs, nor does he seem to have the human compassion of one who is himself deprived. Charity – alms giving – is one of the five fundamental principles of Islam; it is the daily duty of the believer. "The Giver" is one of the 99 names of God,[7] and the exegesis of this attribute leads to a deep commitment to charitable giving, generosity, and willingness to assist others. In this religious context, the carter fails lamentably in his duty. His thoughts at the start of his day, as he gives a ride to the three persons who climb onto his cart, are not at all charitable, and he is particularly bitter in his attitude towards Mommadou, who persists in leaving his home every morning even though he is unemployed.

There is little doubt concerning Borom Sarret's personal bitterness which appears to have eliminated even the most fundamental ethical principles of sharing and community. His frequent prayers to God, the saints and marabouts are mere formulas uttered for the sake of safety, which, ultimately, they do not buy him. His dependency on religious formulas lures him into trespassing in a part of Dakar where carts are not permitted, and consequently he loses his cart.

From a social and economic perspective, Fatima is dependent on her husband, but, from a perspective of initiative and potential, the converse is true. When the carter returns home penniless, it is Fatima who will calmly seek a way out of the hunger that threatens them. In this way, the carter, who roams the streets and various districts of Dakar to hire his labour, is much more circumscribed by his life space than is his wife, who presumably remains in the compound for the greater part of her day. However, the woman has yet to possess a space outside of her husband's vision of her limits, and this in itself gives her ontological potential of a dimension that is not seen in the portrayal of her husband. This potential of Sembene's women characters is clearly seen in his prose fiction, as well as in his films. One has to refer only to the short story and film, *Taaw* (1970), to understand how this aspect of Sembene's ideological enterprise

Xala (1974)

Emitaï (God of Thunder, 1971)

Emitaï (God of Thunder, 1971)

Ceddo (1976)

Mandabi (The Money Order, 1968)

Camp de Thiaroye (*Camp Thiaroye,* 1988)

La Noire de... (*Black Girl,* 1966)

emanates from his work.

The severe limits of the carter's world are best depicted in the scene in which he is leading his horse down a street, away from the European quarter of Dakar. Even though he no longer has his cart, he feels obliged to stop at traffic lights, and remarks on how the lights regulate his life. This recalls a comparable scene in Richard Wright's novel, *Native Son*.[8] However, Wright's novel is firmly within the philosophical tradition of what is known in European thought as "the absurd", and, although Sembene's work shows many aspects of the absurd, these do not appear to be the preoccupations of Sembene's characters; nor is this the theoretical framework in which the director chooses to present his literary or cinematographic work. Sembene's preoccupations are more clearly defined by the basic need to survive whilst adhering to a moral and cultural system which is no longer sustained by even the most elementary economic factors. There is little available employment, even less money, and all of those familiar social structures that supported individual spirituality are falling apart.

Although the carter earns some money during the course of the day, he happily gives it to the *griot*. The carter's gift to the *griot* is an act of pride and a sign of spiritual unity with the ancestors, but it is also a foolhardy act, since the carter is left with no money. Neither God, the saints, divinities or ancestors are of any help; in the end, the carter is humiliated by the policeman who confiscates his cart, and the protagonist's human dignity is in every way trampled upon. He has lost his means of earning a living as well as the instrument – his cart – that identifies him.

In the first scenes of *Borom Sarret*, Fatima is pounding in the mortar as her husband is praying. He concludes his prayer by asking God's protection against unbelievers and the law. We see the justification of the prayer for protection against the law when he is stopped by a policeman in Plateau – the European quarter. As he drives towards Plateau, dominated by the Catholic Cathedral, and makes his way down wide streets between the imposing buildings of the district, we hear European symphonic music which contrasts with the Senegalese music heard up to this point. As he leaves Plateau with his horse, but without his cart, the melody of the Latin hymn, "Ave Verum Corpus",[9] is heard: this music accompanies the carter back to the Sandaga Market and remains with him until he is within sight of the Major Mosque of Dakar, when the music of the kora is heard again. The words towards the end of the great Latin hymn refer to the "hour of our death", and these bars of music coincide with the carter saying that all that is now left for him is his own death.[10]

Is Sembene saying that the new crucified is the African worker trying to battle against hunger? Is the new crucified the African who faithfully implores God to guide, protect and provide for him, and whose prayers go unanswered? On whose cross is the African worker being sacrificed? We must remember that the film begins in the early morning, as we hear the call to prayer from the mosque and see the carter in prayer. Having concluded his prayers, he gives himself additional protection by putting on his gris-gris. However, in the end, what matters is who will bring home something to eat, and the protagonist is not at all successful in his quest.

The power of the message resides in the potential attributed to the woman at the end of *Borom Sarret*. We do not know what she will obtain, how much she will obtain or even if she will return with any food at all. The essential point is her resolve and single-mindedness. There are no dreams, no prayers and no mystifications in her words at the beginning or at the end of the film. Fatima is energy and force in creative movement, and at the end of the film she has taken on a transformational role. It is this potential that defines her Being.

It is evident that one of the messages of *Borom Sarret* is that, since the traditional economic and social structures no longer provide a framework within which individuals can provide for themselves, religion and culture have become mere trappings devoid of great significance.

In *Mandabi* (*The Money Order*, 1968),[11] the ontological question is posed within the framework of personal identity. Ibrahima Dieng exists: he is a man with two wives and several children. He is acknowledged and respected in his urban community. He has an address to which mail is delivered. Yet, when he receives the money order which his nephew has sent to him, he is unable to cash it because he does not have an identity card. His vain quest for the card is the thematic context of the film. When Dieng presents himself at the city hall, he is asked his date of birth, but he knows neither the month nor the precise year, and cannot obtain a birth certificate which is the preliminary to obtaining the identity card. Since he does not exist on an officially sanctioned piece of paper, he has no moral existence and a relatively simple right – the cashing of the money order – becomes an insurmountable obstacle to survival. Dieng's plight recalls that of the father in *Borom Sarret* who could not bury his child because he did not have the correct papers.

Dieng has to endure much humiliation at the hands of the bureaucracy and rogues. He is eventually swindled out of the money order. Ironically, only a small part of the total sum was intended for his own use, but the news of the money order resulted in a succession of begging visitors, headed by the imam. In his quest for his official identity, Dieng learns that there is an absence of trust and integrity in human relations. His own struggle for survival is mirrored by the desperation of those who despise and cheat him. Dieng finally concludes that "honesty is a sin in this country". The postman gives a final message of hope that there will be positive change in the country. However, even at the end of *The Money Order*, the protagonist remains a non-Being whose existence is all that matters to those around him.

Despite his systemic and systematic humiliation, Dieng enjoys all the outward attributes of the head of a household, and at one point he firmly reminds his two wives that good wives must not act independently of their husband's decision. The first family scenes of *The Money Order* portray an aging, well-fed man whose eating habits are disgusting and whose wives are completely subservient to his needs. Dieng is preoccupied with his own authority, the order of his household, and the comfort that his wives can give him; he does not seem to realise that if these external points of reference predominate, the more fundamental cultural, religious and ontological aspects of life are subordinated. During the course of the film, we realise that it is the wives who maintain some sanity and a balanced view of the overall situation, yet Ibrahima Dieng tries to rule his household in a despotic fashion. His social function is that of husband, father, brother and head of a family, with all that these designations imply within the context of authority and responsibility. In fact, he is powerless outside the confines of his home. It is as if the signs themselves have effectively replaced the meaning of those signs. It is only in the last scenes of the film, surrounded by his wives and the postman, that Dieng comes to a deeper realisation of what has been happening to him and to the society in which he lives.

In *Taaw*,[12] the father is a tyrant whose only way of asserting himself is through terrorising his family. The film begins with a scene of the bare buttocks of a young boy being beaten by the father. The mother eventually rushes up to save the child who is loudly accused of being a liar and a degenerate by his father. It is soon obvious that much of what the father expresses concerning the child he has just beaten is meant for another son, Taaw, who is much older. Twenty-year-old Taaw does not even answer as his father insists that he respond. Taaw washes himself and goes off for the day. As he is greeted by his two friends, one of them asks Taaw why he bothered to get up. The hopelessness of these unemployed youths is such that staying in bed or looking for a job is no different. As Taaw lays on a public bench and thinks of his life, he concludes that, since he refuses to beg for his food, the only thing that he can do is to steal. He wonders if eventually he would be incarcerated or committed to a mental hospital, and in his daydreaming he concludes that the best future would be in becoming a politician. It is also indicative of

Sembene's use of irony that the repeated emphasis on stealing occurs as we see an image of the National Assembly on the screen.

A secondary theme of the film is the presence of Taaw's younger siblings at the Qur'anic[13] school. The teacher is a large, well-dressed man who exploits his *talibes*[14] by sending the boys out into the streets to beg. Taaw's young sister is kept back by the Qur'anic teacher to massage his toes. The teacher thanks God with sincere gratitude after the little boys bring him their morning's takings. It is significant that in the first scene in which we see the Qur'anic master, he is teaching the *talibes* to recite the very brief but powerful Sourate 112,[15] which underlines the absolute nature and the oneness of God. Exegesis of this sourate emphasises that no human or other being can usurp the absolute oneness of God, who depends on no one for his absolute nature. This is a sourate of sublime transcendence which leads believers to acknowledge and contemplate their own dependence and insignificance in relation to God.

In *Taaw*, the boy who has already been beaten by his father arrives at Qur'anic school where he is beaten by the Qur'anic master for not reciting the *Fatiha* correctly. This is in itself highly significant. The *Fatiha* is the first sourate of the Qur'an and is frequently used at the beginning of any new enterprise – at the start of the day, a meal, a speech, a class and so on. The reciter submits herself/himself to the protection of God the Merciful. The reciter asks for guidance along the paths of God. However, there is neither mercy nor positive guidance in the methods of the Qur'anic master. In this film, it is clear that there are those – fathers and the Qur'anic master – who consider themselves to be empowered by the omnipotence of God and who seek to exercise a despotic power over those who look to them for shelter, protection and sustenance. The father's violence against his family can only be understood as learned behaviour sanctioned by the society in which he lives. It is in this spiritual context that the Being of the individual finds its essential definition and transcendent force.

Taaw clearly shows that the ontological potential of young people and of women is seriously stifled. The father's desperate adherence to his tyrannical paternal role is reflected in the anachronistic and brutally exploitative model of rote learning of the Qur'an. In neither case is there any positive influence on the inner resources of the younger people. The deontology of community living has given way to the pursuit of expediency, which is itself an expression of lust for power and money. The new spirituality is determined by the need to dominate and exploit the younger and weaker members of society.

The young children gathered around the feet of the Qur'anic master are preparing for the life of the unemployed youths of Taaw's age, whom we see hanging around the street corners listening to popular music. Their lives will not be filled with the fruits of spiritual fulfilment but with the frustration of not being able to realise their potential with the emptiness of desperation and submission to tyranny. The popular music that Taaw's father condemns is the cultural and spiritual continuation of the Qur'anic recitations that the young children are learning.

In *Taaw*, as in other films, Sembene emphasises that the African family he depicts is not necessarily a haven of peace, love and harmonious growth, but a context in which despotic male power is exercised with little to restrain it. Taaw's woman friend, Nafi, seeks refuge at Taaw's home, since she is pregnant and has consequently been expelled from her home by her father. This sets off the *dénouement* of the film, as Taaw confronts his father, takes Nafi by the hand and leaves with her. The last scenes of the film are centred on Taaw's mother being restrained by her husband as she pleads pitifully with Taaw not to leave. One feels that this is the final rupture.

On the one hand, we have the frustrated and despotic father pitted against his equally frustrated and desperate son; on the other hand, we have the powerless mother and the equally powerless mother-to-be. Both women are constrained to behave in ways that are not of their own choosing. In the final scenes of the film, one of the women is being physically held back, whilst the other is being led away like cattle.

There is a fundamental tension in Sembene's work on Africans living in urban centres. Although African society generally emphasises the primacy of the community, the basic urban unit is the nuclear family created through the process of fragmentation that accompanied colonial urbanisation.[16] Similarly, Islam emphasises the concept of the *'umma*, the Islamic community, as a manifestation of spiritual unity under God. Ideally, the social community and the *'umma* exist in a close interdependence that offers maximum social, emotional and psychological security to the individual. The Being of the individual experiences its definition, expansion and fulfilment within the spiritual force of the *'umma*. There is no inherent contradiction between the concept of the *'umma* and African communal living. It should be noted that "a lot of [Sembene's] motion pictures...are shot outdoors in medium or long shots to illustrate the collective, communal aspect of traditional Senegalese life".[17]

In both the social community and the *'umma*, the quest for power and human greed have destroyed the structures that protected the weak and regenerated the community. Religious belief and practice are no longer in harmony with family realities. There is a subsequent ontological dislocation of individuals as they struggle to come to terms with the disintegrated *'umma* and the consequently disintegrated Self.

In *Taaw*, the tyrannical father makes himself ridiculous, instead of projecting the image of a respected adult. The Qur'anic teacher shows himself to be the worst type of hypocrite imaginable. However, both men are well-established in their status and there is evidence in the film to believe that Taaw will mature into the image of his own father.

Taaw is a powerful exposition of the social and economic impotence of men, and one of Sembene's most delicate revelations of their religious bankruptcy. In the absence of the traditional social and economic bases to their power, Sembene's men become quite unsure of themselves and completely unstable. This is one of the essential themes of *Emitaï* (*God of Thunder*, 1971), in which Sembene uses the technique of contrasting scenes of women and men to good effect. In the film, inhabitants of Casamance are faced with the brutality of the French and their African troops kidnapping young men to fight in the Second World War. They are also faced with the colonial administration's attempt to steal the rice of the community as a contribution to the war effort. It is obvious that the abduction of the young men of the community dramatically alters the importance of the women as they continue to perform their traditional economic tasks, as well as replacing the men who have been taken away. The struggle over the rice is a struggle over wealth, and also over a cultural means of expressing fundamental social concepts of appreciation, joy and so on. The economic and cultural importance of the 30 tons of rice demanded by the French is not to be underestimated.

As the young men are being rounded up and taken away, the elders of the community sit in their shrine and discuss. They attempt to appease their divinities, whilst the chief, Djimeko, expresses his serious doubts about the efficacity of traditional religious rites. He is killed in a futile attempt to confront the soldiers, and his defiance against the divinities is seen by his peers as a factor responsible for his death. During the preliminary funerary rites, the shaman evokes the divinities of the Diola, and there ensues an impassioned but inconclusive dialogue between the dead Djimeko and the spirits. The elders, all men, seriously discuss the possibility of capitulation and of handing over the rice to the French. Eventually, one of the men delivers some rice to the French in an attempt to free the women of his family who are being tortured by being held in the sun. The women maintain their solidarity, despite the torture they have to endure. When a young boy is shot by the soldiers, the women free themselves in a spontaneous act of revolt. The women still do not reveal where they have hidden the rice, and eventually it is they who conduct Djimeko's funeral rites. Simultaneously, the men of the community decide to hand over the rice to the French and are subsequently assassinated en masse. Throughout the film, the women have maintained their integrity and demonstrate their strength in and through community. The men are characterised by their lack of focus. They do not possess the interior resources to face major adversity, and therefore have recourse to the world of spirits.

There is, in fact, no ideological point of contact between the men and women of the community. Their respective approaches to the threat diverge. It is therefore appropriate that the women conduct the final funeral rites of Djimeko, since he was the only man who suggested abandoning the appeals to the divinities and facing the threat with courage and reason. The women of the community are driven forward by a sense of justice and pride in themselves. They live and demonstrate the meaning of unity through community, whilst the male leaders offer sacrifices.

However, the goat, the fowl and the libations offered to the divinities are of no avail. The manifestations of the divinities and their interventions fail to save the Diola from their fate at the hands of a modern and foreign inhumanity. The men practise rituals based on a system of traditional beliefs which has not evolved. The collective Being of the women is constantly in dynamic movement according to the problems that present themselves. This is an aspect of Sembene's philosophy that is clearly developed in his novel, *Les Bouts de Bois de Dieu* (*God's Bits of Wood*, 1960),[18] in which the women's movement takes over the strike started by the menfolk. Once the women start out on the path of their own initiatives, they accomplish their immediate sociopolitical objectives and establish a dynamic unity that acknowledges no identifiable leader. It is a unity built on confidence in a common purpose striving for human dignity through action. This is Sembene's most thorough analysis and demonstration of the dynamism of the collective being of women. Thus, Sembene presents us with an important ideological situation in which ontology is clearly defined by gender.

On the surface, the ontological discourse of *Xala* (*The Curse*, 1974) appears to differ from that of the earlier films. El Hadji Abdoukader Beye's impotence has been brought about by the manipulation of spiritual forces. The consultation of various marabouts is of no effective avail. The first marabout, recommended by the President of the Chamber of Commerce, is an obvious charlatan, and is apparently ridiculed by Sembene. Implicitly, however, it is the President of the Chamber of Commerce and El Hadji himself who are ridiculed, particularly when the afflicted man is made to crawl towards his new wife with an animal's tooth between his own.

The second marabout is recommended by Modu, El Hadji's chauffeur, and is to be taken much more seriously because he produced a positive reaction in El Hadji's afflicted penis. Furthermore, because El Hadji's payment cheque bounced, the second marabout takes out his beads and starts praying in order to restore the businessman's impotence. Modu's marabout uses Islam as his overt means of operation whilst the first marabout's use of cowries and various talismans is essentially the process of African shamanism. Eventually, we learn that the businessman's impotence is a result of vengeance by a relative who had been cheated of his inheritance. This relative is none other than the blind beggar who often sat outside El Hadji's business establishment, one of the *déchets humains* – human garbage – so despised by the rich and successful man.

It is the dispossessed relative who organises the ceremony during which an assembly of beggars spits on El Hadji as a means of restoring his sexual powers. It is not uncommon for saliva, in quite modest quantities, to be used in African religious ceremonies. A shaman might spray individuals or objects with liquid – often water, or a mixture of water and herbs – from her or his mouth. Sembene's spitting ceremony is emotional, spiritual and social. El Hadji's first wife cries as she witnesses the disgusting humiliation of her husband, as the group of beggars surrounds him – some of them deeply clearing their throats before expelling large quantities of spittle on the man's head, face and torso. This scene is to be contrasted with the gathering for the wedding reception, where El Hadji was surrounded with wealthy colleagues carefully nurturing their own corruption.

The businessmen form an ideological group whose place of religious worship is the Chamber of Commerce. Their spiritual discourse is to be found in their sycophantic speeches in which they constantly congratulate each other. Their Being is completely wrapped up in their show of power, which depends entirely on the crumbs that foreigners permit them to enjoy. They reject their own language, and value only those customs – polygamy, for example – that satisfy their need to dominate and indulge in themselves.

The spitting ceremony at the conclusion of *The Curse* is also a confrontation between an exploiter and the exploited, the culturally dead and the culturally oppressed. Spiritual healing and valorization through spitting are used here as a means of social regeneration.

El Hadji's impotence so closely coincides with the financial collapse of his business that one feels that the spitting ceremony will indeed lead him to new paths. It appears to be the outward sign of an inner purification that could engender humility. El Hadji undergoes a new pilgrimage in which he "dies" as his former self, with the possibility of a spiritual regeneration of his Self being possible in the deepest social sense.

This apparent spiritual power and the humiliating process to which El Hadji is submitted at the end of the film appear to give credence to powers beyond those of human beings. Despite the title he bears, El Hadji Abdoukader Beye does not appear to exercise the virtues of Islamic charity. On the contrary, he is particularly harsh with those who are less fortunate than him, and on one occasion he does not hesitate to have a group of ragged beggars – including the blind man – removed by the police. In *The Curse*, the closest that El Hadji gets to Islam is a view of the Major Mosque as the cars of the members of the Chamber of Commerce drive past.

In every way, Sembene sets up El Hadji for a great fall. Apart from his marriage to his third wife, who is sufficiently young to be his own daughter, he is intolerant of the use of his own language and culture, and he completely worships everything that is French. In the religious context, he uses his economic power to satisfy his lust, he lacks true sensibility towards those less fortunate than himself, and religious observance becomes a mere ritual shell. He is a man who has abandoned his rootedness in a dual tradition of Africa and Islam, and has exchanged this source of strength for the sacredness of male power symbolised by money and an erect penis.

Although he slaps his daughter Rama when she says to him that all polygamous men are rogues, El Hadji is as meek as a lamb when he appears before his tempestuous and demanding second wife. She is unashamedly materialistic and also a great admirer of Europe, and she attempts to use El Hadji as he has used her. She confronts him as an equal, and speaks to him without the deference always present in the words and attitudes of the first wife. She appears to have fully adopted the existential code of her husband: an extreme egoism that is incompatible with charity, and a preoccupation with material wealth that eliminates ontological depth.

El Hadji's drama reveals the various levels on which fortune and misfortune are interwoven to ensnare him. The unfolding of the financial disaster coincides with the preoccupation of regaining sexual powers. The loss of property coincides with the loss of the second and third wives.

El Hadji has turned his back on his culture and language to embrace what is superficial. In so doing, he has lost all points of meaningful contact with his African environment. To him, African realities are significant only insofar as they can be exploited for personal benefit. He is adrift from his community, his family and his very Self. This ontological dislocation manifests itself through the emptiness of his choices in life. For example, the mother of the third wife, Ngone, encourages El Hadji to straddle the mortar, and place the pestle between his legs before getting into bed with her very young daughter. El Hadji declines, vehemently denouncing superstition and the backwardness of such warnings. Later, Ngone's mother evokes this incident as evidence that men such as El Hadji have become far too European in their outlook.

Significantly, it is his daughter, Rama, who demonstrates the rootedness in her African language and culture, and who attempts to stimulate her mother to revolt. Her self-esteem is perfectly intact, and her ontological imperatives place her in opposition to her father and what he represents. Rama is conscious of injustice within the context of her cultural nationalism, and is guided by its fundamental principles of affirmation of pride and dignity. Rama is a Wolof cultural nationalist, affirming the cultural, moral and linguistic values that have sustained Wolof society through wars, colonialism, famine and many other trials. It is a context in which family pride and dignity are honoured. The actions of one family member are associated with all other family members, living and dead. Rama sees the humiliation and unhappiness of her mother as an integral part of her own experience as a woman. She also understands that her father's third wife is a victim of a system of power relationships that do not in any way consider the human dignity of the woman concerned. Rama is more in contact with her identity and her ancestral past than is her father.

In *Ceddo*[19] (1976), the young Princess Dior Yacine is a very dignified and powerful character who knows who she is and what her place is in the context of her society. When she shoots the imam, who has usurped the royal prerogatives, she eliminates the rot that is reducing her people to thoughtless parrots. Significantly, as in *God of Thunder*, there are scenes of a dead man communicating with Beings beyond this physical world. This interdependence with the world of spirits presumably accounts for the princess's self-assurance even after the death of her own father. In her characterisation, one feels the presence of generations of ancestors who have ruled. Diogo, the spokesman for the warriors – the *ceddo* – defends his people against the tyranny of the king and the pressures of the imam. Diogo is fearless in his opposition to injustice. The *ceddo* openly oppose the king and his court, as well as the imam. They literally have nothing to lose but their chains, and they fully exploit their right of response to the king. Diogo declares to the king: "No faith is worth a man's life".

However, the king's death marks the end of the traditional ways and the few rights enjoyed by the *ceddo*. The imam, who has usurped the throne, condones the slavery that exists in the community and seems to take no notice of the white slave trader and his very open activities.

The forced mass conversion of the *ceddo* is analogous to the sale of the Africans to the white trader. The African-American music that accompanies each of the short episodes devoted to the slaves awaiting transportation introduces a note of profound sadness in this film. The

Catholic priest and his missionary fantasies present us with a dilemma, since the man has no direct influence or contact with the society in which he lives. The missionary's single African convert contrasts with the imam's numerous followers who answer to his call and surround him. Although the *ceddo* discuss among themselves and dare to confront the king, the followers of the imam seem not to be able to act of their own independent accord, and the single Christian convert is no better. The followers of the Book[20] have become mere zombies who have no will of their own, but execute the perverted words of texts that we have no evidence that they understand. The imam's bleating voice introduces all that he says by the first words of the *Fatiha*: "In name of God, Most Gracious, Most Merciful". However, like most professional religious hypocrites, he dares to invoke God whilst serving his own ends. Although the religion he professes stresses the right of the individual to interpret the meaning of the Qur'an, the impression created by the film is that of an imam who considers himself to be the sole interpreter and, indeed, the spokesman of God. Not only has the imam usurped the throne of an earthly king, but also he has usurped the voice of God.

Ceddo thus confirms a consistent theme throughout Sembene's cinema. Men who have social responsibility tend to transform it into psychological, religious and physical power. It is as if male responsibility has to be lived through in the various dimensions of violence against the family. The father, who is also husband and/or lover, forsakes the paths of the ancestors and the cultural imperatives of his society in the interests of his own ego and the preservation of his prerogatives. He is even capable of usurping the prerogatives of his codified and textualised God in order to satisfy the personal lust for power and control of others. The man thus described is therefore a dysfunctional Being who is no longer capable of contextualizing the Self.

The imam orders a *jihad* against unbelievers, and destruction and massacre precede the forced mass conversion. However, the *jihad* is undertaken in order to consolidate the imam's power. Under the leadership of the Princess Yacine Dior, the *ceddo* defy their armed Muslim captors. The *ceddo* therefore become warriors in the pursuit of human dignity and their revolt is an affirmation of Being that terrifies the Muslims.

One of the major characteristics of Sembene's cultural aesthetics is that he "does not make films to entertain his compatriots, but rather to raise their awareness as to the past and present realities of their society".[21] This didactic purpose is essentially a moral imperative which obliges spectators, who are also listeners and thinkers, to reflect on their own place within the context of the diverse dimensions of their society. This type of cinema leads to a fundamental re-evaluation of the quality of one's presence and to a search for a more appropriate accommodation with the Self. The dynamic of social and political organisation has destroyed self-respect, and stifled the Being and ontological potential of individuals striving to survive. For Ibrahima Dieng, Borom Sarret and Taaw, there is the possibility of realising the Self within their social or religious contexts.

Sembene's highly critical treatment of religion is to be understood within the wider context of a struggle against hypocrisy in all its forms. In Sembene's films, hypocrisy, indecision and lack of responsibility are the attributes of men, whilst the women represent a potential force to restore justice, integrity and the respect of culture. These are not merely philosophical questions, since Sembene is careful to construct a socio-economic context within which his characters attempt to evolve. Their search for human dignity is concretised by the hunger and poverty in which many of them live. The carter, Taaw and Ibrahima Dieng live in a context of physical hunger, whilst El Hadji Abdoukader Beye is surrounded by plenty, but is culturally lost. El Hadji is not even aware of his cultural predicament, and it is precisely for this reason that his condition poses serious ontological questions. Similarly, the men of *God of Thunder* display a striking lack of moral courage, and die because they eventually betray their people and their very Selves. It is for similar reasons that the imam is killed by Yacine Dior in *Ceddo*.

Sembene clearly demonstrates that institutionalised religion is often an empty shell of rites and practices, serving to conserve a certain order: the authority and privileges of men. The individual striving for survival turns inwards and attempts to conserve all that he seems to possess. As a result of their preoccupation with power, the men lose all consciousness of the Self within a community. They see themselves as individuals, free of the burdens of responsibility and accountability to those around them. There is no wider or greater vision beyond the individual Self. It is the women of *God of Thunder*, Rama in *The Curse* the wives in *Borom Sarret* and *The Money Order*, as well as the Princess Yacine Dior in *Ceddo*, who demonstrate that reaching out beyond the Self is also a valid strategy for survival. Since Being is sustained by community, those who isolate their individuality in the satisfaction of the solitary Self suffer a moral death which is portrayed by the emptiness of their gestures and the impotence of their acts. They produce nothing, nor do they create anything that is positive, and the human suffering that they engender is ample evidence of their degeneracy.

In an interview with Sada Niang, Sembene discusses refusal – *le refus* – as a concept.[22] Sembene points out that refusal of oppression and humiliation is the act or process of accepting responsibility for one's Self. It is therefore a regenerative process of great significance for the individual and for the collectivity. It is an act of pride and human dignity that signals the rebirth of a people as we see towards the end of *Ceddo*.

Although Ousmane Sembene is not advocating spiritual regeneration within a codified or institutionalised form, his ontological discourse is essentialist in its major perspectives. It is a discourse that emphasises basic African values of community, and the ethical standards that place a value on human dignity.

Notes

[1]   Such an intratextual analysis is a very worthy project. However, Sembene's films which are based on the themes of his prose fiction tend to become very different works. Primary examples of this are *Taaw* (1970) and *The Curse* (1974).

[2]   The exception is *God of Thunder* (1971), in which the Diola society portrayed by Sembene is entirely African in its religious expression. For the purposes of this essay, a distinction is made between African religions on the one hand, and Islam and Christianity on the other.

[3]   In this context, one has to take into account the tradition of the largest Islamic association – the Mourides. Founded by Ahmadou Bamba in the 19th century, the Mourides preach and practise a form of Islam that is particularly Afrocentric, social and essentially economic. See Moriba Magassouba, *L'Islam au Sénégal: Demain les mollahs?* (Paris: Éditions Karthala, 1985): 7-39.

[4]   In this essay, spirituality is interpreted as the expression of any type of belief – cultural, ideological, religious or mystical – that may take on a conceptual, ritual, economic or political form.

[5]   Mbye Cham, "Official History, Popular Memory: Reconfiguration of the African Past in the Films of Ousmane Sembène", in Samba Gadjigo, Ralph Faulkingham, Thomas Cassirer and Reinhard Sander (eds), *Ousmane Sembène: Dialogues with Critics and Writers* (Amherst: University of Massachusetts Press, 1993): 27.

[6]   This incident in *Borom Sarret* recalls Sembene's short story, "Niiwam", published in *Niiwam suivi de Taaw* (Paris: Présence Africaine, 1987).

[7]   In Islam, God has 99 names which could be considered to be 99 attributes. Each one of these names is the subject of much meditation, writing and philosophy.

[8]   Richard Wright, *Native Son* (New York: Harper & Brothers 1940): 63.

[9]   The words of the hymn are as follows: Ave verum Corpus natum de

Maria Virgine: / Vere passum, immolatum in Cruce pro homine. / Cujus latus perforatum fluxit aqua et sanguine: / Esto nobis praegustatum in mortis examine. / O Jesu dulcis! / O Jesu pie! / O Jesu, Fili Mariae! (Hail true body born of the Virgin Mary! / You have truly known suffering, sacrificed on the cross for men. / From your pierced side flowed water and blood. / In the hour of our death be for us our [celestial] food / O good Jesus! / O compassionate Jesus! / O Jesus, son of Mary!)

[10] By listening very carefully to the music, we realise that the synchronisation caused some difficulty, and the end of the melody had to be repeated to coincide with the carter's interior monologue.

[11] The film is based on the short story published in *Véhi-Ciosane, ou Blanche-Genèse, suivi du Mandat* (Paris: Présence Africaine, 1965).

[12] The film version of *Taaw* basically follows the theme of the short story. However, there are very important differences between the two texts.

[13] The words "Koran" and "Koranic" do not give an accurate rendering of the Arabic words referring to the text revealed to the Prophet Muhammed. It has now become more common to transcribe the Arabic as "Qur'an" and "Qur'anic".

[14] The Arabic word simply means "disciple", but, in the Senegalese context, it refers also to the pupils of Qur'anic classes who often spend more time begging in public places than learning to read, recite and write the Qur'anic verses.

[15] Say: He is God. The One and Only; / God, the Eternal, the Absolute; / He does not beget, nor is he begotten; / And there is none like unto him.

[16] There appear to be fundamental differences between the social structures of urban families in precolonial and colonial Africa.

[17] Françoise Pfaff, "The Uniqueness of Ousmane Sembène's Cinema", in Gadjigo et al (eds): 18.

[18] For a discussion of the women in this novel, see Frederick Case, "Workers Movements: Revolution and Women's Consciousness in God's Bits of Wood", *Revue canadienne des études africaines/Canadian Journal of African Studies* 15: 2 (1981): 277-292.

[19] The word "ceddo" means "warrior". It is obvious that, in the context of the film, the *ceddo* are warriors in the fight for their own human dignity and rebels against humiliation.

[20] Since Jews, Christians and Muslims follow a textual tradition that is framed in a discourse that is largely similar, the followers of these three religions are often referred to as people of the Book.

[21] Pfaff: 14.

[22] Sada Niang, "An Interview with Ousmane Sembène by Sada Niang: Toronto, July 1992", in Gadjigo et al (eds): 97.

The creation of an African film aesthetic/language for representing African realities

Nwachukwu Frank Ukadike

In the 1960s, several African directors of the francophone region launched their filmmaking careers. Their films mark the pioneering of genre films that portray Africa through African lenses. The most well-known director among them is Ousmane Sembene, who achieved fame through the prominence of his films, *Borom Sarret* (1963) and *La Noire de...* (*Black Girl*, 1966). As we assess Sembene's film practice, it becomes clear that he is a gifted *griot*, an artist who has developed a unique cinematic method of "Africanizing knowledge"[1] – to paraphrase V Y Mudimbe. Africanization of knowledge hereby implies the creation of indigenous aesthetics, and this aesthetic orientation can be traced to two different traditions: the tradition originating from the conventions of dominant film practices, and that of traditional narrative style indebted to the African oral tradition.

It is these traditions that I will examine in this essay, by probing the impact of ideology and the synthesis of documentary and fiction techniques that led to the articulation of Sembene's own unique pedagogical aesthetics.

Borom Sarret is Sembene's first film, and also the first professional film made by a black African. It achieved international acclaim when it won a prize at the 1963 Tours International Film Festival – the second African film to do so after Mustapha Alassane's *Aouré* (*Marriage*, Niger, 1962). At first glance, it is possible to dismiss *Borom Sarret* for its simplicity and amateurish photography. A closer examination of its structure, however, reveals a uniqueness that is non-Western, non-European and non-conventional, signalling a different mode of representation, and introducing indigenous aesthetics.

Sembene exposes the dichotomy between the urban rich and the urban poor of Dakar by transforming a series of vignettes into a microcosmic representation of African neocolonial society. The film's explicit indictment of neocolonialism, coupled with Sembene's expressively detailed delineation of its virulent impact on society, represents the creation of a unique ethos that has contributed to the film's special place in African film history as an indisputable masterpiece.

105

Sembene juxtaposes a linear chronology of events interspersed with fragmented episodes presented as coded political messages to illustrate and educate. In this encoded structure, we find an intense critique of the new African élite, who are presented as recreant and even more treacherous than the former colonial administrators. Although the specific content is Senegalese, *Borom Sarret* represents an African universe; the same story could have been filmed anywhere in black Africa, because the nature of the socio-economic and geopolitical experiences represented have been a constant feature from the colonial period to the neocolonial present.

Sembene believes that a filmmaker should strive beyond using the medium simply to inform. Rather, a filmmaker should stimulate individual consciousness and political awareness. In effect, the role of film in the African context must be construed as a modern form of enlightenment media capable of transcending, as he puts it, "artificial frontiers and language barriers".[2] Sembene began as a writer, and moved to film as a medium for addressing that part of his audience prevented from experiencing his written works by illiteracy in French. Hence, in *Borom Sarret*, *Black Girl*, and in many sequences of his other films, he appears to appropriate silent film techniques to achieve clarity. This can be seen in his painstaking attention to detail, as when the camera is made to assume the function of sound, a voice-over, or an observer. For Sembene, therefore, cinema is an educational tool, and its content must be made explicit. This strategy of emphasising image over sound, cutting across "artificial frontiers and language barriers",[3] is pertinent to understanding Sembene's coded political messages. By interweaving detailed indigenous images and explicit ideology, Sembene creates a unique aesthetic that his African audiences can claim as their own.

Sembene and other African filmmakers, including Med Hondo, Safi Faye and Souleymane Cissé, believe in the reciprocity of ideas: ideas flowing from the artist to the audience and vice versa, unencumbered by hierarchical barriers. The manifestations of this tangible objective can be seen in Sembene's filmic process. *Borom Sarret* and *Black Girl*, for example, resonate with character-delineation, masterful use of monologue, and documentary voice-over narration. The narrative and stylistic components are fashioned to inspire the audience to participate in the experiences of a typical routine of the cart driver and those of Diouana. By extension, the viewer is compelled also to think about the ironies of the newly-independent Senegal in transition. This is forcefully presented in *Borom Sarret* by Sembene's repudiation of formal closure, compelling the viewer to identify and reflect upon the cart driver's ambiguous life and the rapid dissipation of post-Independence promises. It is worth noting that Sembene leaves the endings of all his films open so as not to impose solutions, and to allow viewers to continue the discussion after the film has ended.

Both *Borom Sarret* and *Black Girl* are structured to produce an emotional impact upon the viewer. This impact, however, derives not only from the historical significance of Sembene's pioneering position, but also from ideology – the African filmmakers' commitment to the use of the film medium as a timely and plausible cultural document for posterity. Since what is documented has an historical and a cultural function, there is concern for accuracy in presenting a realistic view of the continent. This is what makes African film practice different from many foreign cinematographic representations of Africa which only glorify exoticism.

In *Black Girl*, Sembene demonstrates his remarkable narrative expertise by constructing a binary structure that makes the film a case study of black (African) and white (French) relations. Contrasting the African experience in the Medina (the native quarter of Dakar) with the affluent white experience of life in France, the film explores the life of Diouana. At first glance, the story is deceptively simple: Diouana goes to France as a nanny, only to commit suicide after being mistreated and abused by her employers. However, Sembene transforms the diegesis by adding a political subtext that is both historical and sociological in scope. The film confronts the viewer with the reality of Diouana's misery, the travails of daily life and its strains on her physical and spiritual self, but it is not deliberately structured as a metaphysical observation of the human condition or the meaning of suffering. Rather, it uncovers the meaning of being African, the nature of unequal power-relations, and the pervasive hypocrisy, intolerance and inhumanity of even the most well-bred in the French culture of Dakar.

Diouana is only a black girl, an object of no social standing. Stripped of any identity, her silence underlines the sexism and racism pervasive in France. This is illustrated by the scene in which Diouana waits at a corner with a group of other women to be "picked" as a servant by a white French woman in what might be interpreted as a "slave market". She stands not only as an individual, but also as a member of a collective, and this allows the viewer to identify with her as representing both a bevy of women, and an individual being in a world of inequity, unfairness and racism. This allows the structure to peregrinate beyond the agony inflicted on an individual, and into the dysfunction of the entire populace.

Two questions arise here. Does Diouana choose silence over physical resistance? And why does she choose suicide over returning to Africa? The answer, I believe, is that Diouana's silence is an act of resistance, and her "self-deprecating" and "submissive" attitude does not indicate resignation. Before her death, the film had already shown her in Senegal looking for work, meeting her boyfriend, interacting in social circles, and with her family and friends – all serving as a contrast to the inhuman confinement of Diouana's life in France. Her new life epitomizes cruelty and insensitivity, all the more intense and catastrophic when juxtaposed with her life in Senegal. This chronicle of Diouana's dual existence shows her forbearance: the character's progression from one state of mind and actual location to another is neatly constructed to affirm her life as a living person with a sense of purpose, and not as a character flowing out of the imagination.[4] Her suicide is not an act of desperation, but, rather, one of rebellion against servitude, a refusal to continue life under inhuman conditions. On another level, Clyde Taylor's reading of Diouana's suicide also offers an expanded pan-Africanist meaning:

> According to African ritual belief, Diouana is sending her spirit home to her people. It was with such sentiments in mind that thousands of captured Africans threw themselves in the sea rather than be transported in slavery to America. They were sending their spirits back to their ancestral *Omphalos*, or spiritual centre.[5]

During the 1960s, the radicalization of pan-Africanism had begun to influence cultural productions. Filmmakers also intensified their cinematic exploration of the continent's social and contemporary problems: traditional culture vs. alien influences; the dichotomy between urban and rural life; illiteracy; unemployment; corruption; women in society; and polygamy. With the release of *Mandabi* (*The Money Order*, 1968), black Africa's first full-length feature filmed in colour, Sembene can be said to have scrutinized most of these concerns more critically than any other African filmmaker. The film is a caustic comedy of character and situation, touching on numerous societal mores and tribulations. Ibrahima Dieng, the central character, lives contented in his society, until his nephew in Paris sends him a money order. Before the cheque can be cashed, an identification card is required, bearing Dieng's passport photograph and date of birth. When he cannot produce them, he consults one of his relatives, an attorney, who swindles him out of the money. Dieng is illiterate, wallowing in an intricate alien-designed bureaucracy which humiliates him. However, it also forces him to confront the contradictions of neocolonial bureaucracy and the ironies of Africans' appropriating and entrenching an alien culture. In Dieng, Sembene underlines the need to become part of the revolutionary process of inducing change.

The Money Order denounces ineptitude and social injustices. It is from this perspective that Sembene finds the environment in which to critique the petite bourgeoisie and neocolonial bureaucracy that have reversed traditional ways of life. Sembene uses undiluted realism to render his diegesis engaging. The characters in the film are realistic, played not by professional actors, but by ordinary people representative of the oppressed, with whom the majority of the Senegalese people identify. As Sembene has said, "professional actors are simply not convincing as laborers, as ordinary human beings".[6]

It has been suggested that for its humanism and "universal power and appeal",[7] *The Money Order* can be compared to De Sica's *Ladri di biciclette* (*Bicycle Thieves*, 1948). While it can be observed that African filmmakers and neo-realists share the view that film is a political tool, African filmmakers have gone one step further in constructing a cinema of protest and confrontation by infusing their work with relevant cultural codes and political ideology. For example, in *The Money Order*, careful plotting renders the events depicted both political and humanistic, as an inquiring camera follows Dieng everywhere, capturing his verisimilitude and the vestiges of a traumatized man grappling with his changing society. No special effects adorn the narrative. There are no elaborate sets or artificial lighting: natural light is used to give credence to an overexposed "common" man in an environment that is no longer traditional or tranquil. The aesthetic simplicity magnifies the film's undiluted realism, and it is within this structure that the emotional impact resonates.

Filmmakers and critics have long debated linguistic choices for African films. Sembene placed himself in the forefront of this debate by choosing to shoot *The Money Order* in Wolof, the first time that such a project had been attempted. As a result, many filmmakers have been encouraged to produce their films in local languages, instead of using French and English. Sembene and others have also integrated into their narratives two or three local languages with French or English, which can be viewed as a strategy that uses popular culture to hold the audience's attention.

If *The Money Order*'s social commentary struck a responsive chord with the public, *Emitaï* (*God of Thunder*, 1971) further capitalizes on the African project of inflecting cinematic structures with pedagogic/demagogic, if not proselytizing, accreditation. *God of Thunder* delves into one of Africa's repressed histories: set in Senegal during the Second World War, the film deals with the atrocities associated with the French colonial practice of forcibly drafting African males into the Army, and with the imposition of unrealistic rice quotas in order to sustain France's war effort. Sembene uses this structure to foreground the resistance of the village women against the pillaging of the rice supply, underscoring the need to act in solidarity and dignity.

The film is daring in its critical stance. On one level, it exposes the collective endeavour and the determination of the people fighting off the invasion, making it absolutely clear that the women, and not the men, are the ones spearheading the resistance. In the film, women are shown resisting the French forces, while the men hide themselves, invoking the gods to come to their aid. In Sembene's writings and in his films, female subjectivity is usually approached with the utmost care. Since the image of African/black women in Western films and literature is always construed as that of the docile ancillary creature perpetually subservient to men, he feels that women's history and the contributions they have made to African development must be addressed. In demanding respect and empowerment for women, Sembene has also consistently criticised African men. On another level, Sembene uses this critique of colonialism to attack Africa's ideological impotence, by questioning Africa's dependence on the myths of traditional religions. This suggests, of course, the need for adjusting to the realities of the present circumstances. Sembene poses the following question: Why cannot Africa assert its own authority over its own affairs, decisively confront matters of utmost concern, and emerge victorious? This seems to be the central premise in all of Sembene's films.

Third World and African film practices seek to develop an aesthetic deemed appropriate for their own cultural environment. Sembene, for example, usually depends on linear structuring and the explication of minute details, allowing events to happen in a natural time continuum. He has argued that this strategy enables him deliberately to slow the pacing of his films in pursuit of spectator-participation and for the benefit of the audience, who might not experience the full impact of the message if bombarded with a rapid succession of images.[8] It is possible to argue against the above statement, but it is accurate in the case of *God of Thunder* that:

[I]n its manner of photography – almost entirely long shots, never extracting its characters from the environment, but making the environment an integral part of the story – and in its pace. There are no flash or quick shots, the editing is never manipulated to gain speed on events, everything is made ultra-clear, as if the length of the action and the objectivity of the photography were enough to clarify not only the story but Sembene's thought processes behind the story.[9]

In *The Money Order* and *God of Thunder*, Sembene grounds his indigenous aesthetics on a realist base. *Xala* (*The Curse*, 1974) represents a progression in style from his previous works, by presenting an allegorical tale of the corrupt neocolonial bourgeoisie through a biting satire of complex social, economic and political issues. The story revolves around the rise and fall of El Hadji Abdoukader Beye, a member of the Chamber of Commerce, and his colleagues, the ruling oligarchs. To increase his social status, El Hadji feels compelled by his prominence to marry a third wife, but he finds he cannot consummate the marriage because he is afflicted with *xala* (the curse of impotence). After a series of visits to the marabouts, he is told that the source of the disease is a beggar whose land he had fraudulently appropriated. The film denounces the excesses and misplaced priorities of the new African élites, by equating their neocolonial exploitation and ideological bankruptcy with sexual impotence, presented here as a metaphor for Africa's socio-economic impotence. This critique manifests itself by the miserable condition of the multitude of beggars.

The mordacity with which this socio-economic inertia is illustrated exemplifies Sembene's uncompromising narrative technique, and is embodied in the ironic juxtaposition of opposites. Thus, from the very beginning, the film draws the distinction between the two main classes in Africa: the ruling class, representing the exploiters who share money stolen from the government treasury, and the oppressed subject class, who, after dancing in celebration of Independence, soon discover that the cycle of illusion, exclusion and despair continues unabated.

Sembene, who has been criticised for ponderous, lugubrious pacing in earlier films, demonstrates artistic maturity in *The Curse* by employing a blend of static camera work, long takes and contrast cuts of rapid montage to achieve political results. For example, in the ten-minute teaser, a lingering camera reveals attaché cases filled with wads of currency notes being offered to the new members of the Senegalese Chamber of Commerce, and this provides an ironic contrast to the President's exhortation, "We must all work together". In another sequence, a long take is used to draw the spectator's attention to the imported Evian spring water that El Hadji uses to fill the radiator of his Mercedes. Sembene continues his critique of neocolonial commercialism in the scene in which El Hadji cuts a business deal and demands cash, because, according to him, payments made by cheques can easily be traced. Each of these examples demonstrates how Sembene uses the entire breadth of his *mise en scène* to create his political dialogue.

Accelerated cutting is used in the scene where the President of the Chamber of Commerce arrives to hear El Hadji's story of impotence, as well as during the wedding reception, when Kebe, one of the deputies, finds the time to negotiate a business deal. I have noted that

111

this film alternates long sequences, long takes and continuity editing in relation to real time. Close-ups are not at all emphasised, medium shots dominate, and static shots are preferred to camera movements. Sembene's brilliant use of cinematography, impressive editing, montage for contrast, and documentary technique enhance *The Curse*'s didacticism and effectiveness.[10]

In Sembene's next film, *Ceddo* (1976), the religious and cultural syncretism alluded to in *Borom Sarret* and *The Curse* is given full treatment. Depicting Muslim expansionism and European commercial incursion into Africa, *Ceddo* offers Sembene a venue for the uncovering and revelation of ruptures and discontinuities in the African morass. This expansion was pursued with brutal force; the *ceddo*, the traditionalists of the Diola ethnic group who refused to accept colonial rule until 1942,[11] resisted Islamic and, to some extent, Catholic incursions. It is from these struggles that the film derives its title.

Reminiscent of the women in *The Money Order* who protect the family's interests, the heroine of *Ceddo* is Princess Dior, who saves her people from the wrath of the ruthless Muslim imam, but not until after his subjugation of an entire populace.[12] As Sembene has stated in numerous interviews, *Ceddo* does not attack Islam *per se*; rather, the film reflects his "relentless champion[ship] of political independence and African tradition", in Françoise Pfaff's words. Pfaff also observes that, with "the film's verbal richness and its striking presentation of ancient customs, traditional court attire, and battle scenes, *Ceddo* elevated Sembene's cinematic works to a ritualistic art form that exalts collective values through its celebration of an imperialistic past".[13] Again, we find coded political messages contained in the shaving and conversion sequence, where the imam asserts his supreme authority over his subjects, and in the church scene where the cross in the mitre of the Bishop (ironically a *ceddo*) is laced with cowrie shells. Here we see not only creativity, aesthetic excellence and authorial vision, but also an indictment of cultural colonialism and Africa's tepidity towards it.[14]

For Sembene and for most of his colleagues, there still exists the urgency to reassess contemporary issues through the investigation of past history. For example, *Ceddo* represents an uncompromising and daring political document which focuses on the ills of society even in the filmmaker's own cultural "back yard".[15] By contrast, *Camp de Thiaroye* (*Camp Thiaroye*, 1988), co-directed by Sembene and Thierno Faty Sow, probes perceptive lessons offered by history with an acute sense of authenticity and talent.

For African filmmakers, probing the past is a way of exposing Africa's present position on the periphery of world power. This innovative practice includes, together with *Camp Thiaroye*, films such as Med Hondo's *Sarraounia* (1986) and Kwah Ansah's *Heritage... Africa* (1987). All three films are imbued with historical concerns and their objectives are realised with a pedagogical perceptiveness that is gripping and emotionally resonant. The films' messages are pointed: they urge both a re-examination of ruinous policies towards Africa, and respect for the historical value of traditional cultures.[16]

The concern for truth about Africa continues to inform Sembene's narratives; as *Camp Thiaroye* and *Guelwaar* (1992) show, France and the clashes between African customs and Western ways remain for Sembene a deep well-spring of themes that cannot be depleted. *Camp Thiaroye* is based on an actual event, the 1944 massacre by French forces of the African soldiers serving in the French colonial Army (the "tirailleurs sénégalais") stationed at Camp Thiaroye, a few miles outside Dakar. The African infantrymen had revolted against injustices by the French authorities: the issues involved France's refusal to pay them back wages and to exchange their savings at the going exchange rate; the refusal to pay a demobilization allowance; and the lack of adequate clothing. These practices, coupled with racist dehumanization and an inedible food supply, fuelled an atmosphere that was already charged with discontent, an ugly reminder of the iniquitous treatment of the African soldiers who fought to save France, not Africa, during the war.

According to Myron Echenberg, "[t]o the ex-POWs the authoritarian manner in which they were being treated was a bitter reminder that they were returning home to an unchanged colonial system, unappreciative of the great sacrifices they and their fallen comrades had made".[17] This is a powerful statement, but it lacks both the subtlety and the force that *Camp Thiaroye* achieves through its cinematography and historical referents. These qualities correspond with the director's ideology and the way in which he asserts his authorial vision. The facts can be deciphered from the cinematic rendering, specifically in the manner in which Sembene juxtaposes fiction with documentary elements. William F Van Wert, comparing Sembene with Glauber Rocha, observes that they both "deliberately strip the denotative level of their images of the empirical meanings in order to force a cultural, ideological reading at the connotative level".[18] In *Camp Thiaroye*, meticulous plotting, methodological selection of details, and careful dramatisation and characterisation enhance the film's deep emotional impact, as well as compel the viewer to ponder the sociopolitical and historical imperatives of the filmed events.

Camp Thiaroye delineates the colonizer's tactics of subjugating and dehumanizing Africans to explicate Africa's muteness in global power-brokerage situations. In the film, Sembene uses the character of Pays, a mute soldier and former POW at Buchenwald, as an allegory of this unequal relationship. Through him, the viewer learns about the temerity of centuries of colonial exploitation attendant in the contradictions of modern Africa. Pays's comrades were not able to convince him that Senegal is not Buchenwald, as he trembles in shock, feeling trapped by the barbed wire surrounding the camp in Senegal. In this sequence, the lingering camerawork and close-ups reveal Pays's dilemma, but his muteness (an ordeal suffered at the war front) represents the political inertia, economic impotence and dependence that are synonymous with today's Africa.

In another scene, Sembene further illustrates the tragedy of the alliance between the former colonies and France. Towards the end of the film, he shows France's failure to recognise "the degree to which the African ex-POWs had acquired a heightened consciousness of themselves as Africans united by shared experience in suffering".[19] The result of the uprising was calamitous, with the French forces destroying this resilience through a barrage of gunfire. This attack, according to French official figures (which Sembene disputes as being far too low), left "thirty-five Africans...killed, an equal number seriously wounded, and hundreds more or less seriously injured".[20] Carefully orchestrated, the slaughter sequence is Sembene's acerbic denunciation of crimes against humanity and is created with a regenerative aesthetic that is strictly Sembenean. Subdued, instructive lighting conveys the aura of a nightmarish scare. When the attack begins, gun salvoes punctuate the natural serenity of a tranquil, although artificial African villagescape. Sembene employs long takes to emphasise relevant points. For example, as a column of enemy tanks and artillery moves nearer the camp, a static camera positions the viewer to experience a mesmerizing ordeal.

Finally, when the attackers release an unprecedented inferno upon the camp, the camera is confined to close-ups of the tank's guns ceaselessly spitting out fire. The intensity of the scene is heightened by carefully chosen music that runs throughout the sequence, underscoring images of the smoked-out camp. The next sequence is even more emotionally wrought. It reveals the extent of the massacre through a delicate camera panning that seeks out the dead. This is followed by a mass burial shot in medium close-up, and then long shots capturing bodies draped in white linen as they are thrown into mass graves, in a scene reminiscent of Jorge Sanjines's *El Coraje del pueblo* (*The Courage of the People*, Bolivia/Italy, 1971). *Camp Thiaroye* ratifies the contention that it is the colonialist who invests the African with its terrors. Sembene's aesthetic and revolutionary dynamics echo the Africanist liberationist/ideology of using art to reveal, scrutinize, explicate, disturb, and jolt consciousness.

Sembene's most recent film, *Guelwaar*, also makes reference to historical specificities, although these are not necessarily a central point of focus. The scope of *Guelwaar* is deliberately microscopic, limited to the events surrounding a funeral in a tiny Senegalese village. The dead man is Pierre Thioune (Thierno Ndiaye), nicknamed "Guelwaar" or "Noble One" for his accomplishments as an outspoken community leader: "As Pierre's Roman Catholic family gathers to bury him, they discover that his body has disappeared from the local morgue. At first this disappearance raises the possibility that the corpse has been stolen by fetishists, but the truth is even more troubling to the Thioune family: Pierre has been buried in a Muslim cemetery by mistake."[21]

The confusion generated by this mix-up sends the community scrambling to rectify the situation, culminating in a caustic critique of contemporary politics and culture. *Guelwaar*'s plot opens as a critique of contemporary politics by revealing the administrative ineptitude associated with burying Catholic Guelwaar in the Muslim cemetery, but it soon expands to reveal that Guelwaar did not die from natural causes as first suspected. His death is politically motivated by his involvement in the crusade against corruption: Guelwaar speaks out against the leadership's interference with and misappropriation of foreign aid.

Guelwaar was originally based on a newspaper article which outlined the burial mistake, but Sembene broadened the structure to include the critique of foreign aid. As he explains, foreign aid is a burning issue in Africa: "For more than thirty years we've been plagued with foreign aid and food assistance. People can be helped for a little while, but not for thirty years!"[22] Sembene's critique speaks loud and clear of Third World empowerment and self-sufficiency through economic restructuring, not in the IMF way, but as a collectivized political economy geared towards enabling individual people and nations to regain control over their own destinies.

Sembene's works force us to reflect upon the present period, when the Western media continue to expand as an enterprise of acculturation, and to ask: Can Africa be awakened through its own media to recover its own lost cultural heritage? Can this happen when Africans themselves are heartily embracing the cultural assimilation imposed first by colonialism, then by neocolonialism, and now by the Western recolonizing processes in full gear, while vigorously pursued by the predatory claws of the IMF and the World Bank? In other words, how can the screen and other channels of information be completely decolonized to serve African interests? Who and what are the priorities?

Notes

[1] V Y Mudimbe, *The Invention of Africa: Gnosis, Philosophy and the Order of Knowledge* (Bloomington and Indianapolis: Indiana University Press, 1988): 182.

[2] For a more detailed explanation, see Howard Schissel, "Sembène Ousmane: film-maker", *West Africa* 3440 (18 July 1983): 1665-1666.

[3] Ibid: 1665.

[4] Diouana was badly treated, not only by the family she serves, but also by their friends. At the dinner scene, one of them says that Independence has made them (Africans) less human. Another compares Diouana's rice with an aphrodisiac, and even wants to kiss her, because, according to him, he has never kissed a black woman.

[5] Clyde Taylor, "Two Women", in Renee Tajima (ed), *Journey Across Three Continents: Film and Lecture Series* (New York: Third World Newsreel, 1985): 29.

[6] For references to Sembene's interviews, see Françoise Pfaff, *Twenty-five Black African Filmmakers* (Westport, CT: Greenwood Press, 1988): 256-258.

[7] G M Perry and Patrick McGilligan, "Ousmane Sembene: An Interview", *Film Quarterly* 26: 3 (1973): 37.

[8] For a fuller discussion of the topic, see Carrie Dailey Moore, *Evolution of an African Artist: Social Realism in the Works of Sembene Ousmane* (PhD thesis, Indiana University, 1973).

[9] Lyle Pearson, "Four Years of African Film", *Film Quarterly* 26: 3 (1973): 46-47, cited in Françoise Pfaff, *The Films of Ousmane Sembene*, monograph written for the National Gallery of Canada.

[10] For an extended discussion of *The Curse* and the issues presented here, see my book, *Black African Cinema* (Berkeley and Los Angeles; London: University of California Press, 1994).

[11] This information was provided by Sembene in Samba Gadjigo, Ralph Faulkingham, Thomas Cassirer and Reinhard Sander (eds), *Ousmane Sembène: Dialogues with Critics and Writers* (Amherst: University of Massachusetts Press, 1993): 36.

[12] Princess Dior's character as a warrior is reminiscent of the queen (Sarraounia) in Med Hondo's film, *Sarraounia* (1986). This film pays homage to African women for their contribution to liberation struggles (something Hondo frequently emphasises as not usually documented in non-revisionist histories).

[13] Françoise Pfaff, *The Films of Ousmane Sembene* (festival monograph).

[14] For a fuller discussion of this intriguing sequence, see my essay, "African Cinema: a Retrospective and a Vision for the Future", *Critical Arts* 7: 1 & 2

(1993): 43-60.

[15] Sembene is a Muslim who has constantly repeated that he is not against Islam, but against the misuse of its doctrines.

[16] As I write this essay, Nigeria and Cameroon are engaged in a border dispute. As neighbours, and under normal circumstances, the two countries should be able to settle their differences without resulting to warfare. France has been accused by Nigeria for openly meddling in the dispute and pursuing gunboat diplomacy. Instead of initiating a political dialogue and offering to negotiate the dispute, France has rushed its "imperial" troops to Cameroon as a show of force, a situation likely to escalate the tension between the warring neighbours. Still entrenched in a colonial mentality, France cannot claim to be defending Cameroon; rather, it is interested in the recently discovered vast reserves of oil in the disputed Bakassi Peninsula. Such action reminds one of France's past military escapades and interventions in Africa, which were characterised by exploitation and vagrant violation of territorial integrities and the right to self-determination. The point is that the colonies (ex- or not) are valuable only insofar as they bring material benefits to the mother country.

[17] Myron Echenberg, *Colonial Conscripts: The* Tirailleurs Sénégalais *in French West Africa, 1857-1960* (Portsmouth, NH: Heinemann, 1991): 101.

[18] William F Van Wert, "Ideology in the Third World Cinema: A Study of Sembene Ousmane and Glauber Rocha", *Quarterly Review of Film Studies* 4: 2 (spring 1979): 222.

[19] Echenberg: 103.

[20] Ibid: 101.

[21] As in the Detroit Film Theater programme notes 12, 13 and 14 November 1993.

[22] Françoise Pfaff, "*Guelwaar*", *Cineaste* 20: 2 (1993): 48, quoting Sembene.

Language use and representation of the Senegalese subject in the written work of Ousmane Sembene

Ann Elizabeth Willey

While many know the work of Ousmane Sembene primarily through his films, his influence as a writer is undeniable. Through six novels, four novellas, a collection of short stories, and various essays, Sembene has suggested how the modern African writer can fulfil the role of the *griot*, "the pulse of his people".[1] His example of a committed literature drawing from the lives of the majority of the Senegalese people sets a standard for other Senegalese writers who would influence their society. Yet, perhaps because of the socio-economic factors that have helped shape contemporary Senegal, Sembene is better known for his films than for the literature that he produced in the first stages of his career and continues to produce alongside his films.

Much of the criticism of Sembene's written work seeks to make sense of his career trajectory from writer to film director. Critics such as Alioune Tine and Carrie Moore have attempted at great length to show how Sembene's written work addresses the problem of how best to represent the Senegalese- or Wolof-speaking subject in French, a language that makes it difficult to express Wolof subjectivity, by giving up on writing and instead adopting film as a medium. These readings of Sembene's œuvre, tracing how he seeks to fill what Tine calls "the notable absence of a written Wolof",[2] focus on Sembene's use of different languages, his manipulations of French, and his representation of various socio-linguistic groups within his works through his early literature. Tine ends his 1985 article by saying that the progression towards film is logical, in that it allows Sembene artfully to represent Wolof in and of itself. Tine points out, however, that this development of Sembene's career still does not fill the void left by the lack of a written Wolof.

This essay will argue that Sembene has not given up on this search in favour of his film work, but that his efforts to represent a Senegalese subjectivity have also continued in his written work. Most evidently, Sembene has written a novel entirely in Wolof – *Ceddo* – and started a journal dedicated to Wolof-language publishing, *Kaddu*. Perhaps equally significant is what the novel-in-French to film-in-Wolof teleology leaves out: Sembene's increasingly complex representation of a plurivocal Senegalese context in both his films and his novels. Sembene's work expresses a desire to claim both writing and film as mediums within which he can express reality from a Senegalese point of view. Sembene's efforts to speak relevantly to his Senegalese, African and wider audiences have not stopped with the creation of his films mainly in Wolof which continue to avail themselves of the merging linguistic registers of French, Wolof and other languages that comprise the daily language practice of most Senegalese people. The development of Sembene's literary œuvre shows an equally complex representation of the mediation of the many languages in Senegalese life, and a continuing desire to appropriate both the novel and the language of the ex-colonizer as mediums for expressing a committed Senegalese voice. Across the history of his published work, in both their thematics and their style, Sembene's texts show a progressively complex attitude towards the uses of writing, and writing in French.

Language and Senegalese subjectivity in *Le Docker noir*

Sembene's first novel, *Le Docker noir* (*The Black Dockworker*, 1956), is a partially autobiographical novel about the life of African workers in Marseille after the Second World War. The novel tells the story of Diaw Fall, a Senegalese docker who acts as a spokesperson for his fellow African workers who are mistrustful of the white union. At the same time, Diaw also struggles to write and publish his works. After finishing his first manuscript, *Le Dernier voyage du négrier Sirius* (*The Last Voyage of the Slave-ship Sirius*), he gives it to a French author, Ginette Tontisane, who promises to help him get it published, but then passes it off as her own work. Enraged, Diaw goes to Paris, fights with Ginette and knocks her down; in the fall, she is fatally wounded. Diaw is put on trial for murder, but most of the trial seems to be occupied with the question of whether Diaw could have really written the book as he claims.

The Black Dockworker is uneven in style, extremely rough in places, and tending towards clichés in others. However, as Sembene's first novel, it introduces a theme that will occur explicitly or implicitly in most of his other writing: the problems of communicating in the poisoned atmosphere that colonialism created, and of telling the story of colonialism in ways in which Africans can see their own interests represented in the face of great resistance from white cultural institutions.

The novel opens with Diaw Fall's mother, Yaye Salimata, standing on a beach outside Dakar, worrying about the fate of her son who stands accused of murder. Certain that Diaw could not have done such a thing, she returns to her house to look again at the newspaper from the previous day that has her son's picture on the front page. The headline reads: "The Negro Diaw Fall, Murderer of the Famous Author, to be Judged by the Court of the Seine in Three Days".[3] Yaye Salimata has gathered a stack of papers but, the narrator tells us, cannot read a word. However, she recognises the picture of her son in each paper. Yaye Salimata's disbelief that her son could have committed murder begs the question of understanding the newspaper title which she cannot read, and which similarly denies Diaw the right of language. Much as the mother is excluded from participating in the trial of her son, the newspaper's act of attributing, without qualification, the novel in question to Ginette Tontisane keeps Diaw from being considered as a full participant in French culture. Diaw is held to be guilty by the French system that works to keep both him and his mother outside power. The next scene describes how Diaw is the talk of the town (Dakar) in various public venues, such as a *car rapide*.[4] One man, who speaks Wolof, says that Fall may be guilty, but is not the system of colonialism guilty of much more heinous crimes?:

'You see Yaye Salimata? Her son is in France, it seems that he killed a woman, maybe they'll kill him too, or send him to the slammer. He only has one death on his conscience, while the whites who have massacred dozens won't be judged at all...No one will call them to account.'[5]

His neighbour responds: "You're a fool, friend".[6] Switching to French, he then condemns Diaw and excuses the French by drawing a distinction between politics and sadism. The driver, enraged at this defence of the French, stops the car and kicks him out. The offender then threatens to sue the driver who in turn swears back in French.

French in this novel is therefore represented as a language of exclusion: Yaye Salimata is kept from knowing what is happening to her son; the passenger who condemns Diaw excludes him from the questionable right to exercise prerogatives of power inherent in the French system (politics); and the trial itself excludes Diaw from the ranks of "civilised" men deserving of justice, by denying his ability to master the French language. The novel, however, argues that this exclusion comes too late and does not work. The driver of the *car rapide* turns his use of French against the representative of colonialism and, like Caliban, curses him in the language of the colonizing system he seeks to excuse. Similarly, Diaw's novel is a description of the worst horrors of French colonialism, the transatlantic slave-trade. Diaw uses the very same language that seeks to deny his humanity to portray the inhumanity of the French during colonialism and the slave-trade. The desire of the French political and linguistic system to exclude Diaw on the basis of some presumed lesser humanity is undercut by the system itself.

Wolof, on the other hand, is represented to some extent as a symbol of unity for the dockers in Marseille, who form associations according to the native languages of the areas they come from. Diaw reports syndicate news in Saracolé and Wolof during meetings, so that all the dockers may understand. During a confrontation with a dockside supervisor who wants the men to continue unloading ships in a downpour, Diaw convinces the other workers to demand a rest by conferring with them in "Sénégalaise", much to the consternation of the supervisor. Diaw's solidarity with his fellow workers is expressed in the language they use to communicate, Wolof – a language which excludes their French supervisor.

The last chapter of the novel is written in the form of a letter that Diaw writes to his uncle. In reflecting on his trial and contemplating the rest of his life in jail, Diaw thinks back to a poem that he was taught in school in the process of learning a language that he says "is not mine". The poem glorifies the selfless devotion of the "tirailleurs sénégalais" to "la Patrie", and demands that their loyalty be rewarded by full service to the French nation.[7] Diaw seeks to turn this logic of learning French in order to learn how better to serve France against itself by telling a different kind of story in his novel. The story of Diaw's imprisonment can be read as the story of imprisonment within language and the system it represents. He is trapped by a French language that denies the validity of his existence in any circumstance other than that of subservience to an all-encompassing system of power that is best represented by the colonial enterprise. Diaw fails in his efforts to make French tell his story, to make the language his own. The exclusion of language and power is almost total.

Ô Pays, mon beau peuple!

Sembene's second novel takes place in Casamance, the region of Senegal where Sembene was born and spent most of his childhood. This novel recounts the story of Faye Oumar, who is returning to Senegal after serving eight years in the French Military and marrying a French woman, Isabelle. As the protagonist of this novel, Faye manifests many of Sembene's central concerns in Ô Pays, mon beau peuple! (O My Country, My Beautiful People, 1957), especially his desire to transcend the Manichean division between tradition and modernity, or Africa and Europe. Faye incorporates in his person the best of both worlds. He manages to reconcile his years in France, his mastery of the French language, his ties with his indigenous culture, and his desire to help his people: "Faye, in many ways, had perfectly assimilated the ways of thinking and the reactions of whites, all the while preserving in his innermost self the heritage of his people".[8] On the first occasion we see Faye, he is remarking on the landscape of the river to his wife and comparing it to a painting by Rousseau. However, his cultural references to Europe do not preclude Faye from declaring allegiance to his Casamancian people.

In the next scene, the reader sees Faye protecting a group of Senegalese who are being abused by a white man. On the way to Ziguinchor, a scuffle breaks out on the boat when many of the deck passengers seek shelter from a sudden rainstorm in an interior gangway. A European man, beside himself with anger, demands that they return to their place on the deck. The Africans do not understand him and the white man calls a steward over to translate for him. When a translation of his command still fails to move the Africans, the white man resorts to the language of violence. Seeing this, Faye responds in kind and punches the white man, knocking him down. This opening scenario sets the agenda for the rest of the novel, where the problems of communication, tradition and assimilation intersect in the characters of Faye, his wife, his parents and the young people of Ziguinchor.

The distance from his culture which Faye has learned to accept, and which enables him to judge the traditions of the Casamance, rejecting some and cherishing others, is manifested early in the novel by his estrangement from his parents. Isabelle becomes their focus for the change in their son and Faye's mother wonders many times how Faye could have married a white woman. His father, the imam of a local mosque, is so put out by Faye's recent ways that he barely speaks to him. Faye's parents see his departures from tradition as a loss. Faye has indeed returned a different man. He changes languages and habits easily as the situation demands, greeting his family in Wolof and his friends in French. He makes the expected visits to the family of someone long ago betrothed and lowers his eyes in the presence of his father, all according to custom, but the presence of his French wife is a constant reminder that Faye is not coming back as the same dutiful son who left eight years ago.

Isabelle bears the brunt of the family's dissatisfaction with the changes in Faye, especially that of his mother, Rokhaya. Rokhaya ignores Isabelle at first, and, when reminded by her son of the duties of hospitality, she greets Isabelle in "petit-nègre", saying "Bonsour, Madame", and goes on to tell her that she is "Beaucoup solie", adding "Madame, papa, mama, Fransse". Isabelle answers the question that reinforces her own difference. Yes, she is French, to which Rokhaya responds: "Fransse... Loin... Toi, fatiguée?".[9] Rokhaya's initial enmity to her French daughter-in-law, as expressed in her immediate distancing of her, is echoed by the expatriate French community in Ziguinchor, who cannot seem to tolerate Isabelle's transgression of social practice any more than Faye's family can forgive his. One night when Isabelle goes to the cinema by herself because Faye is away on a fishing trip, she is harassed by a man named Jacques, the same man whose mistreatment of the Senegalese constitutes the opening scene of the book. Jacques comes over to sit next to Isabelle at the cinema, and tries to flirt with her. At first, she ignores him, then asks him to leave; he refuses. Isabelle comes back with: "You annoy me. That's French, isn't it?". Jacques understands only too well what Isabelle is asking, but shows her how far outside the "French" community her marriage has placed her by saying: "I thought you only spoke Negro".[10] Jacques slides from discourse to intercourse by suggesting that language communities are racially constituted, and with whom one sleeps determines the language one speaks; Isabelle slaps him. Later in the narrative, Jacques tries to bring Isabelle back into the colour line by attempting to rape her. The rape is a mark of contempt for a woman who has broken a European taboo, and, at the same time, an effort to reclaim Isabelle for the French community. The attempted rape is foiled and Isabelle's presence as a French woman in the African community remains, disruptive and obvious to both sides, but irretrievable.

Despite being rebuffed by both the European community and Faye's family, Isabelle perseveres out of love for Faye, and finds congenial company in the younger citizens of Ziguinchor who begin to congregate at Isabelle and Faye's home. This group is comprised of many different parts of Ziguinchor's community, although most of them have had some education. It is an inclusive group, accepting as members a young white doctor and at least two young women who often bring the discussion around to considering women's status in colonial Senegal. The narrator describes their conversations as taking place in "the most diverse idioms": Diola, Portuguese, Wolof, French. Their openness to languages translates to an openness of dialogue and the possibilities of new ways of doing things. There is, for example, a long discussion about the need to educate women. One of the women declares that the country will not develop unless women are educated, and that male resistance to educating women is based mostly on a desire to perpetuate polygamy. This willingness to interrogate traditional practices such as polygamy, and an openness to other world-views, as shown in the desire to give women formal education, are implicitly linked to the heteroglossic nature of their discussions.

Faye's willingness to break with tradition when there is something to be gained by it is perhaps most obvious in his decision to become a farmer, despite the fact that no one in his family, on either side, has ever been a farmer. Faye not only becomes a farmer, but also tries to establish a system of cooperative farming that would successfully break the monopoly on farm products currently held by the European consortium, Cosono, headed by the infamous Jacques. Faye's challenge to the prevailing system of colonial exploitation provokes a violent reaction in the colonial bureaucrats who respond to this transgression of the rules in the same way that they have since the beginning of the novel – with violence. They ambush Faye one night and fatally beat him. However, the newness and challenge to the closed world-views of both colonialism and tradition that Faye represents, and his ability to break down borders between world-views and to incorporate the best of both sides, continue and become, perhaps predictably, incarnated in the birth of his and Isabelle's child after Faye's death.

O My Country, My Beautiful People, like *The Black Dockworker*, represents one man's struggle to exist in two or more languages and the world-views those languages represent, which would seem to deny the possibility of subjectivity in the other. Unlike *The Black Dockworker*, *O My Country, My Beautiful People* holds out more of a hope for the future, and in turn recognises more often the importance of the indigenous African language and practices. Where *The Black Dockworker* laments the fact that Africans are represented as non-entities in a French language and system that crushes them, *O My Country, My Beautiful People* asks what the French tradition can say to the people of the Casamance. The languages even interact on a textual level. Whereas *The Black Dockworker* contains practically no Wolof phrases, *O My Country* contains several phrases from Wolof or Diola, marking the beginning of Sembene's practices of transcribing indigenous languages into French in such a way that one recognises them as foreign to the French language. Perhaps the best example of this is the representation of greeting rituals, which, among the Senegalese, especially the Muslim portion of the population, are formulaic, involved and quite necessary for any social interaction. *O My Country, My Beautiful People* also marks the first time that Sembene uses a pidgin French (called petit-nègre in the text) and marks the difficulty that Wolof speakers have with some of the French sounds – the soft "j" in "bonjour", for example. Yet, the greetings, which can last several minutes, are left to two or three lines of dialogue, while the rest of the dialogue proceeds in relatively straightforward fashion. In the stories of *Voltaïque* (*Tribal Scars and Other Stories*), published four years later, there is a much different use of the apport of the Wolof tradition.

Tribal Scars and Other Stories

Tribal Scars and Other Stories is a collection of twelve short stories, the most famous of which, "La Noire de..." ("Black Girl"), became Sembene's third film. The collection begins with the story appropriately titled "Devant l'histoire" ("Foreword").[11] "Foreword" is told from the point of view of a young man standing outside a cinema with two friends, trying to decide whether or not they want to see the film. While they debate, they also watch other cinema-goers, especially a young couple who arrive in a taxi. This couple, dressed in the European fashion, is arguing: the woman, whom the narrator recognises as Sakinetou, a schoolteacher from his neighbourhood, would like to see the film, while her companion, Abdoulaye, would not. A long discussion ensues in which Sakinetou accuses Abdoulaye of consistently disregarding her wishes, using the example of having his friends over every Sunday and expecting her to entertain them, when she would rather be out. Their argument is briefly interrupted by the passage of an older man with two wives and five children in tow. The wives remark that they hope there will be singing in this film, but they will watch whatever "oncle" wants to. After the family passes by, Sakinetou says to Abdoulaye: "I'm not an illiterate *fatou*. I can pay for myself."[12] Sakinetou makes as if to buy a ticket, and when Abdoulaye does not follow her she returns to the curb in a huff, hails a taxi and leaves him standing in front of the cinema. After witnessing this altercation, the narrator and his friends remark that the couple has experienced a loss of "balance". They decide to leave the theatre saying: "Suppose we went to see the Toucoleur *kora*-player? It would be a bit of a change".[13] The narrator responds: "Changing your country or your wife doesn't solve any problems. If everyone thought like that...".[14] The three friends then go off to see the kora player, whistling "Soundiata" as they go.[15]

This story has been read variously as an example of the war between the sexes, in which modern men or traditional women lose, or as a harking back to tradition and a mistrust of modernity. However, I believe that the key to this story lies in the narrator's appeal to equilibrium accompanied by change. Sakinetou's problem lies not in demanding the right to pay her own way, nor in refusing to entertain her husband's friends, but in her total dismissal of the traditional world, as shown in her refusal to recognise the narrator, a neighbour, and in her disparaging remarks about illiterate women, such as the polygamous wives who pass in front of her. These wives, on the other hand, are shown as being totally subsumed by their husband. Neither of these family systems is ideal. The presence of "Soundiata" at the end of the story is significant: as the most widely known epic in West Africa, it represents a long-standing and widely available piece of oral tradition. These young men show a familiarity with this tradition while offering a barely coded critique of independence and modernity. If the new bourgeoisie disrespect the majority of the Senegalese population, as the colonialists did, little in the country has changed. One cannot replace one system of marriage with another and assume it will be better, if one does not also change the cultural attitudes that shape those marriages. The same can be said of post-Independence governments.

The remaining eleven stories all develop the interactions between systems without offering easy answers to the questions of which system is "better". "Ses Trois Jours" ("Her Three Days"), for example, is a wrenching critique of polygamy told from the perspective of a woman whose husband, having married a much younger woman, is neglecting her and not keeping to the schedule of wifely visits. After waiting two days for his visit and feeling humiliated by his absence, she expresses her anger to him when he shows up on the third day. "Communauté" ("Community") is a thinly veiled critique of the Referendum of 1958 in the form of an animal fable, in which the cats invite the rats to form a community.[16] "Rue Sablonneuse" ("Sandy Street") is the story of a happy, clean neighbourhood that functions as a well-knit community. The main street is renowned throughout the area for its cleanliness and hospitality. In this happy space two young people fall in love and the entire neighbourhood smiles on the development of their affections. The story takes an abrupt turn, however, when the girl's father exercises his traditional prerogative to choose his daughter's husband and marries her off to one of his friends. Everything sours and the neighbourhood slides down a slippery slope of mistrust, decay and apathy.

While on the thematic level, Sembene's stories are much more critical of tradition than are his earlier works, these stories paradoxically go much further in their efforts explicitly to manifest these traditions and the culture from which they come on a textual level. "Community", for example, takes the form of one of the more well-known genres of storytelling in West Africa, the oral fable as found in Birago Diop's translations of the tales of a famous *griot*, Amadou Koumba.[17] Similarly, the long story, "Lettres de France" ("Letters from France"), offers a look at the uses and abuses of tradition by recounting the letters of Nafi, a young woman who has agreed to marry a man in Marseille based on the picture of a fairly handsome 30-year-old man. When she arrives in France, she is shocked to find that her husband is an old man of nearer 60 who can no longer find work because of his age. In despair, she begins a correspondence with a friend from home who is witness to Nafi's slow reconciliation to her situation and her marriage. In trying to explain her feelings towards the old man whom she has been tricked into marrying, Nafi at several points offers extended references to the fable of the hyena:

> You remember the fable of the hyena? He won the most beautiful female in a competition open to all the animals, and his beaten rivals said to him, 'Hyena, you're much too ugly for her.' And he replied: 'I know. I know I'm not pleasant to look at. But that's because of all of you. When she sees no one but me for weeks and months on end, she'll start to get used to the sight of me and finish by liking me.'[18]

Nafi uses this fable as an extended metaphor to explain why she continues in the marriage even after she realises that she has been tricked by her husband and possibly by her father. This use of the oral tradition as a way of giving shape to narrative in French is first shown in the collection *Tribal Scars and Other Stories*, and suggests new ways of thinking about the final and most famous story, "Black Girl". Whereas Nafi can bring the insights of the oral tradition to bear on the harsh reality of life in France, the heroine of "Black Girl" is so indoctrinated by the colonial system that she fails to see through the illusion of France created by her employer.

Like "Letters from France", "Black Girl" is a story of dissimulation, deception and mistaken appearances. Based on a true story that appeared in the *Nice-Matin* newspaper in 1958, "Black Girl" is surely a story of exploitation, but it couches that exploitation partly in terms of miscommunication. When "Madame" asks her nanny from Dakar, Diouana, if she would like to accompany the family on its holiday to France, the two women speak at cross purposes. Diouana imagines France to be a land of movie stars, great wealth and leisure. For Madame, France may perhaps be the same thing, but Madame knows that this dream comes at the expense of the labour of people such as Diouana. The narrator tells us that, after her last holiday in France, Madame has been carefully planning for this next holiday by cultivating in Diouana dreams of a France that exists only in the imagination:

> Back in Dakar, tired out and deeply annoyed, her pride wounded, she had laid plans for the next leave...for three years she kept dangling the trip to France before Diouana's eyes.[19]

Diouana is fooled by the appearance of the French dream without understanding, as Nafi in "Letters from France" comes to find, that the dream is undergirded by the labour of workers like themselves who, in France, literally have no place in the sun.[20]

Many critics of Sembene have suggested that most of the stories in *Tribal Scars and Other Stories* were written in the 1950s and early 1960s, before *Les Bouts de Bois de Dieu* (*God's Bits of Wood*, 1960). The themes and concerns of the stories therein do indeed share the outlook of Sembene's second novel, *O My Country, My Beautiful People*, in their concern to critique the abuses of traditional culture while maintaining links with that same traditional culture. *Tribal Scars and Other Stories*, however, goes much further than either of Sembene's first two novels in actually working towards expressing those concerns on a textual rather than on a thematic level. *Tribal Scars and Other Stories* also shows a stance towards tradition and modernity that is somewhat more complex than Diaw's total exclusion and exile, or Faye's clear vision of right and wrong with the hope for a happy medium. In the complexity of its social vision, *Tribal Scars and Other Stories* is much more closely linked to Sembene's third novel, *God's Bits of Wood*.

God's Bits of Wood

God's Bits of Wood is Sembene's most famous novel, and for good reason. It is an epic account of the strike of the railway workers on the Dakar-Niger line in 1948. In recounting the genesis and passage of the strike, Sembene shows a variety of characters and situations in at least three cities: Dakar, Thiès and Bamako. The strike leader is a young man named Bakayoko who remains physically absent for most of the novel, while the strikers often call on his knowledge, example or teaching. Bakayoko acts as a link between the union leaders of the three different cities, holding them together across many regional differences and vast spaces. The strike lasts for months, despite the best efforts of the European community to end it: they shut off the water supplies, strong-arm local grocers into refusing credit to the families of strikers, and refuse to let wives of strikers ride the train (operated by scabs imported from Europe) when they are forced to go out of town to find food. The strike ends only after a monumental march by the women of Thiès, who walk all the way to Dakar to protest against the obviously unfair policies of the rail company.

In exploring the impact of such traumatic and dramatic times on the communities of these three cities, Sembene often brings to light the differences between and within communities in their relations to European or indigenous traditions. It is common knowledge, for example, that the peoples of Mali have long considered their Wolof brothers and sisters of the coast to be somewhat frivolous, overly concerned with appearances, and much too involved with the

European community. Most of the characters from Bamako are much more concerned with following traditional ways than are their counterparts in Dakar. Niakoro, the mother of Bakayoko, is one of the older characters from Bamako who wonders at the impetuousness of the strikers and at Bakayoko's role in bringing the strike to pass without consulting her. She thinks to herself:

> Were the ways of the old time gone forever? Ibrahim Bakayoko, her own son, had told her nothing! At the time of that first strike it was true that she had been living in the west, in the country of the *toubabous dyions* – the slaves of the Europeans...Since then she had called the Senegalese 'the slaves,' and when she spoke of her younger son she said, 'He seems like one of the Ouolof [Wolof] people, one of the westerners; he has the bearing, and the manners.[21]

Niakoro is upset not only with her son, but also with her granddaughter, Bakayoko's stepdaughter, Adjibidji. Adjibidji is learning French from her father and accidentally uses the word "alors" in a conversation with her grandmother. Niakoro is incensed and accuses Adjibidji of treating her like a dog. Niakoro's estimation of the French language, as an insult to honest people and not in any way necessary to the functioning of society, is shown throughout the rest of the book to be both right and wrong. Where Niakoro sees French as an intrusion or an insult, Bakayoko suggests that French is indeed a foreign presence, but that it should be seen as no more or less than a tool.

At several points in the novel, we see characters who identify with the French language to the detriment of their identification with their fellow Senegalese or Malian citizens. One such figure is the man who takes the most ribbing in the Dakar Office, a young man named Daouda, who is nicknamed "Beaugosse" ("Pretty-boy") because of his sartorial habits. Beaugosse/Daouda acts as a representative of Dakar in the first meeting with railway directors in Thiès at the beginning of the strike, where he is reprimanded by Bakayoko for speaking to other union members in French. Daouda, jealous of Bakayoko's leadership, as well as of the affections of a young woman named N'Deye Touti, leaves the union before the end of the strike to side with the French administration of the colony. He is begged not to go, since his level of literacy is rare among railway workers and thus very useful, but Daouda cannot be convinced to remain with the union.

N'Deye Touti, the object of Daouda's affection and Bakayoko's inconstant attentions, is similarly shown to be a character misled by her adherence to the French language and cultural values. As with

Daouda, N'Deye Touti's advanced education makes her a resource for the community – she is frequently called on to read and write letters for family, neighbours and friends. Yet, she resents this duty, and dreams only of getting a job as a secretary to a bureaucrat who will marry her so they can spend their holidays jetting off to remote locations. N'Deye Touti's dream world leads her as far as being almost glad when part of her neighbourhood burns down after a riot:

> [S]he found that she was walking in a black dust littered with charred and shapeless refuse. N'Deye Touti had grown up in this very spot; she had played in these tortuous alleyways, these vermin-ridden courtyards and gloomy cabins. The memory was as sharp as the pain of an open wound, and she was almost ready to bless the fire which had destroyed the witnesses to her childhood and her shame.[22]

While N'Deye Touti and Daouda are cautionary cases, Sembene also points to the use of French as a strategic resource, at times for conveying information and at other times for hiding information. When Ramatoulaye, the wife of one of the strike leaders in Dakar, becomes desperate to feed her children, she goes out in a futile search for food, and encounters her brother, accompanied by his legendary spoiled ram, Vendredi.[23] After El Hadji Mabigue refuses to help her and instead recommends that the men go back to work, Ramatoulaye curses him and threatens to kill his ram if it should ever enter her house.

⋅ As expected, a few days later, Vendredi wanders into Ramatoulaye's courtyard and manages to eat the meagre bit of rice that Ramatoulaye has garnered after much searching. True to her word, Ramatoulaye kills Vendredi and boils him up for a feast to which the whole neighbourhood is invited. When the police come looking for Ramatoulaye on a complaint from El Hadji Mabigue, Ramatoulaye's co-wives, Houdia M'baye, Mame Sofi and Bineta, pretend to have just sufficient French to understand the police, but not sufficient to make themselves clear. The police demand Ramatoulaye and "le mouton" ("the sheep"), and in reply the women repeat "the sheep, the sheep", as if they do not understand what the police are looking for. Finally, one of the women says in obviously poor French: "no live here, white mister". Ramatoulaye is eventually brought out and now the women insist that she take along their expert in French, N'Deye Touti, to double-check on the police interpreter. In this situation, French acts as both a shield to the women who pretend ignorance of it, while an actual expertise is used to protect one of their own from the often arbitrary powers of the system that wields it.

Bakayoko makes a similar concession to the use of French in the striker's meeting with the railroad company directors. When the directors assume the use of French in the meeting, Lahbib quickly points out that French will have to do for lack of an intermediary language, and Bakayoko goes even further by saying:

'I am not alone in this strike...but since your ignorance of any of our languages is a handicap for you, we will use French as a matter of courtesy. But it is a courtesy that will not last forever.'[24]

Bakayoko similarly makes French only one of the three languages that he uses to address the crowd at the rally that marks the arrival in Dakar of the women of Thiès. Bakayoko's attitude towards French is reinforced by one of the major organising tropes of this novel: the machine. Throughout the novel, the strikers reflect on their relationship to the machines that they work with, on and for. In asking whether the machines rule them or whether they rule the machines, the strikers redefine themselves and their roles in the production of wealth in the country. Given the passages discussed above concerning characters' attitudes towards the role of language, it appears that Sembene thinks along similar lines. French in this novel, therefore, is a tool that can be effective when used in the proper circumstances and with recognition of a worker's proper relation of mastery to it.

In the writing of this novel, Sembene offers some examples of what this redefined relationship to French might be. His narrative is certainly comprehensible to anyone who reads French and yet it is not the same as any other narrative in French. As with the stories in *Tribal Scars and Other Stories*, Sembene brings the weight of another tradition to bear on the French language and calls on it to carry the burden of representing Senegalese and Malian realities. The exclamations, proverbs and phrases that are repeated throughout this text are characteristically defined once in a footnote and then repeated without explanation. The epic sweep of the novel, set out in an episodic pattern that emphasises connections, repetitions and relations of certain heroes to wider groups of people, reminds one of the structure of West African epics such as "Soundiata", which Sembene has invoked elsewhere.

The transition to film

God's Bits of Wood was the last novel Sembene wrote before he began to make films. Most critics have read this transition as a recognition of the shortcomings of the novel as a medium for addressing all Senegalese audiences. In reading Sembene's career in this way, critics have tended to focus on the question of language (the novels are in French, and the films in Wolof or Diola), and emphasise that Sembene's switch to film was prompted by his unfailing desire to be a committed artist. Indeed, there is much evidence to suggest that Sembene's first forays into film were prompted by the realisation that not many of the people he had wanted to reach were reading his novels. In many interviews, Sembene has stressed the relatively greater accessibility of film than literature: one does not have to be literate, films are much cheaper, and in the crowded urban spaces and communally organised homes and villages of most of Senegal, the solitude necessary for reading is not available. Cinema, as a communal activity, has no such prerequisites.

The issue of language is a compelling part of the question of why Sembene moved into filmmaking. Whereas *God's Bits of Wood* examines French as a tool that may soon be no longer necessary in the Senegalese world, Sembene's films make that leap into the world where French is used only part of the time, and certainly not most of the time. However, to talk of Sembene's films as being strictly Wolof or Diola does something of a disservice to the complexity of the language problem that Sembene illuminates in his films. In *Mandabi* (*The Money Order*, 1968), for example, it is precisely the main character, Dieng's, ignorance of French that makes the civil service worker's use of French so telling of his attitudes towards Dieng. Similarly, in *Camp de Thiaroye* (*Camp Thiaroye*, 1988), we see the main character expressing himself in Wolof, English, "petit-nègre" and a French that is even more correct than that of the French officer who is trying to pull rank on him.[25] This makes the hero a character parallel to Oumar Faye in *O My Country, My Beautiful People*: he remains a man of the people who uses his knowledge of French to advance the interests of the people he comes from.

Perhaps more interesting, however, are the questions that Alioune Tine poses in his 1985 article. Does the advent of his filmmaking in mostly indigenous languages leave a void in Sembene's artistic practice? Is film just a substitute for the novel that Sembene would really like to write, but cannot in French? Again, in many interviews, Sembene has denied that he has abandoned writing, and insists at several points that "for Africa, I would prefer that there were more readers than cinema fans".[26] He has continued to produce novels and short stories in French, some of which form the basis of film scripts; however, others exist independently of Sembene's film work. In an interview published in 1972, he explained:

I prefer literature because I find it a bit more rich than film – a richer medium for expressing oneself. You can go more deeply into things...In film you show everything. You impose your subject on the viewer. Nothing is left to thought. You can't stop the picture so that the viewer can reflect on a certain point. You can stop a book. You can turn the page, close the book, think about it and come back to it later – whereas, in the film, it is continuous. Once you start, you can't stop until it's over.[27]

In 1975, in another interview, Sembene acknowledged that his preference for literature is indeed an indulgence or luxury. In calling the novel a luxury, Sembene points to its limits in the society of which he sees himself and his work as a part. He goes on to point out, however, that this does not mean that the written word has no place in Senegal:

Even if the African author cannot directly address his people, the echoes of his writings spread across Africa and Africans (even if they can't read) stand behind what the author says. There are many instances of people who don't know how to read but buy books and give them to their children to explain to them.[28]

Sembene has also sought to make Wolof a more accepted language for written texts. In 1971, Sembene and several friends, including the linguist Pathé Diagne, began a small journal entitled *Kaddu*, written in Wolof and covering general issues of cultural interest. In the beginning of the first few issues, they copied a chart of Wolof typography and pronunciation in an effort to codify Wolof as a written language. This group also translated several different works of literature, including the Communist Manifesto. Sembene went on to produce a novel entirely in Wolof, *Ceddo*, the basis of the film of the same name (1976); as with the film, however, the novel was quickly banned, and little has been seen or heard of this manuscript. After the quiet death of *Kaddu* and the less quiet disappearance of *Ceddo*, Sembene has returned to writing in French, perhaps, like Bakayoko, in the interest of better communication and as an act of politeness that will not last forever.

L'Harmattan

Sembene's first major written work produced after he started making films is the novel, *L'Harmattan*. *L'Harmattan* is structured somewhat along the lines of *God's Bits of Wood*, employing a large cast of characters and taking place in at least two different settings: the political activists' headquarters, and a hospital for locals directed by Doctor Tangara, a West African. *L'Harmattan* was originally envisioned by Sembene as the first of a three-part series exploring recent West African history. The subtitle of this novel is "Référendum", referring to the Referendum of 1958 – although Sembene shies away from the directly referential history of *God's Bits of Wood* by setting his story in an unnamed and otherwise unspecified country. In this novel, Sembene paints a portrait of the various groups within West Africa that militated for or against a "No" vote in the 1958 Referendum. Throughout this work, Sembene questions the role not only of various social groups in the history of Independence, but also of the writer in political action.

The book begins with an "Avertissement de l'Auteur" ("Author's Note") in which Sembene explains:

> I am not proposing a theory of the African novel. On the other hand, I remember that in what passes for classical Africa, the griot was not only a dynamic element in his tribe, clan, or village, but also the manifest witness to every event. It was he who recorded, laid out for all underneath the talking-tree the words and actions of everyone. The conception of my work flows from that teaching: to remain close to the people.[29]

This search for the appropriate role of the author and the text, and the unasked question of the language in which this text is written, is worked out in the story through the character of Lèye, the former writer, now turned painter, who is active in campaigning for a "No" vote. Lèye had great success with his recent collection of poetry, entitled *Garce d'Afrique (African Tramp)*, but has since decided to stop writing, declaring that painting carries with it less ideological baggage than writing in a European language. As a member of the group fighting for rejection of the French proposal of community, Lèye's politics are obviously valued in the text, and his mural, *L'Harmattan*, is described as a sweeping, profoundly moving commentary of the history of Africa. However, Lèye's decision to move to painting, the language of no country, does not go unchallenged.

One of the other militants in Lèye's group asks him to attend the first meeting of the conference of "Ecrivains d'Asie et d'Afrique", to take place in Taškent. Lèye resists by arguing:

> 'I have renounced writing in French. Not because I no longer wish to express myself, but because I am enriching a foreign

language. A language that is not that of the people! Our people! Drawings, okay, it is a language open to all.'[30]

However, one of Lèye's friends points out that this is utopian thinking in a situation that demands pragmatic attitudes. Attignon replies:

'And because a car may be a French make, do you refuse to ride in it?...Take your drawings...who buys them? The Greek, in order to resell them! Who looks at them? Petit-bourgeois Africans and European tourists in search of the exotic.'[31]

Attignon then offers the counter example of Lèye's last collection of poems which was so popular that it was translated into a hundred languages from the Congo to Mauritania to Benin, thus aiding in the important task of unifying Africa. Lèye eventually decides to go to Taškent, acknowledging French as a useful tool for international communication.

The other major character in this novel, Doctor Tangara, makes the opposite journey of Lèye. Tangara is comfortable in his Western-style knowledge and the use of it, and speaks mostly French at home with his children without a second thought. He is, however, profoundly ambivalent towards the activities of Lèye and his group. Tangara has worked hard to achieve the position of responsibility that he now occupies, and he owes his directorship of the hospital to his past courage in denouncing a corrupt European who was the former chief administrator. Tangara feels an unreasoned suspicion of Communism, the taint that has been left at the activists' doorstep by the media and the administration of the colony. At the same time, Tangara understands that the needs of the people must be respected. He speaks Wolof to his staff when necessary, and both his children speak Wolof fluently, despite conversing in French most of the time.

Tangara is forced to examine his own attitudes and politics when he is removed from his position as director because of his friendship with Lèye. Tangara is outraged that he can be removed from power by a ministerial decree and humiliated when he is replaced by Colonel Luc, the same corrupt, incompetent white man whom he had chased from the hospital years ago. Tangara, having what the narrator describes as a typical liberal belief in the justice of the system, goes from one government office to the next seeking redress or at least an explanation. On one of these trips, a now-flustered Tangara forgets his wallet; as he arrives at his first destination, he tells the taxi-driver to wait for him and he will pay him on the return trip. The taxi-driver is incensed by this, calls him a slacker, and gets the attention of a police officer.

What follows is the longest of any of Sembene's written passages that seek to represent the confusion of languages between an indigenous language, the so-called "petit-nègre", and French. The taxi-driver swears at Tangara: "What do you take me for? For a sucker huh! If you were anything like a doctor, you'd be better dressed."[32] Tangara tries to reassure the man by showing him his letter of demission to which the taxi-driver replies: "You really think I'm a sucker. I can't read", and adds in argotic French: "I don't want to hear any more. Pay up or I smash your face. Understand?"[33] The taxi-driver here speaks in the indigenous language, transliterated into French by the author with the inclusion of a Wolof exclamatory, then switches to petit-nègre and French slang. The situation becomes progressively worse as the spahi[34] – with even less French than the taximan – gets involved, and carts them all down to the police station. Tangara is relieved to see a friend there who is in a position to straighten things out, but the police chief refuses to let Tangara explain the situation to the spahi in the local language, the only way it seems that all parties will understand the whole story.

By the end of the novel, Tangara has had to re-evaluate his belief in the liberal system, partly because of this confusion that could have been easily solved had the chief of police not enforced a rigid and stratifying elitist language policy. Tangara's faith in the liberal system and the nominal independence offered in the French system of "Community" is shaken by this obvious example of how indigenous practices and people are placed at the bottom of a hierarchy dominated by the French. He becomes more and more convinced that Lèye and his Communist friends may be closer to true independence and democracy.

Whereas Lèye reconsiders his linguistic practice because his politics calls for him to continue to use French to communicate with wider groups, Tangara reconsiders his political practice when he is forced to realise how much language practices such as his own are implicated in politics that he finds personally abhorrent. The sticky wicket on which Sembene's characters find themselves when it comes to defining the politics of personal language practices is perhaps most appropriately outlined here, in his first novel produced after the medium of film had become available to him.

Véhi-Ciosane, Le Mandat (The Money-Order), Xala (The Curse)

Sembene's next three publications, all novellas, will be treated together here, as all three were produced as films shortly after they appeared in writing, and are thus discussed elsewhere in this book. Sembene's return to the short story or novella form has been welcomed by critics who find *L'Harmattan* not on a par with Sembene's best novel, *God's Bits of Wood*. Indeed, Sembene's work seems to be most striking in the novella format. In these three novellas, Sembene continues to question traditional mores, especially those that pertain to nobility of blood and to status symbols, including the use of language.

Véhi-Ciosane is the story that provided the basis for the film, *Niaye* (1964). It is a tale of the decline of one the most renowned families of a remote village, as manifested in the incestuous union of a father, Guibril Guedj Diob, with his daughter. As *Véhi-Ciosane* is set in the *niaye* (the scrubland that forms the border between the sahel and the ocean), far from urban centres such as Dakar, the presence of the French language is less of an issue than it may be in the other two stories. However, language and its uses still act as indicators of cultural changes and challenges.

Sembene begins the novella by explaining that the word *niaye* is singular in Wolof, but that the French colonialists had written it in the plural. While this may seem to be an insignificant piece of information, Sembene is foregrounding the effects and processes of colonialist discourse. On the most obvious level it points to the inability of the French properly to understand local languages. Sembene's insistence on the particularity of the place and its local referents continues throughout the story, when markers of time, place or setting are given to the reader in Wolof, defined only the first time they are used. Time of day is marked by the nearest prayer, discussions take place in the *peinthieu* (village square), and the passage of time is marked by changing seasons such as *Navet*, *Loli* or *Thorone*. The dialogues and characters are also more identifiably Wolof than any others Sembene had previously created. Their patterns of speech echo the often circular, implied messages of Wolof speech, and the full import of the Islamic tradition, with its exclamations, curses and greetings, is represented in the dialogue of the characters.

Sembene also shows how changes within the Wolof language system mirror wider social changes engendered by French colonialism, such as urbanisation, which brought about the exodus of younger populations to the cities. When the old men gather around the palabre tree, they do not have words adequate to describe their current situations:

> They would have liked to speak, to express their feelings, the pain they felt in their hearts each time one of them went away, but they lacked the words...Long years of servitude break a man, deprive him of the aristocratic use of words. In other countries, the ability to embellish language is the preserve of the high-bred.[35]

The ultimate example of this loss of language as an indicator of challenges to a previously coherent world-view is that of Tanor Diob, the son of Guibril Guedj Diob. Tanor has served in the French Army, and returned mentally unbalanced. He marches around the village, marshalling the village children into parade formations, and calling out steps to them in his pidgin French. Tanor's physical alienation from the village continues with his linguistic alienation from the community, his mental alienation from himself, and his final moral alienation in the act of killing his father. Tanor's immersion in the French system profoundly disrupts his world-view to the point where he can no longer function in society. The old men feel the effects of a similar disruption, although less drastically, when their world-view is challenged by the creation of urban centres and wage labour that draw the young men from the village. They are literally at a loss for words to describe this new situation.

Similarly, in *The Curse*, Sembene points to the loss of language traditions as the by-product of an increasingly Westernized and corrupt society. However, as in *Véhi-Ciosane*, it is not the loss of the tradition that disturbs Sembene, so much as the loss of the sense of the artistic and varied uses of language. For the old men of *Véhi-Ciosane* to have lost the noble way of speaking is sad, not because they have lost a part of their nobility (an idea that Sembene mocks throughout the story), but because they are losing an effective way of using their own language. In *The Curse*, the main character, El Hadji, is shown to be morally corrupt through most of his actions, including the taking of a third wife, N'Gone, to assuage his male ego, even though in order to marry he must spend far beyond his means, "borrowing" from a collective enterprise money to which he is not entitled. He so enjoys the chase that he cannot see that he is the one being chased. When N'Gone's aunt, anxious to have her married, first sets her eyes on El Hadji, she takes the girl into El Hadji's store and begins a very traditional word-game:

> 'El Hadji, this is my daughter N'Gone. Take a good look at her. Could she not be a kind of measure? A measure of length or a measure of capacity?' 'She is gentle. A drop of dew. She is ephemeral too. A pleasant harbour for the eyes,' replied El Hadji, who had been accustomed to using this kind of language since attaining manhood.[36]

Meanwhile, the narrator tells us that N'Gone, "the child of national hymns and flags", cannot follow a word of this arcane conversation. The other love affair in the novel, that of El Hadji's daughter, Rama, and her beau, Pathé, shows a diametrically opposed use of the Wolof language. Rama disagrees with her father about many things, and he often chides her for her insistence on using Wolof instead of French. Rama and Pathé belong to a group that is trying to rehabilitate Wolof as a language of culture, and Sembene places his own journal, *Kaddu*, in Rama's hands in the story. Rama and Pathé have made a pact to speak only Wolof to each other. In a reversal of the colonial policy of punishing schoolchildren who speak their indigenous languages, Pathé and Rama agree to a forfeit each time they lapse into French.[37] There is no slight irony in the fact that El Hadji, who has been initiated into the many traditions of Wolof language, uses it for selfish and deluded ends, whereas Rama and Pathé are trying to gain access to the language that her father knows so well, in order to denounce the very kinds of actions in which El Hadji is engaged – especially the polygamous marriage that Rama feels is an insult to her mother. While *The Curse* is perhaps less affected by the oral tradition on a textual level than is *Véhi-Ciosane* or *The Money-Order*, Sembene shows how, even in the midst of the bourgeois, corrupt lifestyle that El Hadji represents, the question of language is multi-layered.

The Money-Order attacks questions of status, language and tradition from the other end of the social spectrum. The motivation for the plot resides precisely in the fact that French has become the language of business in Senegal, thus excluding a fair number of Senegalese citizens from engaging in the business of everyday life in any effective or empowering way. Dieng, the main character, is stymied at every turn by his unfamiliarity with French, and with the everyday rituals of business and money in Dakar that are transacted in the French language. In his efforts to cash a money-order sent from France, Dieng is cursed in French by various clerks for being slow, and cheated by a photographer who also insults him in a panoply of languages garnered from French detective novels, Indian films and American television. Moreover, in a metaphor for the larger functioning of the bureaucracy of Senegal, Dieng is robbed of his last cent by his relative, M'Baye, who is described simply as a businessman having a hand in many different enterprises. It is irresistible to read M'Baye as an example of the ruling bourgeoisie that constantly fleeces the largely illiterate population, represented by Dieng, by positioning themselves as intermediaries between the population and international business.

The Money-Order, *Véhi-Ciosane* and *The Curse* all point to how language reinforces social hierarchies both in French and in Wolof. To paraphrase the narrator of "Foreword", changing a language means nothing if people do not change the way they think. That these novellas were produced during the growing fame of Sembene's film career points to the fact that Sembene is seeking to change the way people think through his writing, as well as through his films. According to his own theories of the relative merits of films and written texts, Sembene continues to use French as a medium for reflection on the questions of uses of tradition, language and status on a level that he feels cinema does not encourage.

The non-filmic texts of 1981-87

From the suppression of the Wolof novel, *Ceddo*,[38] in 1976 until the present, Sembene has published one long novel and two novellas. The novellas were published together in 1987, although the first story, "Niiwam", was written in 1977, while the second, "Taaw", bears the date of 1986. "Taaw" is one of the more interesting anomalies of Sembene's career: while his other novellas provided the basis for simultaneously released films, "Taaw" is an expanded version of Sembene's 1970 film of the same name. In 1981, Sembene's latest novel, *Le Dernier de l'Empire* (*The Last of the Empire*, 1981), was published to little or no critical notice, although not through any fault of literary workmanship. Sembene suggests that there was an unofficial ban on it by the Senegalese cultural establishment.[39] These works show a continued interest in representing the plurivocality of Senegalese language practice and its relationship to questions of social hierarchy and status.

"Niiwam"

"Niiwam" is the story of a man, Thierno, from an outlying village who has come to Dakar with his sick child, Niiwam, to seek medical help. Niiwam is too ill to be cured and dies after one night in the hospital. Alone in the city, Thierno and his wife are at loss as to how to bury their son. A merchant who buys the clothes of the newly dead takes pity on Thierno, tells him how to get to the cemetery by bus, gives him the bus fare, and then provides an old, stained sheet for a shroud. The rest of the story is a slightly surreal narrative of the passage of Thierno and the corpse of his son through the city and suburbs of Dakar. Thierno, unfamiliar with the city, feels lost and alone and is unsure about how to conduct himself on the bus. Sembene uses the bus as a device to probe Dakar society through Thierno's eyes, introducing to the reader businessmen, bourgeois women in traditional and European dress, pickpockets, and even religious leaders.

Thierno is particularly apt at noticing the signs of status that abound in the urban society of Dakar. At one stop, a large, well-dressed man seats himself next to Thierno, to the latter's dismay:

His eyes crept slowly up, taking in the well-polished brown ankle-boots, the neat pleats of the trousers. The European clothes were associated for him with the world of chiefs, bosses, well-off people. The proximity of the man irked him, put him on edge. Wary, he kept his distance. His 'neighbour' was an important person.[40]

Perhaps more important to Thierno than the clothes, however, is the fact that his neighbour is reading:

The neighbour spread out his newspaper aggressively. Its rustling sound made Thierno tremble: it evoked in his religious consciousness that myth of writing as the consecration of all knowledge, which imparts authority to all who possess it.[41]

Thierno's discomfort at the presence of this man is aggravated by the man's "aggressive" display of his self-felt importance and difference from Thierno. The symbol of his literacy, the newspaper, literally becomes a shield between him and Thierno.

Thierno's awe in the face of symbols of power such as traffic lights, policemen or newspapers echoes Dieng's confusion in *The Money-Order*, when he is forced to brave the bustle of downtown Dakar to accomplish his task of cashing the money-order. Moreover, like Dieng, Thierno is lightly chided by the narrator for his fatalism based on religious attitudes in the face of these exercises of power and exclusion. Thierno's exclusion from the social rituals of Dakar, however, is mitigated slightly at the end of the story, when one of the irreducible factors of human life, death, equalizes the relations between Thierno and his fellow passengers.

When Thierno finally asks one of the passengers where the cemetery is, the woman guesses the nature of Thierno's bundle, and screams out, in what Sembene describes as an atavistic terror, that there is a corpse on the bus. A general uproar ensues, in which some of the passengers demand that Thierno descend immediately, while a few others sympathetically question him. Obviously an outsider to the city, the first question they ask Thierno is whether he speaks Wolof. Although he does, Thierno still reveals himself as a stranger to the city with no one to help him bury his son. Having pity on him once his secret is discovered, some of the passengers convince the driver to take Thierno to the next stop where they disembark and accompany Thierno to the cemetery to help him bury his son. With this story, Sembene continues to question how power is encoded through a confluence of language, literacy, religion and status, and suggests that the social trappings of power become meaningless in the end.

"Taaw", published together with "Niiwam", is perhaps one of the most interesting examples of the importance of reading Sembene's work as more than the trajectory of written in French to filmed in Wolof. Originally a film in Wolof, "Taaw" became a story in French – and a very unusual French – more than nine years later. The written version of "Taaw" varies from the film version mainly in the presence of two main sub-plots: Taaw's abuse at the hands of his relatives, and Taaw's antagonism towards his father caused by his father's abuse of his mother. The emphasis of these two plot-lines in the written story highlights Sembene's continuing engagement in a critique of the arbitrary exercises of power, whether traditionally sanctioned or not.

The story begins with Taaw waking up to the sound of his little brother being harshly punished by his father. When he emerges from his hut, Taaw's mother is afraid that Taaw will step in and strike his father, as he had done before when his father was beating his mother. Taaw's father tries to provoke him into similar actions, but Taaw resists, mainly because of the urgent pleas of his mother not to dishonour his father. Taaw leaves the house, joins up with several other unemployed friends, and they all go off in search of breakfast. It is here that we begin to see Sembene's most unusual use of language to date. Taaw and his friends, partially educated and existing on the margins of many different levels of society, converse amongst themselves in an argotic language that incorporates French, Wolof and English. When Taaw tells his friends that he wants to go down to the Employment Office and look for a job, they react with disbelief: "Hey, boy, you cracked or something? You better watch out for your old lady, she's witchdoctored you. The only thing you can say is 'work', 'work'."[42] When comparing their grievances about their fathers, one of Taaw's friends recommends that he ignore his father, saying: "Hey boy, you should do what I do. As soon as the dinosaur starts up his old record again, I just tune into reggae in my head."[43] Their mixture of French, "franglais", Wolof and English represents the uncertain status of these young men. They exist on the margins of an older society, represented by their fathers who cannot understand their sons' actions, and a newer society that does not seem to care much about them.

Taaw's only partial mastery of the French language is due in part to an interruption in his school career occasioned by the cruelty and jealousy of his two aunts. Although Taaw is still young when his family moves to the outskirts of Dakar, he proves to be a promising student. However, the twice-daily commuting back and forth from Dakar (to school in the morning; home for lunch; back to school; and finally home to the suburbs) is too tiring for Taaw. In an effort to ease the strain on Taaw, his mother asks her brother and his two wives to feed Taaw lunch during the school year; in return, he will tutor their children. When Taaw excels in school while his cousins remain mediocre students, his aunts become jealous and start to see in Taaw's position as the favoured nephew a challenge to the inheritance of their children. In their spite, they begin to neglect Taaw. They feed him leftovers and scraps of such dubious hygienic state that Taaw soon becomes ill, almost to the point of death.

Taaw eventually returns to school but refuses any longer to visit his uncle's house, preferring instead to give up his lunch and spend his free time wandering the streets of Dakar. Missing lunch and going hungry affects his school work adversely, and, in a no-win situation, Taaw quickly loses enthusiasm for school, resulting in poor marks and the end of his scholastic career. Taaw ends up living with his mother, at odds with his father because of his unemployment, and with a pregnant girlfriend with whom he is on the verge of disavowing any connection.

The written version of Taaw's story therefore offers much more of an exploration of the circumstances in which Taaw finds himself at the beginning of the novella than does the film: he is not just another faceless, unemployed, street-roaming youth. We find that he is an intelligent young man placed in an unfortunate situation through the vagaries of a life removed from the centre, hampered by petty jealousies, at odds with the traditional patriarchal order of authority, and at wit's end when faced with the responsibility of imminent fatherhood while chronically unemployed. Eventually, Taaw lands a job at the port after bribing a minor port official, and returns to his mother's house; on the way, however, he meets up with his girlfriend, Catherine, whom he accuses of lying about the paternity of the baby. Later that afternoon, when Catherine arrives at Taaw's house saying that her father has disowned her, Taaw's father becomes enraged and threatens to throw both of them out into the street. Taaw leaves in a rage and only then does his mother finally take a stand. Aggravated by years of abuse, worried about her sons, and feeling compassion for Catherine, Taaw's mother kicks her husband out and claims the right to rule her own household. She sends her younger son after Taaw to tell him to come home and take care of his family.

The story of Taaw becomes a triumph in the end when he takes responsibility for his actions by behaving as a "proper man", as his mother urges him – but being a proper man in his case means respecting a woman by recognising his responsibility to his girlfriend. Furthermore, Taaw's actions are only effective in the presence of his mother's revolutionary act of rejecting his father and the prevailing social norms. Despite the prevailing mores that would keep her in an abusive relationship, she rejects her husband and sanctions the union of her son by allowing the unmarried couple to live with her long as Taaw recognises his duties towards his pregnant girlfriend.

With "Taaw", Sembene takes advantage of the literary style that encourages a more complicated exploration of Taaw's present circumstances, by bringing many stories to bear on him. His mother's emancipation from her abusive marriage and her decision to forgo social norms in order to help her son are integral to Taaw's ability to act responsibly. Taaw's decline is also made more complicated by the need of a certain socio-economic class to move to the outskirts of the city, by his aunts' jealousy, based on a model of family interactions that is obviously corrupted by an idea of individual wealth, and by the increasingly difficult job situation in which young, half-educated men such as Taaw find themselves. By coming back to this story nine years after making the film, Sembene offers his readers a chance to reflect on the ambiguous and shifting positions that a person such as Taaw or his mother occupies in a changing Senegalese environment – and he does so in a language which reflects those changes.

The Last of the Empire

At first glance, Sembene's most recent novel, *The Last of the Empire*, seems to have little in common with its predecessors. The characters are all educated, urban and élite. The main concern of the novel is with the policies and actions of a government that is out of touch with the majority of the Senegalese population. Sembene also uses an extremely satiric tone, full of hyperbole, and the novel is set in the near future of the time it was written. This departure from the social-realist nature of his other texts (the slice-of-life scenarios drawn from parts of the underclass of Senegal) is a striking development for this author, who consistently claims to be a *griot* for the common man – the storyteller who bears witness to the life of the people in an accurate and truthful manner.[44]

The Last of the Empire is a thinly disguised and slightly exaggerated *roman-à-clef* that seems to portray the late years of Senghor's presidency in Senegal. The elderly president, Léon Mignane, is on the verge of retirement, but is not sure how he can effect his departure in a manner sufficiently dramatic to cap off his tenure as one of the most popular (at least with the donor nations) African presidents. In Léon's efforts to maintain and consolidate his power, he has seated a council of ministers that includes only two politicians of his own generation, including the Minister for Justice, Cheikh Tidiane Sall, complemented by a bevy of younger politicians who revere Léon, referring to him only as "the Venerable One". Léon has appointed as his prime minister a young technocrat, Daouda, who is quite happy to work under Léon's shadow. Léon Mignane has spent the last twenty years playing one member of his cabinet against another (such as his constant manipulating of the antagonism between Daouda and the Minister of Finance, Mam Lat Soukabé). When Léon suddenly disappears one Thursday night, the cabinet is in turmoil and emotions run high.

Through most of the story, the narrative voice remains linked to the point of view of Cheikh Tidiane Sall. Sall is from the old school: he was brought up in the liberal French tradition of assimilation, and he once thought of himself as being French before being Senegalese. Sall's evolution, from an assimilated Frenchman to a Senegalese nationalist to a critic of the neocolonial system, forms the basis for the narrative and for the reader's understanding of the reactions to Léon's disappearance, which brings about a sudden loss of direction and conflict among the ruling élite in Dakar. In the ensuing power struggle, Cheikh Tidiane Sall acts as the reader's guide to the powers that influenced the current dilemma.

The Last of the Empire's language practice is much less complex than that of "Taaw", for example, partly because the élite of Dakar speak French most of the time. However, questions of language complexity and hierarchy are even more subtly constructed here than anywhere else in Sembene's work. One of the more notable elements of this novel is Sembene's frequent use of Wolof phrases that are translated only once for the reader in a footnote, or sometimes not translated at all. For the scenes that occur inside Cheikh Tidiane Sall's home, Sall is always referred to as "Joom Galle", master of the house. While walking down the street one day, Sall overhears two friends exchange greetings and news of a death in a conversation punctuated with the phrase "Ndey san". This phrase is not translated, either in a footnote or in the narrative.[45]

In another passage, we are presented for the first time with an entire Wolof proverb written in Wolof in the middle of the text.[46] These intrusions of the Wolof language into the French text seem much less obvious than in earlier works, when phrases were repeated in two languages or transliterated into French. Sembene also uses more English in this novel than previously, incorporating words such as "walkie-talkie" and "freelance". The increasing prominence of the American influence in Senegal, as well as the French desperation to retain the myth of a united Francophonie, is lampooned through a conversation between the journalist, Kad, and Badou, one of Sall's sons. Kad is presented as a trustworthy source, a journalist renowned for his integrity and courage to say the whole truth.[47]

Kad is also the only character who can piece together the whole story of Léon's disappearance and the attempted coup at the end of the novel. Badou is also a sympathetic character, as shown in his resistance to the fawning nature of Léon's advisors, and in his objections to the continued relationship between France and Senegal. It is odd therefore that we find Badou, a professor of modern literature, worried about the purity of the French language. When Badou asks Kad what kind of work he currently does, Kad responds quite naturally: "freelance". However, Badou corrects him automatically with the word, "temporaire".[48] Perhaps Badou's attachment to the proper use of the French language at the same time that he resents France's interference in an independent Senegal is similar. to his father's attachment to the enlightenment ideals of citizenship, despite the ideological poverty of the current system.

One of the most pointed comments on the status of language offered by Sembene in this text occurs during a small incident towards the end of the novel. Cheikh Tidiane Sall discovers that Léon's disappearance is part of a plot organised by several persons that call their operation "Caaf da Xëm".[49] The French accomplices of this plot have their own label for it, "Opération Jaron", but the French in this novel have as much trouble with the Wolof as the Wolof speakers have with French in Sembene's other works. When the French government hesitates in its promise to aid the plotters of the coup, a French commander becomes enraged and sputters out: "Operation... Ja...Ja...Damn it. (He had trouble pronouncing the word *Jaron* in Wolof) Damn...Operation Dolphin is under way..."[50] In a deliciously ironic reversal of petit-nègre (perhaps we could call it *touti-toubab*?), a French speaker is represented as obviously deficient in his or her attempts to speak another language. It is the French commander who looks childish here in his inability to wrap his tongue around a Wolof word of two syllables.

On another level, it can be argued that *The Last of the Empire* represents a shift in direction in its rendering of Senegalese subjectivity by incorporating the Senegalese reader as an (almost) precondition for reading the text itself. One of the arguments consistently made about the African writing in French is that this choice implies a desire to reach a non-indigenous or metropolitan audience. The argument is as follows: because the Senegalese population has a literacy rate of only about 20%, most of whom do not read for leisure, these books in French cannot be intended for a Senegalese audience, but instead must be oriented towards a European readership.

There is another argument, however, that has been made by several African authors and intellectuals.[51] Jonathan Ngate argues that, beyond the level of language, African authors have looked for ways to ground their texts in indigenous practices and contexts, even if the language they use is French. Ngate constructs his argument around the theories of heteroglossia and reader-response. There is, he argues, in the latest generation of francophone African texts a real move to anticipate an African audience as the intended reader of a text. This can be seen in the ways in which the text supplies or holds back information and in the gaps it leaves for the reader to fill in.[52] If we take Ngate's argument and look at Sembene's latest novel in terms of the reader that the text assumes, we can safely say that this novel is even more situated in and aimed at the Senegalese contexts than are any of his earlier novels. The amount of Senegalese history needed to fully limn this text is beyond that of the casual observer or recent initiate to Senegal.[53] A *roman-à-clef* always demands a certain amount of background knowledge to make it understandable, and, in this case, certain characters, such as Léon Mignane, are easily recognisable.

However, Sembene goes far beyond the parody of Senghor into offering critiques of characters as diverse as Blaise Diagne, the institution of Dakar's daily paper, *Le Soleil*, or even the deposed Minister of Finance, Mamadou Dia. In ranging from the well-known to the lesser-known, and from the past to the present, and even portraying institutions of everyday life such as the newspaper, Sembene constructs a narrative that is imbricated with Senegalese reference points. The Senegalese reader cannot but be more "at home" in this text than any French person.

Conclusion

Sembene's written work continues to rise to the goal he has set for himself: to be a faithful witness to the concerns of his people by continuing to engage in the process of questioning how power is constructed in the Senegalese context. Through his explorations of power, religion, tradition, literacy and multivocal language practices, Sembene asks his readers, increasingly imagined as saturated in Senegalese subjectivity, to think through the practices of language and power in contemporary Senegal in all its manifestations. While this exercise is not always a pleasant one, it is necessary. In the introduction to his novella, *Véhi-Ciosane*, Sembene defends his choice to tell such an unsavoury story of incest, patricide and madness by saying that he is not worried about how others perceive him, and that a strong society comes together and faces its own problems in public. The story is at least partly dedicated to the child in the story and others like her:

> Perhaps when you are old enough to go to school, you will
> find a place and later you will read these lines. More probably,
> like thousands of others of your generation, you will never

read them. The present symptoms of our society do not permit me to predict a better life for you. When you reach the age of awareness, you will rebel, like thousands of others as anonymous as you, but, whether it is individual or collective, it will be a futile revolt because it will be badly directed. Your mother, our contemporary, illiterate in French as well as Arabic, will have no chance to read these pages. She lives alone; it is a way of clothing herself in her drama. As for you, VEHI-CIOSANE NGONE WAR THIANDUM, may you prepare the genesis of our new world.[54]

Sembene writes for the people of Senegal and for the future of Senegal in the belief that French can act as a tool of communication and unification when used in appropriate ways. Throughout his written works, he gives examples of what those modes of writing might be: through his analogy of the railroad in *God's Bits of Wood*, with the influence of the oral tradition as shown in the short stories of *Tribal Scars and Other Stories*, and with the awareness of the constantly evolving and changing nature of the language itself in the Senegalese context as shown in "Niiwam", "Taaw" and *The Last of the Empire*. French-language writing, Senegalese-style, continues to be an integral part of Sembene's efforts to be truly "the pulse of the people".

Notes

[Translations from *Le Docker noir*, *L'Harmattan: Référendum* and *Ô Pays, mon beau peuple!* (which have not been published in English editions) are mine.]

[1]   Translated from the French: "la pulsation du peuple". Carrie Dailey Moore, *Evolution of an African Artist: Social Realism in the Works of Ousmane Sembene* (PhD thesis, Indiana University, 1973): 215.

[2]   Alioune Tine, "Wolof ou français: le choix de Sembène", *Notre Librairie* 81 (1985): 49-50.

[3]   Translated from the French: "LE NEGRE DIAW FALLA, ASSASSIN DE LA CELEBRE ROMANCIERE SERA JUGE DANS TROIS JOURS PAR LA COUR D'ASSISES DE LA SEINE". Ousmane Sembene, *Le Docker noir* (Paris: Présence Africaine, 1973): 14. The novel was first published by Éditions Debresse in 1956.

[4]   A form of public transportation in Dakar consisting of vans that can hold approximately fifteen passengers and that travel mainly from the suburbs to the city centre.

[5]   Translated from the French: "Tu vois Yaye Salimata? Son fils est en

France, paraît qu'il a assassiné une femme, peut-être qu'on va le tuer aussi ou l'envoyer au bagne. Lui, il n'a qu'un meurtre sur la conscience, les Blancs viennent de massacrer des dizaines d'hommes, ils ne seront même pas jugés... Personne ne leur demandera de comptes." Sembene: 17.

[6]   Translated from the French: "Tu es bête mon vieux". Ibid.

[7]   "'Le dévouement des tirailleurs sénégalais / Pour leurs chefs, est digne d'admiration. / Ces braves gens se donnent tout entier / A celui qui les commande...' / J'abrège (faute de mémoire). / '...L'officier ne peut pas oublier le regard / Que jettent ces hommes une fois tombés / Pour ne plus se relever. C'est une vraie / Troupe... Française... que nous avons / Il est impossible de l'employer autrement / Qu'au service de la Patrie.'" Ibid: 214.

[8]   Translated from the French: "Faye, sur de nombreux points, avait parfaitement assimilé les modes de pensée, les réactions des blancs, tout en ayant conservé au plus profond de lui l'héritage de son peuple". Ousmane Sembene, *Ô Pays, mon beau peuple!* (Paris: Le Livre Contemporain, 1957): 15.

[9]   Ibid: 35-36.

[10]   Translated from the French: "Ne voudriez-vous pas reprendre votre place? Votre présence me dérange." "Tout doux, beauté. Ici, chacun a payé sa place." "Vous m'ennuyez. C'est du français, non?". "Je pensais que vous parliez nègre". Ibid: 74-75.

[11]   Len Ortzen, translator of the 1987 edition of *Voltaïque*, entitled *Tribal Scars and Other Stories* (London: Heinemann, 1987), renders the title of this story as "In the Face of History". What this translation emphasises is the narrator's eventual commentary on the role of history in building present-day attitudes and identities. Unfortunately, what is lost is the pun on the placement of this story as the first in the French edition, hence before the other stories, and thus the double play on the word "histoire" as both history and story.

[12]   Ibid: 20. *Fatou* is a common name for women of traditional backgrounds in Senegal.

[13]   Ibid: 21.

[14]   Ibid.

[15]   "Soundiata" is the foundational epic of the empire of Mali. "Soundiata" (sometimes spelled Son-Jara), recounts the consolidation of the empire of Mali under its strongest leader. The epic is still very much a part of West African culture and forms the centre-piece of an annual gathering of the most esteemed *griots* in Mali.

[16]   The Referendum of 1958 was proposed by De Gaulle as a means of ensuring the French community. All French colonies were given the opportunity to vote "Yes" and stay in the French Community, or "No", thus gaining their complete independence. Only one French colony, Guinea,

voted "No". The French pulled out of Guinea, taking with them everything that they could carry. What they could not carry they threw into the ocean. Guinea was subsequently entirely cut off from French aid, and France worked actively to keep Guinea excluded from international societies such as the United Nations. Two years later, in 1960, the "Community" was dissolved in favour of independence for all the African countries within a framework of "special relations" with France.

[17] Sembene has remarked in interviews that he much admires Diop, and that he is the only person that Sembene knows of that can truly pass from French to Wolof without losing anything in either language.

[18] Sembene (1987): 65.

[19] Ibid: 89.

[20] Diouana's break with indigenous tradition is made more explicit in the film, when she is shown to be obsessed with the image of France in her wearing wigs and pasting up pictures of film stars, while the importance of her reclaiming her tradition is shown in the end of the film when she takes back a mask that she has given Madame before she commits suicide. This mask does not occur in the story.

[21] Ousmane Sembene, *God's Bits of Wood*, translated by Francis Price (London: Heinemann, 1970): 12-13.

[22] Ibid: 161.

[23] With this name, Sembene adds salt to the wound of his critique of Islam. "El Hadji" is the title given to devout Muslims who have accomplished a pilgrimage to Mecca. Not only is El Hadji Mabigue a toady to the local colonial administration in preaching to the strikers to go back to work, but also he shows the utmost contempt for his sister's starving children by parading around with a fattened ram named after the Islamic holy day, Friday.

[24] Sembene (1970): 247.

[25] Manthia Diawara recounts how a crowd at a FESPACO showing of the film applauded during this scene. Manthia Diawara, "Camp de Thiaroye", *Black Film Review* 6: 3 (1991): 15.

[26] Translated from the French: "pour l'Afrique, j'aurais préféré qu'il y ait davantage de lecteurs que de cinéphiles". Paulin Soumanou Vieyra, *Ousmane Sembene, Cinéaste: Première période 1962-1971* (Paris: Présence Africaine, 1972): 188, quoting Sembene, interviewed in *France Culture* April 1967.

[27] "Ousmane Sembene at the Olympic Games", *American Cinematographer* 53: 11 (November 1972): 1276, 1322.

[28] Translated from the French: "Même si l'écrivain africain n'avait pas la possibilité de s'adresser à son peuple, les échos de ses écrits retombaient sur

l'Afrique et l'Afrique se sentait solidaire – (Même s'ils ne lisaient pas) à ce que ce type disait. Il nous est arrivé beaucoup d'exemples des gens qui achetaient des livres africains ne sachant pas lire pour les donner à leurs enfants pour se faire expliquer ces livres." Moore: 239.

[29] Translated from the French: "Je ne fais pas la théorie du roman africain. Je me souviens pourtant que jadis, dans cette Afrique qui passe pour classique, le griot était non seulement l'élément dynamique de sa tribu, clan, village, mais aussi le témoin patent de chaque événement. C'est lui qui enregistrait, déposait devant tous, sous l'arbre du palabre, les faits et gestes de chacun. La conception de mon travail découle de cet enseignement: rester au plus près du réel et du peuple." Sembène Ousmane, *L'Harmattan: Référendum* (Paris: Présence Africaine, 1980): 9.

[30] Translated from the French: "J'ai renoncé à écrire en français. Non parce que je ne peux pas m'exprimer, mais parce que j'enrichis une langue étrangère. Une langue qui n'est pas celle du peuple! De notre peuple! Les dessins, d'accord! Le dessin est une langue ouverte à tous." Ibid: 140.

[31] Translated from the French: "Sous prétexte que les voitures sont de marques françaises ou autres, tu refuses de voyager dedans?...Prenons tes dessins!...qui les achète? Le Grec, pour les revendre! Qui les regarde? Les demi-bourgeois africains et les touristes européens par exotisme." Ibid: 141.

[32] Translated from the French: "Tu me prends pour qui? Pour un con, yo! Si tu avais de quoi être un médecin, tu serais mieux habillé." Ibid: 262.

[33] Translated from the French: "Tu me prends vraiment pour un con. Je ne sais pas lire", and adds "Pas de 'coute frère! Tu payes ou je te casse la gueule. Compris?" Ibid.

[34] Indigenous policeman under the colonial system.

[35] Sembène Ousmane, *The Money-Order* with *White Genesis*, translated by Clive Wake (London: Heinemann, 1972): 34. This was originally published as *Véhi-Ciosane ou Blanche-Genèse, suivi du Mandat* (Paris: Présence Africaine, 1965).

[36] Ousmane Sembene, *Xala*, translated by Clive Wake (London: Heinemann, 1976): 7.

[37] African literature is replete with the tales of colonial schools which forbade the speaking of indigenous languages. Several authors have recounted the story of schools under the colonial system in which the first student caught speaking their indigenous language would be given a token (a button, a rod, and so on), which they then had to pass on to the next person whom they heard speaking a local language, and so on. At the end of the week, the schoolmaster would ask the last boy with the token who had given it to him and the next the same question until the token had been traced to the first boy caught by the schoolmaster himself. Ngũgĩ wa Thiong'o tells a version of this story in his *Decolonising the Mind: The Politics of Language in African Literature* (London: James Currey, 1986), and Sembene uses a version of it in *L'Harmattan*.

[38] Remarkably little evidence of this text exists. Tine alludes to it in his article, and personal experience in Senegal showed there to be a rumour of its existence, but the manuscript seems to have been so effectively buried that one begins to doubt its existence.

[39] In a 1992 interview with Fírinne Ní Chréacháin, Sembene is asked why his latest novel does not seem to be widely read in Senegal. He responds: "It's not talked about in Senegal. Even the critics haven't reviewed it" (245), and goes on to detail the instances of censorship directed towards *The Money Order*, *The Curse* and *Ceddo*. Ousmane Sembene, "'If I Were a Woman, I'd Never Marry an African'", interview by Fírinne Ní Chréacháin, *African Affairs* 91 (1992): 241-247. Some critics theorize that *Ceddo* was censored by the government because the film criticises the presence of Islam in Senegal as a form of colonialism, and the government cannot afford to alienate powerful Muslim leaders.

[40] Sembene Ousmane, *Niiwam and Taaw* (Claremont, South Africa: David Philip/Africasouth New Writing, 1991): 8.

[41] Ibid.

[42] Ibid: 38.

[43] Ibid.

[44] See Sembene's foreword to *L'Harmattan*.

[45] Elsewhere in his work Sembene has used this phrase with the editorial explanation that this is a phrase used to convey deep sympathy in Wolof.

[46] "Cëb lëkë bënë na ngi-cibir". Ousmane Sembene, *The Last of the Empire* (London: Heinemann, 1983): 186.

[47] It is tempting to read this name as a version of the initials of Cheikh Anta Diop, one of the great thinkers of Senegalese history, who is best known for writing historical treatises that sought to describe the true nature of Senegalese society before colonialism and the African roots of Egyptian culture. Kad (or Cad), with his desire to lay bare the true workings of power, becomes like Cheikh Anta Diop in his quest for historical truth in Africa.

[48] Sembene (1983): 114.

[49] Interestingly, the French version of this novel offers a translation of this as "Les cacahuèttes grillés sont calcinées", but the English version offers no translation of this phrase at all. To say that "the roasted peanuts are burnt" in Senegal is probably very close to the English saying, "the goose is cooked".

[50] Sembene (1983): 195.

[51] In an interview with the Senegalese author Boubacar Boris Diop (1991) I asked for whom he thought he was writing. "The Senegalese", he answered without hesitation. I then asked how he reconciled that with the

fact that most Senegalese could not read French. He answered firstly that he hoped that his books would be taught to upper-level school students, a substantial proportion of the reading public in Senegal, and secondly that, as levels of education increased, there would be more and more readers of French in Senegal. He was in effect writing for whoever could read him now, and counting on an even wider readership in the future.

[52] Jonathan Ngate, *Francophone African Fiction: Reading a Literary Tradition* (Trenton, NJ: Africa World Press, 1988).

[53] Craig Vincent Smith makes a similar argument in "Utopia and Necessity: The Crises of Nationalism in African Literature" (PhD thesis, University of Pennsylvania, 1993): 178-233. Smith argues that the contradiction between the intended Senegalese audience and the French language is subsumed by the fact that it is precisely the francophone élite at whom this novel is aimed. I would like to suggest that this is partly true but unnecessarily limiting to Sembene's intentions. It is, after all, the students who are most ready for revolution in this novel and it is students who in reality represent the largest part of Sembene's reading audience in Senegal. Elsewhere it has been said that it is ironic that Sembene's *God's Bits of Wood* is always taught in the same university that bemoans the students' tendencies to go on strike to claim redress for their grievances.

[54] Sembene (1972): 6.

Ousmane Sembene: filmography

Compiled by Sheila Petty

The following abbreviations have been used:

OS	Ousmane Sembene	m	mins
		m	music
ad	art direction	*p*	producer
bw	black and white	*pc*	production company
col	colour	*ph*	cinematography
d	director	*pm*	production manager
dist	distributor	*sc*	scriptwriter
ed	editing	*sd*	sound

[ ] around an English title indicates a literal translation in the cases where there is no official English title.

L'Empire Songhaï
[The Songhaï Empire]
Mali 1963 20m bw 16mm in French
d OS
[A documentary on the history of the Songhaï empire. This film has never been commercially distributed.]

Borom Sarret
[The Cart Driver]
[Le charretier]
Senegal/France 1963 20m bw 16mm fiction
In French with English subtitles
pc Les Actualités Françaises (France)/Les Films Domirev (Senegal)/ Participation of Ministère Coopération (France) *d* OS, assisted by Ibrahima Barro *sc* OS *ph* Christian Lacoste *ed* André Gaudier
main cast Abdoulaye Ly (Borom Sarret), Albouarah (the horse).
dist New Yorker Films (USA), Metro (UK)
awards Prix de la Première Œuvre – Tours 1964; Prix Spécial – Film Africain et Malgache 1964.

Niaye
Senegal/France 1964 35m bw 35mm fiction in French and Wolof
pc Les Films Domirev (Senegal)/Les Actualités Françaises (France)/
Participation of Ministère Coopération (France) *d* OS, assisted by
Ibrahima Barro *sc* OS *based on a short story by OS*, "Véhi-Ciosane"
ph Georges Caristan *ed* André Gaudier
main cast Serigne Sow (the *griot*), Astou N'Diaye (the woman *griot*),
Mame Dia (Ngoné War Thiandum), Modou Sene (the soldier), the
people of the village of Keur Haly Sarrata (the villagers).

La Noire de...
Black Girl
Senegal/France 1966 65m bw 35mm fiction feature
In French with English subtitles
pc Les Films Domirev (Senegal)/Les Actualités Françaises (France)/
Participation of Ministère Coopération (France) *d* OS, assisted by
Ibrahima Barro and Pathé Diop *sc* OS *based on a story from*
Voltaïque, a collection of short stories by OS *ph* Christian Lacoste
ed André Gaudier
main cast Thérèse M'Bissine Diop (Diouana), Momar Nar Sene (the
young man), Anne-Marie Jelinek (Madame), Robert Fontaine
(Monsieur), Ibrahima (young boy with mask).
dist New Yorker Films (USA), AUDECAM (France), Metro (UK)
awards Tanit d'or – Journées Cinématographiques de Carthage, 1966;
Grand prix – Festival Mondial des Arts Nègres, 1966; Prix Jean Vigo,
1966.

Mandabi
The Money Order
[Le mandat]
Senegal/France 1968 105m (Wolof version) 90m (French version)
colour 35mm fiction
The Wolof version is available with English subtitles
pc Les Films Domirev (Senegal)/Comptoir Français du Film (France)/
Participation of Ministère Coopération (France) *d* OS, assisted by
Ababacar Samb-Makharam *sc* OS *based on the short story, "The Money*
Order" by OS *ph* Paul Soulignac *ed* Bernard Lefèbre, Gillou Kikoine
sd Henry Moline, assisted by El Hadji M'Bow
main cast Makhourédia Gueye (Ibrahima Dieng), Younousse N'Diaye
(Méty, the first wife), Issa Niang (Aram, the second wife), Serigne Sow
(the imam), Moustapha Touré (M'barka, the shopkeeper), Medoune
Faye (the postman), Moussa Diouf (the nephew), Thérèse Bass
(Dieng's sister), Christophe N'Doulabia (the water-seller).
dist New Yorker Films (USA), AUDECAM (France), Metro (UK)
awards Prix de la Critique International – Venice Film Festival, 1968;

Prix des Cinéastes Soviétiques – Taškent Film Festival, 1968; Best Foreign Film – Atlanta Film Festival, 1969.

Polygamie
[Polygamy]
1969
[A short film made for European television (no documentation available)]

Problème de l'Emploi
[Unemployment Problems]
1969
[A short documentary film made for European television (no documentation available)]

Taaw
Senegal 1970 24m colour 16mm fiction
In Wolof with English subtitles
pc Broadcasting Film Commission, National Council of the Church of Christ *d* OS, assisted by Pap Sow *sc* OS *ph* Georges Caristan *m* Diabaré Samb *ed* Mawa Gaye *sd* El Hadji M'Bow *pm* Paulin Soumanou Vieyra
main cast Amadou Dieng, Mamadou M'Bow, Fatim Diagne, Coumba Mané, Yoro Cissé, Mamadou Diagne, Christophe N'Doulabia.
dist New Yorker Films (USA), Metro (UK), International Tele-Film Enterprises (Canada)
awards Golden Lion – Asmara Film Festival, Ethiopia, 1971; Golden Eagle – United States Council, 1972.

Emitaï
God of Thunder
[Dieu du tonnerre]
Senegal 1971 95m colour 35mm fiction
In Diola and French with English subtitles
pc Les Films Domirev (Senegal)/Participation of Ministère Coopération (France) *d* OS, assisted by Pap Sow *sc* OS *ph* Georges Caristan *ed* Gilbert Kikoine *sd* El Hadj M'Bow *pm* Paulin Soumanou Vieyra
main cast Robert Fontaine (the Commandant), Michel Renaudeau (the Lieutenant), Pierre Blanchard (the Colonel), Andoujo Diahou (the Sergeant), Fodé Cambay (the Corporal), Thérèse M'Bissine Diop, Ibou Camara, Ousmane Camara, Josephy Diatta, Dji Niassebanor, Sibesalang, Kalifa (the villagers).
dist New Yorker Films (USA), Metro (UK), International Tele-Film Enterprises (Canada)
award Silver Medal – Moscow Film Festival, 1971.

Jeux Olympiques de Munich
[The Munich Olympic Games]
1972
[OS participated in the production of a medium-length, two-part documentary film on the 20th Olympic Games]

Xala
[Temporary Sexual Impotence]
[The Curse]
[L'impuissance temporaire]
Senegal 1974 116m colour 35mm fiction
In Wolof and French with English subtitles
pc Société Nationale de Cinématographie (Senegal)/Les Films Domirev (Senegal)/Participation of Ministère Coopération (France)
d OS *sc* OS, *based on Xala*, a novel by OS *ph* Georges Caristan
ed Florence Eymon *sd* El Hadj M'Bow *pm* Paulin Soumanou Vieyra
main cast Thierno Leye (El Hadji Abdoukader Beye), Seun Samb (Awa, the first wife), Younousse Seye (Oumi, the second wife), Dieynaba Dieng (Ngone, the third wife), Miriam Niang (Rama), Douta Seck (Gorgul, the blind beggar), Fatim Diagne (secretary), Moustapha Touré (the client), Ilimane Sagnan (the chauffeur), Makhourédia Gueye (the President), Abdoulaye Seck (the Minister), Doudou Gueye (the Deputy Minister), Farba Sarr (the banker).
dist New Yorker Films (USA), Contemporary Films (UK)
awards Special Jury's Prize – Karlovy Vary (Czechoslovakia), 1976; Silver Medal – Festival Figueira da Foz (Portugal), 1976.

Ceddo
Senegal 1976 120m colour 35mm fiction
In Wolof with English subtitles
pc Les Films Domirev (Senegal)/Participation of Ministère Coopération (France) *d* OS, assisted by Moussa Bathily and Ousmane M'Baye
sc OS *ph* Georges Caristan *m* Manu Dibango *ed* Florence Eymon
main cast Tabara N'Diaye (Princess Dior Yacine), Moustapha Yade (Madi Faim Fall), Ismaïla Diagne (the kidnapper), Goure (the imam), Makhourédia Gueye (the King), Oumar Gueye (Jaraaf), Mamadou Diagne (Prince Biram), Nar Modou Sene (Saxewar), Ousmane Camara (Diogamay), OS (a *ceddo* renamed Ibrahima).
dist New Yorker Films (USA), British Film Institute (UK), M H Films (France).
awards Paul Robeson Prize – Los Angeles, 1978; Screened at the Quinzaine des réalisateurs/Directors' Fortnight – Cannes Film Festival, 1977 and the Berlin Film Festival, 1977.

Camp de Thiaroye

Camp Thiaroye
Senegal/Tunisia/Algeria 1988 153m colour 35mm fiction
In Wolof and French with English subtitles
pc Société Nationale de Production Cinématographique (SNPC)
(Senegal)/SATPEC (Tunisia)/ENAPROC (Algeria)/Participation of Les
Films Domirev (Dakar) and Films Kajoor (Thiès) *d* OS and Thierno
Faty Sow *sc* OS and Thierno Faty Sow *ph* Ismaïl Lakhdar Hamina
m Ismaïla Lo *ed* Kahena Attia-Riveill *sd* Rachid Bouafia
main cast Sijiri Bakaba, Ibrahima Sane, Mohamed Dansogho Camara,
Ismaïla Cissé, Ababacar Sy Cissé, Moussa Cissoko, Eloi Coly, Ismaïla
Lo, Jean Daniel Simon, Gabriel Zahon, Pierre Orma, Gaston
Ouedraogo.
dist New Yorker Films (USA), Metro (UK) [available on video].
awards Special Jury Prize – Venice Film Festival, 1988; Prix Institut
des Peuples Noirs – Festival Panafricain du Cinéma et de la
Télévision, Ouagadougou 1989; Special Jury Prize and Prix OUA
(Organisation de l'Unité Africaine) – Journées Cinématographiques de
Carthage, 1988.

Guelwaar

Guelwaar: an African Legend for the 21st Century
Senegal/France 1992 115m colour 35mm fiction
In Wolof and French with English subtitles
p OS and Jacques Perrin *pc* Les Films Domirev (Senegal)/Galatée
Films/FR3 Films Production (France)/Channel 4 (UK)/WDR
(Germany) *d* OS, assisted by Clarence Delgado and Amadou Thior
sc OS *ph* Dominique Gentil *m* Baaba Mall *ed* Marie-Aimée Debril
ad François Laurent Sylva and Moustapha Ndiaye *sd* Ndiouga Mactar
Ba *pm* Papa Wongue Mbengue
main cast Omar Seck, Mame Ndoumbe Diop, Thierno Ndiaye,
Ndiawar Diop, Moustapha Diop, Isseu Niang, Joseph Baloma Sane,
Abou Camara, Samba Wane, Coly Mbaye, Marie Augustine Diatta,
Myriam Niang.
dist New Yorker Films (USA), IDERA (Canada).

Samori

[The Almany Samory Touré]
[A fiction film in progress, comprising two parts each of 90 minutes:
"Faamaya Syla" and "Faama". Both parts focus on Samory, the famous
Mandingue chief, who successfully resisted the French and British
colonial armies and united all West Africa.]

Ousmane Sembene: selected bibliography

Compiled by Sheila Petty

The intention of this selected bibliography is to provide a list of major resources written primarily in English and in French.

Primary bibliography

A: Writings by Sembene

Le Docker noir (Paris: Nouvelles Éditions Debresse, 1956).

Ô Pays, mon beau peuple! (Paris: Le Livre Contemporain, 1957).

"La Mère" (short story). *Présence Africaine* 17 (December 1957-January 1958): 111-112.

Les Bouts de Bois de Dieu (Paris: Le Livre Contemporain, 1960) [published in English as *God's Bits of Wood*, translated by Francis Price (New York: Doubleday, 1962; London: Heinemann, 1970)].

Voltaïque (Paris: Présence Africaine, 1962) [published in English as *Tribal Scars and Other Stories*, translated by Len Ortzen (London: Heinemann, 1974)].

L'Harmattan (Paris: Présence Africaine, 1964).

Véhi-Ciosane ou Blanche-Genèse, suivi du Mandat (Paris: Présence Africaine, 1965) [published in English as *The Money Order, with White Genesis*, translated by Clive Wake (London: Heinemann, 1972)].

Xala (Paris: Présence Africaine, 1974) [published in English as *Xala*, translated by Clive Wake (Westport, CT: Lawrence Hill and Co; London: Heinemann; 1976)].

"*Borom Sarret*, un film d'Ousmane Sembène", *l'Avant-Scène du Cinéma* 229 (1 June 1979): 35-42 [script].

Le Dernier de l'Empire, two volumes (Paris: L'Harmattan, 1981) [published in English as *The Last of the Empire*, translated by Adrian Adams (London: Heinemann, 1983)].

Niiwam suivi de Taaw nouvelles (Paris: Présence Africaine, 1987) [published in English as *Niiwam and Taaw* (Cape Town, South Africa: David Philip/Africasouth New Writing, 1991)].

B: Interviews and statements

(i) In books

Gabriel, Teshome H. "Interview with Ousmane Sembene", in *Third Cinema in the Third World: The Aesthetics of Liberation* (Ann Arbor, MI: UMI Research Press, 1982): 112-116.

Ghali, Noureddine. "An Interview with Sembene Ousmane", *Cinema 76* 208 (April 1976), translated in John D H Downing (ed), *Film & Politics in the Third World* (New York: Autonomedia, 1987): 41-54 [Ghali's interview first appeared in *Cinéma 76* 208 (April 1976): 83-95, translation and notes by the editor].

Jensen, Monika. "The role of the filmmaker: an interview with Ousmane Sembene", in John Tulloch (ed), *Conflict and Control in the Cinema* (Melbourne: Macmillan Company of Australia, 1977): 486-491 [reprint of "The role of the filmmaker: three views – interview with Ousmane Sembene", *Arts in Society* 10: 2 (summer-autumn 1973): 220-225].

Niang, Sada. "An Interview with Ousmane Sembène by Sada Niang: Toronto, July 1992", in Samba Gadjigo, Ralph Faulkingham, Thomas Cassirer and Reinhard Sander (eds), *Ousmane Sembène: Dialogues with Critics and Writers* (Amherst: University of Massachusetts Press, 1993): 87-108.

Sembene, Ousmane. "Préface: Cinéma école du soir/Preface: Cinema as Evening School", in FEPACI (ed), *L'Afrique et le Centenaire du Cinéma/ Africa and the Centenary of Cinema* (Paris; Dakar: Présence Africaine, 1995): 9-14.

Vieyra, Paulin Soumanou. "Sembène, Ousmane: Retrouver l'identitié africaine" (comments collected by Ignacio Ramonet, March 1979), in *Le Cinéma au Sénégal* (Brussels: OCIC/L'Harmattan, 1983): 151-153.

(ii) In journals

"African Cinema Seeks a New Language – Sembene Ousmane, Writer and Film Director (Senegal)", *Young Cinema and Theatre* 3 (1983): 26-28.

Arbois, Janick. "Ousmane Sembène: L'indépendance ça sert à quoi?", *Télérama* 987 (15 December 1968): 54.

Armes, Roy. "Ousmane Sembene: Question of Change", *Cine Tract* (summer-autumn 1981): 71-77.

Arora, K L. "Africa Speaks Out", *Film World* 16: 3 (March 1979): 67-69.

Berruer, André. "Un Cinéaste africain: Ousmane Sembène", *Pas à Pas* 142 (March 1964): 31-34.

Bonnet, Jean-Claude. "Ousmane Sembène", *Cinématographe* 28 (June 1977): 43-44.

Bosséno, Christian. "Entretien avec Ousmane Sembène", *La Revue du Cinéma/Image et Son* 342 (September 1979): 116-118.

Bowie, Geoff. "Ousmane Sembene interview", *POV (Canadian Independent Film Caucus)* 19 (autumn 1992): 11-13.

Cheriaa, Tahar. "Ousmane Sembène: Carthage et le chemin de la dignité africaine et arabe", *Cinémarabe* 4-5 (November 1976): 15-17.

——————. "Ousmane Sembène, Carthage et le cinéma africain", *Cinéma-Québec* 3: 9-10 (August 1974): 51-52.

——————. "Problématique du cinéaste africain: l'artiste et la révolution", *Cinéma-Québec* 3: 9-10 (August 1974): 13-17.

Cheriaa, Tahar and Férid Boughedir. "Jeune Afrique fait parler Sembène Ousmane", *Jeune Afrique* 795 (2 April 1976): 54-55.

Delmas, Jean and Ginette. "Ousmane Sembène: Un Film est un Débat", *Jeune Cinéma* 99 (December 1976-January 1977): 13-17.

Diallo, Siardiou. "Jeune Afrique fait parler Sembène Ousmane", *Jeune Afrique* 29 (27 January 1973): 44-49.

Diop, Ousseynou. "L'Organisation traditionnelle africaine ne correspond plus à l'Afrique nouvelle: Entretien avec Sembène Ousmane", *Cinébulles* 12: 4 (autumn 1993): 28-31.

Dury, Hélène. "Un Entretien avec Sembène Ousmane", *Lutte Ouvrière* 454 (14 May 1977): 20.

Fanon, Josie. "Au nom de la tolérance – un entretien avec Sembène Ousmane", *Demain l'Afrique* 32 (30 July 1979): 72-73.

"Film-makers and African Culture", *Africa* 71 (July 1977): 80.

Fiofori, Tam. "Film Realities", *West Africa* (27 April 1987): 820.

Gadjigo, Samba and Sada Niang. "Purity Has Become a Thing of the Past: an interview with Ousmane Sembène", *Research in African Literatures* (special issue on African cinema) 26: 3 (summer 1995): 174-178.

Ghali, Noureddine. "Ousmane Sembène", *Cinéma 76* 208 (April 1976): 83-95.

Gregor, Ulrich. "Interview with Ousmane Sembene", *Framework* 7-8 (spring 1978): 35-37.

Grelier, Robert. "Ousmane Sembène", *La Revue du Cinéma/Image et Son* 322 (November 1977): 74-80.

Gupta, Udayan, Deborah Johnson, and Nick Allen. "Seven Days Interview: Sembene", *Seven Days* 10 March 1978: 26-27.

Haffner, Pierre. "Sembène Ousmane à Kinshasa", *Recherche, Pédagogie et Culture* 37 (1978): 42-48.

Hennebelle, Guy. "Ousmane Sembène: En Afrique noire nous sommes gouvernés par des enfants mongoliens du colonialisme", *Les Lettres Françaises* 1404 (6 October 1971): 16.

————. "Ousmane Sembène: Pour moi le cinéma est un moyen d'action politique, mais...", *L'Afrique Littéraire et Artistique* 7 (1969): 73-82.

————. "Pour ou contre un cinéma africain engagé?", *L'Afrique Littéraire et Artistique* 19 (October 1971): 87-93.

————. "Sembène Ousmane", *L'Afrique Littéraire et Artistique* 49 (1978): 114-26.

"J. A. fait parler Sembène Ousmane", *Jeune Afrique* 976 (19 September 1979): 72-75.

James, Emile. "Je n'utilise pas de vedettes ça coûte trop cher", *Jeune Afrique* 499 (28 July 1970): 39-42.

Jensen, Monika. "The role of the filmmaker: three views – interview with Ousmane Sembene", *Arts in Society* 10: 2 (summer-autumn 1973): 220-225.

Mabrouki, Azzedine. "Le pouvoir, la parole, la liberté", *Les Deux Ecrans* 12 (1979): 19-21.

Marcorelles, Louis. "Ousmane Sembène, romancier, cinéaste poète", *Les Lettres Françaises* 1177 (6 April 1967): 24.

Medeiros, Richard de. "Dialogue à quelques voix", *Recherche, Pédagogie et Culture* 17-18 (May-August 1975): 39-42.

Morellet, Jean-Claude. "Sembène Ousmane: pour un congrès des cinéastes africains", *Jeune Afrique* 386-387 (27 May 1968): 70.

Ndaw, Aly Kheury. "Sembène Ousmane et l'impuissance bourgeoise", *Jeune Afrique* 694 (7 April 1974): 20.

Nee Owoo, Kwate. "The language of real life: Interview with Ousmane Sembene", *Framework* 36 (1989): 83-85.

Ní Chréacháin, Fírinne. "'If I Were a Woman, I'd Never Marry an African'", *African Affairs* 91 (1992): 241-247.

"Ousmane Sembene at the Olympic Games", *American Cinematographer* 53: 11 (November 1972): 1276, 1322.

"Ousmane Sembene on the State of African Cinema", *Black Film Bulletin* 3: 2/3 (summer/autumn 1995): 3-5.

Pâquet, André and Guy Borremans. "Ousmane Sembène: les francs-tireurs sénégalais", *Cinéma-Québec* 2: 6-7 (March-April 1973): vii-xii.

Perry G M and Patrick McGilligan. "Ousmane Sembene: An Interview", *Film Quarterly* 26: 3 (1973): 36-42.

Pfaff, Françoise. "Entretien avec Ousmane Sembène à propos de *Ceddo*", *Positif* 235 (October 1980): 54-57.

Prelle, François. "Ousmane Sembène à batons rompus", *Bingo* 222 (July 1971): 56-60.

Richter, Rolf. "Ich will mit meinem Volk reden: Gespräch mit Ousmane Sembène", *Film und Fernsehen* 2 (1978): 32-34.

V C. "Un Film dont on parle et dont on parlera longtemps: Le mandat de Ousmane Sembène", *Bingo* 195 (April 1969): 41-42.

Weaver, Harold D Jr. "'Filmmakers Have a Great Responsibility to Our People': An Interview with Ousmane Sembene", *Cineaste* 6: 1 (1973): 27-31.

—————————. "Interview with Ousmane Sembène", *Issue* 2: 4 (1972): 58-64.

(iii) In newspapers

A B. "Sembène Ousmane: les cinéastes ne sont pas des martyrs", *Fraternité Matin* 13-14 March 1982: 16.

Diedhiou, Djib. "Sembène Ousmane – mon prochain film: Samory", *Le Soleil* 4 July 1984: 2-3.

Lemoine, Jacqueline. "Sembène: le théâtre est un accouplement de tous les soirs", *Le Soleil* 1 March 1984: 4-5.

N A P. "Sembène Ousmane nous dit: j'ai été témoin d'un drame, dans un village sénégalais. J'ai voulu en faire un roman... et puis ce fut un film", *Dakar-Matin* 1 March 1966: 4.

Ramonet, Ignace de. "Ousmane Sembène: retrouver l'identité africaine", *Le Monde Diplomatique* March 1979: 29.

Traoré, Biny. "L'artiste a le devoir de donner à refléchir...", *Sidwaya* 25 March 1987: 5.

Secondary bibliography

A: Books and theses devoted to Sembene

Bestman, Martin T. *Sembène Ousmane et l'esthétique du roman négro-africain* (Sherbrooke, Quebec: Éditions Naaman, 1981).

Gadjigo, Samba, Ralph Faulkingham, Thomas Cassirer and Reinhard Sander (eds). *Ousmane Sembène: Dialogues with Critics and Writers* (Amherst: University of Massachusetts Press, 1993).

Minyono-Nkode, Mathieu-François. *Comprendre "Les bouts de bois de Dieu" de Sembène Ousmane* (Issy les Moulineaux, France: Les Classiques Africains, 1979).

Moore, Carrie Dailey. *Evolution of an African Artist: Social Realism in the Works of Sembene Ousmane* (PhD thesis, Indiana University, 1973).

Moriceau, Annie and Alain Rouch. *"Le mandat" de Sembène Ousmane: Étude critique* (Paris: Fernand Nathan/Nouvelles Editions Africaines, 1983).

Ode, Okore. *The Film World of Ousmane Sembene* (PhD thesis, Columbia University, 1982).

Pfaff, Françoise. *The Cinema of Ousmane Sembene: A Pioneer of African Film* (Westport, CT: Greenwood Press, 1984).

Tekpetey, Alphonse Kwawisi. *Social and Political Commitment in the Works of Ousmane Sembene* (PhD thesis, University of Wisconsin, 1973).

Vieyra, Paulin Soumanou. *Ousmane Sembene, Cinéaste: Première période 1962-1971* (Paris: Présence Africaine, 1972).

B: Special journal issues devoted to Sembene

CinémAction 34 (1985)
Contents: "Préface: Qu'on l'admire ou qu'on le dénigre...", by Férid Boughedir (4); "Préambule: Un 'inconnu' nommé Sembène Ousmane...", by Daniel Serceau (5-7); "Biographie" (10-11); "Sembène Ousmane, écrivain", by Jacques Chevrier (12-16); "La thématique", by Antoine Kakou (17-19); "Éléments pour un autoportrait magnétique", by Pierre Haffner (20-24); "Sembène parle de ses films", by Guy Hennebelle (25-29); "*Borom Sarret*, la fiction documentaire", by Maxime Scheinfeigel (32-34); "*Niaye*, l'Afrique sans masque", by Michel Serceau (35); "*La Noire de...*, premier long métrage africain", by René Prédal (36-39); "*Le Mandat*, un film catalyseur des relations sociales", by Michel Serceau (40-42); "*Émitaï*, l'échec d'une transposition dramatique", by Daniel Serceau (43-45); "*Xala*, une fable sur la bourgeoisie africaine", by Michel Serceau (46-50); "La polygamie au Sénégal", by Abdoulaye Bara Diop (51-54); "*Ceddo*, la barbarie à visage

divin", by Daniel Serceau (55-57); "Contrepoint: *Ceddo*, entre l'Histoire et les mythes", by Jean Copans (57-59); "Les gris-gris d'un conteur", by Antoine Kakou (62-65); "La recherche d'une écriture", by Daniel Serceau (66-72); "Du masque au mandat: tradition et modernité", by Michel Serceau (72-79); "La place de la femme", by Catherine Ruelle (80-83); "Sandy et Bozambo, entretien avec Jean Rouch sur Sembène", by Pierre Haffner (86-94); "Filmographie" (95-96).

The Films of Ousmane Sembène/Les Films d'Ousmane Sembène (festival monograph) with an essay entitled "Ousmane Sembène: Pioneer African Filmmaker/Ousmane Sembène: Pionnier du cinéma africain", by Françoise Pfaff (Ottawa: National Gallery of Canada/Musée des beaux-arts du Canada, 10-15 July 1992).

C: Chapters or sections on Sembene and his work in books

Armes, Roy. *Third World Film Making and the West* (Berkeley; Los Angeles; London: University of California Press, 1987): 281-292.

Berrian, Brenda. "Through Her Prism of Social and Political Contexts: Sembène's Female Characters in 'Tribal Scars'", in Carol Boyce Davies and Anne Adams Graves (eds), *Ngambika: Studies of Women in African Literature* (Trenton, NJ: Africa World Press, 1986): 195-204.

Boughedir, Férid. *Le Cinéma Africain de A à Z* (Brussels: OCIC, 1987): 57-73 (analysis of *Borom Sarret*).

Cham, Mbye Baboucar. "Les Œuvres de Ousmane Sembène", in OCIC and FESPACO (eds), *Tradition Orale et Nouveaux Médias* (Brussels: OCIC, 1989): 171-189.

Diakité, Madubuko. *Film, culture, and the black filmmaker* (New York: Arno Press, 1980) [chapter on Sembene].

Diawara, Manthia. *African Cinema: Politics & Culture* (Bloomington and Indianapolis: Indiana University Press, 1992): selected pages.

Gabriel, Teshome H. *Third Cinema in the Third World: The Aesthetics of Liberation* (Ann Arbor, MI: UMI Research Press, 1982): 77-89, 25-26 and selected pages.

Gardies, André. *Cinéma d'Afrique Noire Francophone: l'espace-miroir* (Paris: Editions L'Harmattan, 1989): selected pages.

Haffner, Pierre. *Palabres sur le cinématographe* (Kinshasa: Les Presses Africaines, 1978).

Harrow, Kenneth. "*The Money Order*: false treasure or true benefice", in Kofi Anyidoho, Abioseh M Porter, Daniel Racine and Janice Spleth (eds), *Interdisciplinary Dimensions of African Literature* (Washington, DC: Three Continents Press, 1985): 75-87.

Ilboudo, Patrick G. *Le Fespaco 1969-1989 – Les Cinéastes Africains et leurs Œuvres* (Ouagadougou: Editions La Mante, 1988): 375-382.

Jacquemain, Jean-Pierre. *Comparaison de l'écriture littéraire et cinématographique chez Sembène Ousmane* (Kinshasa: Université Louvanium, 1970).

Makward, Edris. "Women, Tradition, and Religion in Sembène Ousmane's Work", in Kenneth W Harrow (ed), *Faces of Islam in African Literature* (Portsmouth, NH: Heinemann, 1991): 187-199.

Moore, Gerald. "Sembène Ousmane: The Primacy of Change", in *Twelve African Writers* (London: Hutchinson, 1980): 68-83.

Mortimer, Mildred. "Catalyst for Change", in *Journeys Through the French African Novel* (Portsmouth, NH: Heinemann, 1990): 69-103.

Peters, Jonathan A. "Aesthetics and Ideology in African Film: Ousmane Sembène's 'Emitai'", in Eileen Julien, Mildred Mortimer and Curtis Schade (eds), *African Literature in Its Social and Political Dimensions* (Washington, DC: Three Continents Press, 1986): 69-75.

Petty, Sheila. "Le geste plus important que la parole: *Emitaï* d'Ousmane Sembène", in Michel Larouche (ed), *Films d'Afrique* (Montreal: Editions Guernica, 1991): 9-19.

Pfaff, Françoise. *Twenty-five Black African Filmmakers: A Critical Study, with Filmography and Bio-Bibliography* (Westport, CT: Greenwood Press, 1988): 237-266.

Pommier, Pierre. *Cinéma et développement en Afrique noire francophone* (Paris: Pédone, 1974): 114-139, 171-181.

Relich, Mario. "Sembene Ousmane as film-maker", in Angus Calder et al (eds), *African Fiction and Film* (Milton Keynes: Open University Press, 1983): 28-33.

Stratton, Florence. *Contemporary African Literature and the Politics of Gender* (London; New York: Routledge, 1994): 41, 42-44, 137-138.

Ukadike, Nwachukwu Frank. *Black African Cinema* (Los Angeles: University of California Press, 1994): 90-104 and selected pages.

Vieyra, Paulin Soumanou. *Le Cinéma au Sénégal* (Brussels: OCIC/ L'Harmattan, 1983): selected pages.

Zell, Hans M, Carol Bundy and Virginia Coulon (eds). *A New Reader's Guide to African Literature* (London: Heinemann, 1983): 457-459 [Sembene's entry is listed under "Ousmane"].

D: Articles in journals and magazines

Aje, S O. "L'Importance de l'écriture en tant qu'institution sociale dans

L'Argent (Emile Zola), *Le roi des Aulnes* (Michel Tournier) et *Le mandat* (Ousmane Sembène)", *Neohelicon* 16: 1 (1989): 237-255.

Akpadomonye, Patrick. "La parodie et la ré-écriture chez Sembène Ousmane: Problèmes textologiques", *Neohelicon* 16: 2 (1989): 211-219.

Allen, Tom. "Pleasure over Pain: The Good, Better and Best", *Village Voice* 1 January 1979: 39.

──────. "The Third World Oracle", *Village Voice* 20 February 1978: 40.

Anyidoho, Kofi. "African Creative Fiction and a Poetics of Social Change", *Komparatistische-Hefte* 13 (1986): 67-81.

Atkinson, Michael. "Ousmane Sembène: 'We are no longer in the era of prophets'", *Film Comment* 29: 4 (July-August 1993): 63-69.

Auguiste, Reece. "Sembene Ousmane and Afrikan [sic] Political Cinema", *Frontline* 2: 4 (1983): 114-116.

Aumont, Jacques and Sylvie Pierre. "Huit fois deux", *Cahiers du Cinéma* 206 (November 1968): 30.

Bayo, Ogunjimi. "Ritual Archetypes: Ousmane's Aesthetic Medium in 'Xala'", *Ufahamu* 14: 3 (1985): 128-138.

Binet, Jacques. "Le sacré dans le cinéma négro-africain", *Positif* 235 (October 1980): 44-49.

Bontemps, Jacques. "Semaine de la critique: *La Noire de...* de Ousmane Sembène", *Cahiers du Cinéma* 179 (June 1966): 48.

Boughedir, Férid. "The Blossoming of the Senegalese Cinema", *Young Cinema and Theatre* 4 (1974): 14-20.

Broz, Martin. "The Birth of African Cinema", *Young Cinema and Theatre* 1 (1968): 37-43.

Cancel, Robert. "Epic Elements in '*Ceddo*'", *Current Bibliography on African Affairs* 18: 1 (1985-86): 3-19.

Case, Frederick. "Workers Movements: Revolution and Women's Consciousness in God's Bits of Wood", *Revue canadienne des études africaines/Canadian Journal of African Studies* 15: 2 (1981): 277-292.

Castiel, Elie. "Ousmane Sembène: le patriarche de la mémoire" *Séquences* 165 (1993): 40-41.

Cervoni, Albert. "*Le Mandat*, si Dakar m'était conté", *Cinéma 69* 134 (March 1969): 119-21.

Cham, Mbye Baboucar. "Art and Ideology in the Work of Sembene Ousmane and Haile Gerima", *Présence Africaine* 129 (1984): 79-91.

——————. "Islam and the Creative Imagination in Senegal", *American Journal of Islamic Studies* August 1984: 1-22.

——————. "Ousmane Sembene and the Aesthetics of African Oral Traditions", *Africana Journal* 13: 1/4 (1982): 24-39.

——————. "The Creative Artist, State and Society in Africa", *Current Bibliography on African Affairs* 17: 1 (1984-85): 17-28.

Cnockaert, André. "*Véhi-Ciosane*, recit clé dans l'œuvre de Sembène Ousmane", *Zaïre-Afrique* 28: 222 (1988): 109-121.

Coad, Malcolm. "Ousmane Sembene and *Ceddo*", *Index on Censorship* 10: 4 (1981): 32-33.

Dagneau, Gilles. "*Xala*", *La Revue du Cinéma/Image et Son* 305 (April 1976): 102-105.

Débrix, Jean-René. "Le Cinéma africain", *Afrique Contemporaine* 38-39 (July-October 1968): 7-12.

Delmas, Jean. "Sembène Ousmane", *L'Afrique Littéraire et Artistique* 49 (1978): 111-113.

Echemin, Kester. "Sembène Ousmane et le mythe du peuple messianique", *L'Afrique Littéraire et Artistique* 46 (1978): 51-59.

Enagnon, Yénoukoumé. "Sembène Ousmane, la théorie marxiste et le roman", *Peuples Noirs, Peuples Africains* 11 (September-October 1979): 92-127.

Engelibert, Anne-Marie and Françoise Martin. "Sembène Ousmane: une œuvre, deux moyens d'expression", *Aujourd'hui l'Afrique* 3 (1975): 36-41.

Feuser, Willfried F. "Richard Wright's *Native Son* and Ousmane Sembene's *Le docker noir*", *Komparatistische-Hefte* 14 (1986): 103-116.

Fischer, Lucy. "Xala: A Study in Black Humour", *Millennium Film Journal* 7/8/9 (autumn/winter 1980/1981): 165-172.

Gabriel, Teshome H. "'*Xala*': A Cinema of Wax and Gold", *Présence Africaine* 116 (1980): 202-214 [reprinted in *Jump Cut* 27 (1982): 31-33].

Gardies, René. "Jeune cinéma d'Afrique noire", *La Revue du Cinéma/ Image et Son* 212 (January 1968): 16-18.

Gérard, Albert. "Afrique invisible: les littératures méconnues du Sénégal", *L'Afrique Littéraire et Artistique* 58 (1982): 83-89.

Gérard, Albert and Jeannine Laurent. "Sembene's Progeny: A New Trend in the Senegalese Novel", *Studies in Twentieth Century Literature* 4: 2 (spring 1980): 133-145.

Glinga, Werner. "The Ceddo's Ghost: History and Fiction in Senegal", *Ufahamu: Journal of the African Activist Association* 16: 2 (1988): 45-59.

Goldfarb, Brian. "A Pedagogical Cinema: Development Theory, Colonialism and Post-Liberation African Film", *Iris* 18 (spring 1995): 7-24.

Gueye, A Mactar. "Spelling It Out", *Index on Censorship* 8: 4 (July-August 1979): 57-58.

Haffner, Pierre. "Radiographie du cinéma sénégalais", *Filméchange* 18 (spring 1982): 41-48.

Hall, Susan. "African Women on Film", *Africa Report* (January-February 1977): 15-17.

Harrow, Kenneth W. "Art and Ideology in *Les bouts de bois de Dieu*: Realism's Artifices", *The French Review* 62: 3 (February 1989): 483-493.

—————————. "*Camp de Thiaroye*: Who's That Hiding in those Tanks, and How Come We Can't See Their Faces?", *Iris* 18 (1995): 147-152.

—————————. "Sembène Ousmane's '*Xala*': The Use of Film and Novel as Revolutionary Weapon", *Studies in Twentieth Century Literature* 4: 2 (spring 1980): 177-188.

Hennebelle, Guy. "Ousmane Sembène", *L'Afrique Littéraire et Artistique* 20 (1972): 202-208.

Hennebelle, Guy, Férid Boughedir, Mohand Ben Salama and Abdou Achouba Delati. "Le Cinéma de Sembène Ousmane", *Ecran 76* 43 (15 January 1976): 41-50.

Hill, Allan. "African Films and Filmmakers", *Essence* July 1978: 18-24.

Huannou, Adrien. "L'Islam et le christianisme face à la domination coloniale dans *Les bouts de bois de Dieu*", *Nouvelles du Sud* 6 (1986-87): 41-48.

—————————. "Sembène Ousmane, cinéaste et écrivain sénégalais", *L'Afrique Littéraire et Artistique* 31 (1975): 24-28.

Ibrahim, Jibo. "Teaching Africa Through Sembene", *Concord Weekly* 48 (1985): 38.

Ijere, Muriel. "Victime et bourreau: l'Africain de Sembène Ousmane", *Peuples Noirs, Peuples Africains* 35 (September-October 1983): 67-85.

Iyam, David Uru. "The Silent Revolutionaries: Ousmane Sembène's 'Emitai', 'Xala', and 'Ceddo'", *African Studies Review* 29: 4 (December 1986): 79-87.

Kindem, Gorham H and Martha Steele. "*Emitai* and *Ceddo*: Women in Sembene's films", *Jump Cut* 36 (1991): 52-60.

Landy, Marsha. "Political Allegory and 'Engaged Cinema': Sembene's *Xala*", *Cinema Journal* 23: 3 (spring 1984): 31-46.

——————. "Politics and Style in *Black Girl*", *Jump Cut* 27 (July 1982): 23-25.

Lee, Sonia. "The Awakening of the Self in the heroines of Sembène Ousmane", *Critique* 17 (1975): 17-25.

Linkhorn, Renée. "L'Afrique de demain: Femmes en marche dans l'œuvre de Sembène Ousmane", *Modern Language Studies* 16: 3 (summer 1986): 69-76.

Lüsebrink, Hans-Jürgen. "De l'incontournabilité de le fiction dans la connaissance historique: questionnements théoretiques à partir de romans historiques contemporains de Alejo Carpentier, de Yambo Ouologuem et d'Ousmane Sembène", *Neohelicon* 16: 2 (1989): 107-128.

Lyons, Harriet D. "The Uses of Ritual in Sembene's *Xala*", *Canadian Journal of African Studies* 18: 2 (1984): 319-29.

Makolo, Muswaswa. "La solidarité africaine hier, aujourd'hui et demain, dans *Le Mandat* de Sembène Ousmane", *Zaïre-Afrique* 145 (1980): 289-300.

Maxwell, Richard. "The Reality Effect of Third World Cinema: Ethnography in '*Ceddo*' and '*Ramparts of Clay*'", *Cresset* 43: 3 (January 1980): 21-22.

McCaffrey, Kathleen. "African Women on the Screen", *Africa Report* 26: 2 (March-April 1981): 56-58.

——————. "Images of Women in West African Literature and Film: a Struggle Against Dual Colonization", *International Journal of Women's Studies* 3: 1 (1980): 76-88.

Mermin, Elizabeth. "A Window on Whose Reality? The Emerging Industry of Senegalese Cinema", *Research in African Literatures* 26: 3 (1995): 120-133.

Mortimer, Robert A. "Ousmane Sembene and the Cinema of Decolonization", *African Arts* 5: 3 (spring 1972): 26, 64-68, 84.

Mowitt, John. "Sembene Ousmane's *Xala*: Postcoloniality and Foreign Film Languages", *Camera obscura* 31 (January-May 1993): 73-94.

Mpembele, N M. "Sembène Ousmane, le combat par la plume et l'image", *Zaïre* 486 (1977): 34-35.

Mpoyi-Buatu, Th. "'*Ceddo*' de Sembène Ousmane et '*West Indies*' de Med Hondo", *Présence Africaine* 119 (1981): 152-164.

Mulvey, Laura. "*Xala*, Ousmane Sembene (1974): The Carapace That Failed", *Camera obscura* 31 (January-May 1993): 49-70.

Mzamane, M V. "Three Novelists of the African Revolution", *Heritage* 3 (1979): 54-57.

Niang, Sada. "Modes d'écriture dans *L'aventure ambigue* et *Xala*", *Revue francophone de la Louisiane* 8: 1 (1994): 77-91.

N'Noruka, M. "Une Lecture de *Xala* de Sembène Ousmane", *Peuples Noirs, Peuples Africains* 36 (November-December 1983): 57-76.

Novicki, Margaret A and Daphne Topouzis. "Ousmane Sembene: Africa's Premier Cineaste", *Africa Report* 35: 5 (November 1990): 66-68.

Ojo, S Ade. "Revolt, Violence and Duty in Ousmane Sembène's *God's Bits of Wood*", *Nigeria Magazine* 53: 3 (July-September 1985): 58-68.

Ostor, Akos. "Cinema and Society in India and Senegal: The Films of Satyajit Ray and Ousmane Sembene", *Cinewave* (Calcutta) 7 (October 1984-March 1985): 8-18.

Pearson, Lyle. "Four Years of African Film", *Film Quarterly* 26: 3 (1973): 42-47.

Peters, Jonathan A. "Sembène Ousmane as Griot: *The Money Order with White Genesis*", *African Literature Today* 12 (1982): 88-103.

Pfaff, Françoise. "Cinema in Francophone Africa", *Africa Quarterly* 22: 3-4 (1983): 41-48.

————. "Film and the Teaching of Foreign Languages and Cultures", *College Language Association Journal* 22: 1 (September 1978): 24-30.

————. "Myths, Traditions, and Colonialism in Ousmane Sembène's '*Emitaï*'", *College Language Association Journal* 24: 3 (March 1981): 336-346.

————. "Notes on Cinema", *New Directions* 6: 1 (1979): 26-29.

————. "Ousmane Sembene: His Films, His Art", *Black Art* 3: 3 (1979): 29-36.

————. "Three Faces of Africa: Women in *Xala*", *Jump Cut* 27 (1982): 27-31.

Pouillaude, Jean-Luc. "L'emblème sur 'Ceddo'", *Positif* 235 (October 1980): 50-53.

Rashidi-Kabama, Margaret. "Senegal's Master Filmmaker", *Share* 18: 1 (13 April 1995): 7, 10.

Robinson, Cedric. "Domination and Imitation: *Xala* and the Emergence of the Black Bourgeoisie", *Race and Class* 22: 2 (1980): 147-158.

Ropars-Wuilleumier, M C. "A propos du cinemá africain: la problématique culturelle de *La Noire de...*", *Recherche, Pédagogie et Culture* 17-18 (May-August 1975): 10-15.

Rosen, Philip. "Making a Nation in Sembene's *Ceddo*", *Quarterly Review of Film and Video* 13: 1-3 (1991): 147-172 [reprinted in Hamid Naficy and Teshome H Gabriel (eds), *Otherness and the Media: The Ethnography of the Imagined and the Imaged* (Chur, Switzerland: Harwood Academic Publishers, 1993): 147-172].

Scharfman, Ronnie. "Fonction romanesque féminine: Rencontre de la culture et de la structure dans *Les bouts de bois de Dieu*", *Ethiopiques* 1: 3-4 (1983): 134-144.

Schissel, Howard. "Sembène Ousmane: film-maker", *West Africa* 3440 (18 July 1983): 1665-1667.

Sembene, Carrie D. "Cinema in Africa: the Senegalese experience", *International Development Review* 17: 2 (1975): 32-35.

Sevastakis, Michael. "Neither Gangsters Nor Dead Kings: Ousmane Sembene's five fatalistic films", *Film Library Quarterly* 6: 3 (summer 1973): 13-23, 40-48.

Shaka, Femi Okiremuete. "Vichy Dakar and the Other Story of French Colonial Stewardship in Africa: A Critical Reading of Ousmane Sembène and Thierno Faty Sow's *Camp de Thiaroye*", *Research in African Literatures* 26: 3 (1995): 66-77.

Smyley, Karen. "Ousmane Sembène: Portraitist of the African Woman in the Novel", *The New England Journal of Black Studies* (1981): 23-29.

Smyley-Wallace, Karen. "'*Les Bouts de Bois de Dieu*' and '*Xala*': A Comparative Analysis of Female Roles in Sembène's Novels", *Current Bibliography on African Affairs* 17: 2 (1984-85): 129-136.

Spass, Lieve. "Female Domestic Labor and Third World Politics in *La Noire De...*", *Jump Cut* 27 (July 1982): 26-27.

Taylor, Clyde. "Shooting the Black Woman", *The Black Collegian* 9: 5 (May-June 1979): 94-96.

——————. "Two Women", in Renee Tajima (ed), *Journey Across Three Continents: Film and Lecture Series* (New York: Third World

Newsreel, 1985): 28-31.

Tenaille, Frank and Charles Lemaire. "Samory Touré à l'écran", *Nouvelle Afrique* 1939 (17 September 1986): 18-19.

Tine, Alioune. "Wolof ou français: le choix de Sembène", *Notre Librairie* 81 (1985): 43-50.

Turvey, Gerry. "*Xala* and the Curse of Neo-colonialism: Reflections on a Realist Project", *Screen* 26: 3-4 (May-August 1985): 75-87.

Van Wert, William F. "Ideology in the Third World Cinema: A Study of Sembene Ousmane and Glauber Rocha", *Quarterly Review of Film Studies* 4: 2 (spring 1979): 207-226.

Vast, Jean. "Ousmane Sembène et Maxence Van der Nerech: même combat pour la justice", *Unir Cinéma* 18: 125 (May-June 1985): 4-5.

Vignal, D. "Le Noir et le Blanc dans *Voltaïque* de O. Sembène", *Peuples Noirs, Peuples Africains* 36 (November-December 1983): 96-116.

—————. "Sembène Ousmane, Nouvelliste", *Peuples Noirs, Peuples Africains* 19 (1981): 141-147.

X. "*Ceddo* ou le poids des mystifications en Afrique", *Peuples Noirs, Peuples Africains* 12 (November-December 1979): 37-46.

E: Selected reviews

General

Bass. "Je ne milite dans aucun parti, je milite à travers mon œuvre, nous affirme Ousmane Sembène", *Dakar-Matin* 11-12 April 1966: 1.

"Caméra et fusil – Ousmane Sembène", *Cinéma 72* 162 (January 1972): 20.

"Dakar: Sembene's Railway Strike on Stage", *Afrika* 25: 8-9 (1984): 40.

Diawara, Manthia. "The Perpetual Rebel", *Village Voice* 6 April 1993: 56, 58.

Flatley, Guy. "Senegal is Senegal, Not Harlem", *The New York Times* 2 November 1969: D17.

Gupta, Udayan. "The Watchful Eye of Ousmane Sembene", *N.Y. Amsterdam News* 11 February 1978: B12.

Hobson, Sheila Smith. "In the Senegalese filmmakers's Will to Succeed, a Lesson for All", *N.Y. Amsterdam News* 11 February 1978: B12.

Mabrouki, Azzedine. "Londres: un hommage à Ousmane Sembène", *Les Deux Ecrans* 35 (June 1981): 33-34.

Ndaw, Aly Kheury. "Ousmane Sembène tel qu'en lui-même: I –
cinéaste proche du peuple", *Le Soleil* 24 July 1984: 8.

——————. "Ousmane Sembène tel qu'en lui-même: II –
Plaidoyer du militant", *Le Soleil* 25 July 1984: 12.

Niang, Sada. "Ousmane Sembene Retrospective", *African Arts* 16: 1
(January 1993): 83-85, 103.

Nwagboso, Maxwell. "West African Film Festival: Sembene Rides High",
Africa Now June 1985: 63.

Randal, Jonathan C. "An African Director Reaching the People", *The
Washington Post* 17 June 1976: B1, B4.

Ruelle, Catherine. "Sembène Ousmane, un cinéaste hors du commun",
Actuel Développement 46 (January-February 1982): 44.

"Toujours Sembène", *Le Soleil* 31 December 1985-1 January 1986: 12.

Turan, Kenneth. "Out of the Real Africa: Acclaimed Senegalese director
Ousmane Sembene gets a rare retrospective at the Nuart", *The Los
Angeles Times* 1 January 1995, Calendar Sec.: 30, 33-36.

Guelwaar

Brown, Georgia. "Seers and Soothsayers", *Village Voice* 6 April 1993:
56, 58.

Maslin, Janet. "From Out of Africa, a Generation of Film Makers
Deserving Attention", *The New York Times* 2 April 1993: The Living Arts
Sec: B10.

Pfaff, Françoise. "*Guelwaar*", *Cineaste* 20: 2 (1993): 48-49.

Stratton, David. "Guelwaar", *Variety* 30 November 1992: 76.

Camp Thiaroye

"*Le camp de Thiaroye*", *Unir Cinéma* 135 (1987): 25-26.

Diawara, Manthia. "Camp de Thiaroye", *Black Film Review* 6: 3 (1991):
14-15.

Leahy, James. "Camp de Thiaroye (Camp Thiaroye)", *Monthly Film
Bulletin* 56: 668 (September 1989): 270-271.

Ndaw, Aly Kheury. "Sembène Ousmane tourne '*Le Camp de Thiaroye*'",
Le Soleil 24 March 1987: 10.

——————. "Thiaroye à l'écran", *Le Soleil* 22 April 1987: 1, 13.

Pym, John. "Soldiers Pay: *Camp de Thiaroye*", *Sight and Sound* 58: 4
(autumn 1989): 280.

QSF. "Camp Thiaroye", *Screen International* 719 (26 August-1 September 1989): 34.

Yung. "Camp de Thiaroye", *Variety* 5 October 1988: 154.

Ceddo

Allen, Tom. "The Third World Oracle", *Village Voice* 23: 8 (1978): 40.

Amengual, Barthelemy. "*Ceddo*, de Sembène Ousmane (Sénégal)", *Positif* 195-196 (July-August 1977): 83.

Amiel, Mireille. "*Ceddo*, de Sembène Ousmane (Sénégal)", *Cinéma* 77 223 (July 1977): 75.

──────────. "*Ceddo*, Ousmane Sembène", *Cinéma* 79 249 (September 1979): 92-93.

Armah, Ayi Kwei. "Islam and *Ceddo*", *West Africa* 8 October 1984: 2031.

Armes, Roy, "16mm/Ceddo (1977)", *Films and Filming* 329 (February 1982): 36

Ayari, Farida. "Les hommes de refus", *Jeune Afrique* 966 (1979): 66.

Bassan, Raphael. "*Ceddo*", *Ecran* 79 83 (September 1979): 62-63.

Bonnet, Jean-Claude. "*Ceddo*", *Cinématographe* 28 (June 1977): 44.

Bosséno, Christian. "*Ceddo*", *La Revue du Cinéma/Image et Son* 342 (September 1979): 114-116.

Boujut, Michel. "*Ceddo* de Sembène Ousmane, film sénégalais", *Les Nouvelles Littéraires* 2695 (12 July 1979): 28-29.

Canby, Vincent. "Film: *Ceddo*, a Pageant from Sembene's Africa", *The New York Times* 17 February 1978: C8.

Daney, Serge. "*Ceddo* (O. Sembène)", *Cahiers du Cinéma* 304 (October 1979): 51-53.

Decaux, Emmanuel. "*Ceddo*", *Cinématographe* 15 (October 1979): 48-49.

Dione, Sakhewar. "*Ceddo* – recouvrer l'héritage négro-africain", *Le Soleil* 19 July 1984: 8.

Diouf, Bara. "*Ceddo* ou la résistance à l'islamisation", *Le Soleil* 10 July 1984: 7.

Gabriel, Teshome H. "*Ceddo*: a revolution reborn through the efforts of womanhood", *Framework* 15-17 (1981): 38-39.

Gupta, Udayan. "*Ceddo*", *Cineaste* 8: 4 (summer 1978): 37-38.

Hobson, Sheila Smith. "*Ceddo*: An Epic Masterpiece", *N.Y. Amsterdam News* 11 February 1978: B12.

Kebzabo, Salek. "*Ceddo* ou l'homme du refus", *Jeune Afrique* 812 (30 July 1976): 60-61.

Leahy, James. "Ceddo", *Monthly Film Bulletin* 49: 576 (January 1982): 5.

Mabrouki, Azzedine. "*Ceddo* – période négrière et pénétrations religieuses", *Les Deux Ecrans* 12 (April 1979): 18.

Mosk. "*Ceddo*", *Variety* 1 June 1977: 18.

Nave, Bernard. "*Ceddo*", *Jeune Cinéma* 104 (July-August 1977): 43-44.

Oster, Jerry. "African Portrait: *Ceddo* – Film from Senegal", *New York Tribune* 17 February 1978: 28.

Pascaud, Fabienne. "*Ceddo*", *Télérama* 1540 (18 July 1979): 72.

The Curse

Arbois, Janick. "*Xala*", *Télérama* 1365 (10 March 1976): 82.

Arnold, Gary. "*Xala*: The Curse of Storytelling Impotence", *The Washington Post* 29 September 1977: D9.

B, A J. "*Xala, Ceddo* et les autres...", *Le Soleil* 4 July 1984: 3.

Bilbow, Marjorie. "*Xala*", *Screen International* 62 (13 November 1976): 21.

Cyclope, Le. "*Xala*, Rut Barre d'Ousmane Sembène", *Le Soleil* 27 February 1975: 11.

Delmas, Jean. "*Xala*", *Jeune Cinéma* 93 (March 1976): 30-32.

Dubroux, Danièle. "Exhibition (Xala)" *Cahiers du Cinéma* 266-267 (May 1976): 72-74.

Eder, Richard. "Film Festival: Cutting, Radiant *Xala*", *The New York Times* 1 October 1975: 62.

Forbes, Jill. "Xala", *Monthly Film Bulletin* 43: 515 (December 1976): 260-261.

Ghali, Noureddine. "*Xala*, histoire symbolique d'une déchéance", *Cinéma 76* 208 (April 1976): 95.

Gross, Linda. "Africa's *Xala* and *Sambizanga*", *The Los Angeles Times* 23 September 1977: 14-15, part IV.

Hennebelle, Monique. "*Xala* une impuissance sexuelle bien symbolique", *Afrique-Asie* 79 (1975): 63-64.

Holl. "Xala (Impotence)", *Variety* 20 August 1975: 19.

Malcolm, Derek. "*Xala*", *The Guardian* 4 November 1976: 10.

Masson, Alain. "Mascarade à Dakar (Xala)", *Positif* 182 (June 1976): 54-56.

Ngara, John. "*Xala* – An Allegory on Celluloid", *Africa* 64 (December 1976): 51.

Niang, Mamadou Leye. "Le fond et la forme", *Le Soleil* 2 May 1975: 4.

Robinson, David. "The Nasty Spell of Success", *The Times* 5 November 1976: 9.

Serre, Olivier. "*Xala*", *Téléciné* 207 (April 1976): 24.

Siskel, Gene. "*Xala* a potent Senegalese film", *Chicago Tribune* 11 June 1976: Sec. 3, 3.

Winsten, Archer. "*Xala* – A Senegalese Fable", *New York Post* 6 October 1975: 23.

"*Xala*", *Film Library Quarterly* 16: 4 (1983): 67-68.

God of Thunder

Afrique Nouvelle. "Ousmane Sembène à l'honneur", *Afrique Nouvelle* 1254 (1971): 11.

Chevallier, Jacques. "*Emitai*, Dieu du Tonnerre", *La Revue du Cinéma/ Image et Son* 320-321 (October 1977): 97.

Cluny, Claude-Michel. "*Emitai* de Sembène Ousmane", *Cinéma 72* 165 (April 1972): 40-42.

Delmar, Rosalind. "Emitaï", *Monthly Film Bulletin* 40: 475 (August 1973): 167.

Diack, Moktar. "*Emitai* or Africa Arisen", *Young Cinema and Theatre* 4 (1972): 27-29.

Dury, Hélène. "*Emitai* de Sembène Ousmane", *Lutte Ouvrière* 454 (14 May 1977): 20.

Farès, Tewfik. "Les Gris-gris de Ousmane Sembène", *Jeune Afrique* 602 (22 July 1972): 66.

Ghali, Noureddine. "*Emitai*, la vrai nature du colonialisme", *Cinéma 76* 208 (April 1976): 94.

Jouvet, Pierre. "*Emitaï*", *Cinématographe* 27 (May 1977): 40.

Marcorelles, Louis. "Les Vérités premières de Sembène Ousmane", *Le Monde* 7 May 1977: 1, 33.

Mosk. "*Emitaï*", *Variety* 12 July 1972: 28.

Pouillaude, Jean-Louis. "*Emitaï*", *Positif* 195-196 (July-August 1977): 120-121.

The Money Order

Andrews, Nigel. "Mandat, Le (The Money Order)", *Monthly Film Bulletin* 40: 469 (February 1973): 30-31.

Arbois, Janick. "*Le Mandat*", *Téléciné* February 1969: 29.

—————. "*Le Mandat*", *Télérama* 987 (15 December 1968): 57.

B F. "*Le Mandat*", *Le Film Français – La Cinématographie Française* 1270 (13 December 1968): 17.

Bonitzer, Pascal. "L'argent-fantôme", *Cahiers du Cinéma* 209 (February 1969): 57-58.

Bory, Jean-Louis. "*Le Mandat*", in *Dossiers du cinéma, films I* (Paris: Casterman, 1971): 137-139.

Capdenac, Michel. "*Le Mandat*, film sénégalais de Sembène Ousmane", *Les Lettres Françaises* 1259 (27 November 1968): 22.

Chauvet, Louis. "*Le Mandat*", *Le Figaro* 4 December 1968: 28.

Ciment, Michel. "*Mandabi*", *Positif* 100-101 (December 1968-January 1969): 45.

Diouf, Bara. "*Le Mandat*, film d'Ousmane Sembène", *Dakar-Matin* 7 December 1968: 8.

Frazer, John. "*Mandabi*", *Film Quarterly* 23: 4 (summer 1970): 48-50.

Gauthier, Guy. "*Le Mandat*", *La Revue du Cinéma/Image et Son* 224 (January 1969): 99-100.

Greenspun, Roger. "*Mandabi*, bitterly comic film, returns", *The New York Times* 30 September 1969: 41; 27 March 1970: 22.

"*Le Mandat*", *l'Avant-Scène Cinéma* 90 (March 1969): 147-150.

Marcorelles, Louis. "*Le Mandat*, Sénégal", *Les Lettres Françaises* 1256 (6 November 1968): 19.

Taratt, Margaret. "*The Money Order*", *Films and Filming* 20: 4 (January 1974): 45, 48.

Black Girl

"*Black Girl/La Noire de...*" *Film Library Quarterly* 16: 4 (1983): 54-56.

Duvigneau, Michel. "*La Noire de...*", *Téléciné* 134 (August-September 1967): 46.

Ellovich, Risa. "Review of *Black Girl*", *American Anthropologist* 79: 1 (1977): 198-200.

Gardies, René. "*La Noire de...*", *Image et Son/Revue du Cinéma* 210 (November 1967): 132-133.

Garidou, R. M. "Le symbolisme du masque dans *La Noire de...*", *Ciné Qua Non* 2 (1972): 10-12.

Marcorelles, Louis. "Ousmane Sembène romancier, cinéaste poète", *Les Lettres Françaises* (6 April 1967): 24.

Mosk. "La Noire De... (The Negro Woman From...)", *Variety* 11 May 1966.

"*La Noire de...*" *Dossiers Art et Essai* 23 (29 March 1967): 37.

Pennec, Claude. "La Noire, d'Ousmane Sembène", *Arts et Loisirs* 80 (5 April 1967): 52.

Veysset, Marie-Claude. "Un Film, deux visions", *Jeune Cinéma* 34 (November 1968): 10-11.

Niaye

"Un cinéaste qui croit encore à quelque chose: Sembène Ousmane", *Dakar-Matin* 15-16 August 1966: 5.

"*Niaye* de Sembène Ousmane", *Dakar-Matin* 9 July 1965: 4.

Borom Sarret

A M. "Le cinéma africain se cherche", *Afrique Nouvelle* 836 (1963): 15.

Andrews, Nigel. "Borom Sarret", *Monthly Film Bulletin* 40: 469 (February 1973): 40.

Marchal, Pierre A. "'*Borom Sarret*' un court métrage d'Ousmane Sembène", *Afrique Nouvelle* 872 (1964): 19.

Weiler, A H. "Screen: 2 from Senegal", *The New York Times* 13 January 1969: 31.

Index

181

Notes on contributors

Roy Armes is Professor of Film at Middlesex University. He has published widely on the cinema during the past 30 years, and his current interest in African filmmaking is reflected in such recent publications as *Third World Film Making and the West* (1987), *Arab and African Film Making* (co-authored with Lizbeth Malkmus, 1991), and the bilingual *Dictionary of North African Film Makers/Dictionnaire des Cinéastes du Maghreb* (1996). His current project is a study of Merzak Allouache's Algerian film, *Omar Gatlato*, for the *Cinetek* series.

Frederick Ivor Case is Professor of French and teaches African and Caribbean literature at the University of Toronto. Apart from several publications on Sembene's writing, he is the author of numerous articles on Caribbean literature and on Islamic discourse in African literature. Among his more important works are *Racism and National Consciousness* (1979) and *The Crisis of Identity: Studies in the Guadeloupean and Martinican Novel* (1985).

Sada Niang is Associate Professor of African and Caribbean Literature at the University of Victoria, British Columbia. He is the author of numerous articles in internationally known journals, and the co-author of two monographs: *Elsewhere in Africa* (1978) and *African Continuities* (1989).

Sheila Petty is Associate Professor of Film and Video at the University of Regina, Canada. She is the author of numerous articles on African cinema in various journals and was a contributor to *Films d'Afrique* (1991) and to *International Women's Writing: New Landscapes of Identity* (1995). She is currently preparing a book and exhibition project on Quebec, Brazilian and African television series.

Philip Rosen is Associate Professor of Modern Culture and Media at Brown University. He is editor of *Narrative, Apparatus, Ideology: A Film Theory Reader* (1986) and co-editor of *Cinema Histories/Cinema Practices* (1984). He is the author of several articles on the concept of national cinemas and a forthcoming book, *Past Present: Cinema, Theory, History*.

Nwachukwu Frank Ukadike teaches film and cultural studies in the Program in Film and Video Studies and the Center for Afroamerican and African Studies at the University of Michigan, Ann Arbor. He is the author of *Black African Cinema* (1994), and guest editor of *Iris* 18 (special issue on African cinema). He is currently working on a book tentatively titled, *A Questioning Cinema: Conversations with African Filmmakers*.

Ann Elizabeth Willey received her PhD from Northwestern University's Program in Comparative Literature and Theory in 1993. She is currently Assistant Professor of English at the University of Louisville. Her work focuses on the representations of nations as communities in both francophone and anglophone African literatures. She has published articles in *Passages* and *Selected Papers of the 1992 African Literature Association*, and has an essay in the forthcoming *Studies in Twentieth Century Literature* and *Interventions: Feminist Dialogues on Third World Women's Literature and Film*.